Code/Space

Software Studies

Matthew Fuller, Lev Manovich, and Noah Wardrip-Fruin, editors

Expressive Processing: Digital Fictions, Computer Games, and Software Studies
Noah Wardrip-Fruin, 2009

Code/Space: Software and Everyday Life
Rob Kitchin and Martin Dodge, 2011

Programmed Visions: Software and Memory
Wendy Hui Kyong Chun, 2011

Code/Space

Software and Everyday Life

Rob Kitchin and Martin Dodge

The MIT Press
Cambridge, Massachusetts
London, England

First MIT Press paperback edition, 2014
© 2011 Massachusetts Institute of Technology

This book was set in Stone Sans and Stone Serif by Toppan Best-set Premedia Limited.

Library of Congress Cataloging-in-Publication Data

Kitchin, Rob.
Code/space : software and everyday life / Rob Kitchin and Martin Dodge.
    p.   cm. — (Software studies)
Includes bibliographical references and index.
ISBN 978-0-262-04248-2 (hardcover : alk. paper) — 978-0-262-52591-6 (paperback)
1. Computers and civilization. 2. Computer software—Social aspects. I. Dodge, Martin, 1971– II. Title.
QA76.9.C66K48   2011
303.48'34—dc22

                                                    2010031954

Contents

Foreword

To trace software through the figuration of space is to take both in significant new directions with many interesting twists and turns.

Computing's key problem has often been presented as one of time, how fast a complex calculation can be carried out. In part computing has achieved results through the literal compression of space, making work that once took equipment the size of a room happen in the landscape of a chip. *Code/Space* takes another route, by showing how software expands out of the computer, becoming spatially active. In doing so software generates behaviors and opportunities, and traffics in meanings, readings, and interpretations. In assembling this book, the authors also provide a set of means by which computing itself may be opened up to hitherto tricky spaces and understandings—where traditional questions of control, monitoring, and ordering are entangled with power, ethics, and experience.

What *Code/Space* shows is that the ways in which software interpolates, mixes with, and takes part in the generation of new kinds of space is incredibly rich and requires attentive means to understand it. The numerous cases discussed here—from travel, home life, consumption, social control—all emphasize the authors' call for a sustained and differentiated empirical study of software as parts of particular sites, and as something that weaves them together. The way in which software invests the mundane with capacities for logging, tracking, and reporting lacks sustained and detailed attention, and which in turn is experienced differentially according to multiple dimensions of relationality suggest new means of understanding and studying software and its places in contemporary life.

So this is another thing that this book does, if it provides a means of recognizing the spatialities of software—not simply linking the screen, register, and algorithm with roads, rooms, and runways, but showing how such things in turn transduce each other—*Code/Space* brings in turn the social sciences into forceful relation with software studies.

Matthew Fuller
Centre for Cultural Studies, Goldsmiths, University of London

Preface

It is very difficult to avoid the effects—the work—of software in the world, especially in the developed West, because of the difference it makes to the constitution and practices of everyday life. Indeed, to varying degrees, software conditions our very existence. Living beyond the mediation of software means being apart from collective life: not appearing in government records; not employing any utilities such as water and electricity or banking services; not using the many kinds of household appliances that rely on digital code to control functions, ranging from bathroom scales to washing machines; not watching or taking part in commercial entertainment or recreational activity (e.g., watching television, reading a newspaper); excluding oneself from professional health care, avoiding all manner of everyday activities such as shopping (thereby eluding the significant role of software in barcode systems, computerized cash registers, credit cards, and the like); and not traveling anywhere by any mode of transport (pedestrians are registered on digital surveillance camera networks). In fact, even nonparticipation is often still logged; passivity is as easily monitored by software as activity is.

The means through which this book was bought into being amply demonstrate how so many practices are mediated and augmented by software. It was composed using word processing applications, with drafts e-mailed back and forth between us. When we met to discuss the text face-to-face, we booked plane tickets online with credit cards and traveled through an air travel assemblage that enrolls a complex ecology of software to make safe and affordable flying possible (route scheduling and yield management software, checking in, security screening, aircraft systems, air traffic control). The manuscript was designed and typeset using desktop publishing applications; physically manufactured on a computer-controlled printing press; and marketed, distributed, and tracked using sales management systems. When the book was sold, it was almost certainly done so using either an Internet e-commerce system or a software-driven checkout register, and it is likely that a credit card was used to facilitate the transaction. Even if the book was purchased for cash, there is no escaping the fact that the sale was processed using software, thereby being recorded in the store inventory and sales database. Revenue for the sale was then credited back to MIT Press accounts, and ultimately, a small percentage was registered electronically against our names for annual payment of author royalties. Of course, you may even be reading it as an e-book, in which case the words you are seeing now are a visible manifestation of the work of software in the world.

Software, then, is having a profound influence on the world. Understanding this ongoing and growing influence, its underlying logics, and long-term implications, requires a thoroughly social and spatial analysis. Software is shaping societal relations and economic processes through the automatic production of space (Thrift and French 2002) that generates new spatialities and the creation of software-sorted or machine-readable geographies that alter the nature of access and governmentality (how societies are organized and governed to fulfill certain aims; Graham 2005). *Code/Space* examines in detail these new spatialities of everyday living and new modes of governance and empowerment through an exploration of the dyadic relationship between software and space: the production of space is increasingly dependent on code, and code is written to produce space—hence our title, *Code/Space*, with the slash symbolically binding together the code and space into one dyadic concept. In so doing, we develop a set of conceptual tools for identifying and understanding these relationships, illustrating our arguments through rich, contemporary empirical material relating to different types of everyday activities that depend on software in varying degrees: traveling, homemaking, and consuming.

The principal concepts we detail are transduction and automated management. Through the concept of transduction, we theorize space and spatialities as ontogenetic in nature—as constantly in a state of becoming. Software, through its technicity—its ability to do work in the world—transduces space, that is, it enables space to unfold in multifarious ways. We formulate the concept of automated management to think through the various ways that new software systems survey, capture, and process information about people and things in automated, automatic, and autonomous ways, making judgments and enacting outcomes algorithmically without human oversight. We are sensitive, however, to the fact that software is not simply deployed to discipline people, that is, act or perform in a way prescribed by the rules encoded in its algorithms; it is at the same time also empowering, bringing into being spaces and social activities that qualitatively improve daily life for many people. These processes of regulation and empowerment are sometimes hard to discern because they are often opaque or else they operate from spaces several steps removed from the places of embodied experience. Nonetheless, given their increasingly widespread deployment, it is essential to tease them out and think them through.

Ultimately *Code/Space* makes the case that software matters. It is extensively and intimately woven into the fabric of people's lives in diverse and significant, though often banal, ways. Software is thus actively shaping sociospatial organization, processes, and economies, along with discursive and material cultures and individuals' construction of identities and personal meanings. And its effects are set to become increasingly pervasive as more and more everyday practices and tasks are augmented or automated by code. Clearly, trying to understand the nature, roles, and implications of software on the unfolding spatialities of daily life is important. We hope that *Code/Space* is a productive step in that direction.

Acknowledgments

Code/Space builds on and significantly extends ideas we have developed over the past few years and published in a number of internationally refereed journals and book chapters. It also elaborates new conceptual tools for understanding the relationship of software, digital technologies, space, and everyday life. In developing our work, we have benefited enormously from the feedback we have received from referees and scholars at a number of multidisciplinary workshops and seminars we have attended around the world, as well as international conferences including the several meetings of the Association of American Geographers. We thank those who have challenged our ideas and helped to shape our thinking; they have led us to a much stronger thesis and richer text. In particular, we thank Mark Jayne and Martin Hess at the University of Manchester; Alex Singleton and Mike Batty at University College London; and Matt Zook at the University of Kentucky and www.floatingsheep.org. Graham Bowden, in the Cartography Unit at the University of Manchester, skillfully redrew some of the figures for us. We also thank Doug Sery and Katie Helke at the MIT Press for their patience and faith in this project.

We hope that *Code/Space* has utility for the broad range of scholars working across the social sciences who are examining the work of software in the world, including those working in human geography, science and technology studies, media studies, software studies, cyberculture, anthropology, and sociology.

I   Introduction

1 Introducing Code/Space

Software is everything. In the history of human technology, nothing has become as essential as fast as software.
—Charles Fishman

Our civilization runs on software.
—Bjarne Stroustrup

Over the past thirty years, the practices of everyday life have become increasingly infused with and mediated by software. Such are the capacities and growing pervasiveness of software that it has become the lifeblood of today's emerging information society, just as steam was at the start of the industrial age. Software, like steam once did, is shaping our world—from the launch of billion-dollar spacecraft to more mundane work such as measuring and displaying time, controlling traffic lights, and monitoring the washing of clothes. Indeed, whatever the task—domestic chores, paid work, shopping, traveling, communicating, governing, playing—software increasingly makes a difference to how social and economic life takes place. In short, software matters, and this book documents how and why it does. We detail how software produces new ways of doing things, speeds up and automates existing practices, reshapes information exchange, transforms social and economic relations and formations, and creates new horizons for cultural activity. And we do so by explicitly making software the focus of critical attention rather than the technologies it enables.

Software

As we explore in more detail in chapter 2, software consists of lines of code—instructions and algorithms that, when combined and supplied with appropriate input, produce routines and programs capable of complex digital functions. Put simply, software instructs computer hardware—physical, digital circuitry—about what to do (which in turn can engender action in other machinery, such as switching on electrical power, starting a motor, or closing a connection). Although code in general is hidden, invisible inside the machine, it produces visible and tangible effects in the world.

Software is diverse in nature, varying from abstract machine code and assembly language to more formal programming languages, applications, user-created macros, and scripts. One way to consider these forms is as a set of hierarchically organized entities of increasing complexity that parallel that of organic entities (figure 1.1). Software takes form in the world through multiple means, including hard-coded applications with no or limited programmability (embedded on chips), specialized applications (banking software, traffic management systems), generic user applications (word processors, Web browsers, video games), and operating systems (Windows, Mac

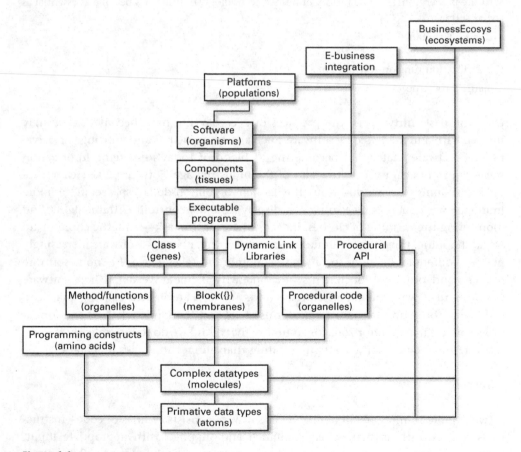

Figure 1.1
A hierarchical conceptualization of different scales of software. The approximate parallels with biological entities are indicated in parentheses. (Redrawn from Nguyen 2003, 10)

OS, Linux), that run on a variety of hardware platforms (embedded chips, dedicated units, PCs, workstations) and can generate, distribute, monitor, and process capta (capta are units that have been selected and harvested from the sum of all potential data, where data are the total sum of facts in relation to an entity; in other words, with respect to a person, data is everything that it is possible to know about that person, capta is what is selectively captured through measurement—see glossary) and information flows across a range of infrastructures (printed circuit boards, coaxial and fiber-optic cables, wireless networks, satellite relays) using a variety of forms (electrical, light, microwave, radio).

The phenomenal growth in software creation and use stems from its emergent and executable properties, that is, how it codifies the world into rules, routines, algorithms, and captabases (a collection of capta stored as fields, typically within a tabular form, that can easily be accessed, managed, updated, queried, and analyzed; traditionally named a database, it has been renamed to recognize that it actually holds capta not data) and then uses these to do work in the world. Although software is not sentient and conscious, it can exhibit some of the characteristics of being alive. Thrift and French (2002, 310) describe it as "somewhere between the artificial and a new kind of natural, the dead and a new kind of living" having "presence as 'local intelligence.'" This property of being alive is significant because it means code can make things do work in the world in an autonomous fashion—that is, it can receive capta and process information, evaluate situations, make decisions, and, most significant, act without human oversight or authorization. When software executes itself, it possesses what Mackenzie (2006) terms *secondary agency*. However, because software is embedded into objects and systems in often subtle and opaque ways, it largely forms a technological unconscious that is noticed only when it performs incorrectly or fails (Thrift 2004b, Graham and Thrift 2007). As a consequence, software often appears to be "automagical" in nature in that it works in ways that are not clear and visible, and it produces complex outcomes that are not easily accounted for by people's everyday experience.

The things that software directs are themselves extremely diverse, varying from simple household items to complex machines and large systems that can work across multiple scales, from the local to the global. In some cases, software augments the use of existing, formerly "dumb," electromechanical technologies such as washing machines and elevators; in other cases, it enables new technological systems to be developed, such as office computing, the Internet, video games, cell phones, and global positioning systems. We see software as embedded in everyday life at four levels of activity, producing what we term *coded objects, coded infrastructures, coded processes*, and *coded assemblages*.

Coded objects are objects that are reliant on software to perform as designed. As we discuss in chapter 3, such objects can be divided into several different classes. Coded machine-readable objects might not have any software embedded in them but rely on external code to function; DVDs and credit cards are examples. Unless they are worked on by software, they remain inert pieces of plastic, unable to provide entertainment or conduct financial transactions. Other coded objects are dependent on the software embedded within them to perform. Here, software enhances the functional capacity of what were previously dumb objects, such as an electronic scale, or enables objects to be plugged into distributed networks, such as networked vending machines, or underpins the invention of entirely new classes of digital objects, some of which have an awareness of themselves and their relations with the world and record aspects of those relations for future use (examples are MP3 players and mobile devices) (see chapters 3 and 8).

Coded infrastructures are both networks that link coded objects together and infrastructures that are monitored and regulated, fully or in part, by software. Such coded infrastructure includes distributed infrastructures, such as computing networks, communication and broadcast entertainment networks (mail, telephone, cell phones, television, radio, satellite), utility networks (water, electricity, gas, sewer), transport and logistics networks (air, train, road, container shipping), financial networks (bank intranets, electronic fund transfer systems, stock markets), security and policing networks (criminal identification captabases, surveillance cameras), and relatively small-scale and closed systems such as localized monitoring (say, fire and access control alarms and HVAC performance within one building complex), and small but complex systems such as an individual automobile. The geographical extent of distributed infrastructures varies from the global, as with satellite-based global positioning systems (which literally can be accessed from any point on the planet), to more localized coverage, such as a network of traffic lights in a city center.

Coded processes consist of the transactions and flows of digital capta across coded infrastructure. Here, the traffic is more than rudimentary instructions to regulate coded objects within an infrastructure; rather, the flows are structured capta and processed information. Such flows become particularly important when they involve the accessing, updating, and monitoring of relational captabases that hold individual and institutional records that change over time. Such captabases can be accessed at a distance and used to verify, monitor, and regulate user access to a network, update personal files, and sanction a monetary payment, for example. An example of a coded process is the use of an ATM. Here, capta in terms of transaction events are transferred across the coded infrastructure of the bank's secure intranet based on access using a coded object (the customer's bank card), verifying the customer based on a personal identification number (PIN), determining whether a transaction will take place, instructing the ATM to complete an action, and updating the user's bank account. Part of the power of relational captabases is that they hold common fields that allow several captabases to be cross-referenced and compared precisely by software. Other coded processes center on captabases relating individuals and households to bank accounts, credit cards, mortgages, taxation, insurance, medical treatments, utility use, service contracts, and so on, all of which can be accessed across open or, more commonly, closed networks. Although coded processes are largely invisible and distant, they are revealed to individuals through the fields on official form letters, statements, bills, receipts, printouts, licenses, and so on, and through unique personal identification numbers on the coded objects used to access them (bank and credit cards, library cards, transportation cards, store loyalty cards) and increasing requirements to use passwords. Many of these processes relate to everyday consumption practices and are discussed in chapter 9.

Coded assemblages occur where several different coded infrastructures converge, working together—in nested systems or in parallel, some using coded processes and others not—and become integral to one another over time in producing particular environments, such as automated warehouses, hospitals, transport systems, and supermarkets. For example, the combined coded infrastructures and coded processes of billing, ticketing, check-in, baggage routing, security screening, customs, immigration, air traffic control, airplane instruments, and so on work together to create a coded assemblage that defines and produces airports and passenger air travel (see chapter 7). Similarly, the coded infrastructures of water, electricity, gas, banks and insurers, commodities, Internet, telephone, mail, television, government captabase systems, and so on work in complex choreographies to create an assemblage that produces individual households (see chapter 8). These assemblages are much greater than the sum of their parts, with their interconnection and interdependence enabling the creation of highly complex systems with high utility, efficiency, and productivity.

Computation

That such coded objects, infrastructures, processes, and assemblages exist widely and do work in the world is itself a function of the rapid advances in hardware and the exponential growth in digital computation at increasingly reduced costs, along with the ability to access such computation at a distance through reliable communication technologies. Although the focus of this book is not computer and communications technologies per se, it is important to acknowledge the extent to which computing power has multiplied dramatically in terms of operating speed since the first modern computers were built during World War II, enabling the widespread distribution of software-enabled devices. It is estimated that over the past hundred years, there has been a 1,000,000,000,000,000-fold fall in the cost of computation (Computing Research Association 2003), most of which has occurred in the past fifty years. Nordhaus (2002) calculates that there was approximately a 50 percent increase in computational power each year between 1940 and 2001. In addition, as new electronic and solid-state hardware technologies for processing have been developed, the cost per million units of computation declined steeply during this period (see figure 1.2).

Computer memory and storage have grown significantly, in tandem with the tremendous improvements in processing power. Gilheany (2000), for example, estimated that since the introduction of the first commercial magnetic disk by IBM in 1956, the cost of storage per gigabyte has fallen by a factor of 1 million to 1. The growth in storage density, as measured in bits per inch on magnetic disks, has even outpaced the upward curve of Moore's law (that the number of transistors on a CPU doubles every two years) and shows few signs of slowing in the near future. The physical space required for data storage has also shrunk dramatically as hard drives and flash memory have become smaller and the density of packing has increased. This growth in storage capabilities enables radically different strategies of information management: deletion of old information is becoming unnecessary, continuous recording is a possibility, and individuals can carry with them enormous amounts of capta in a tiny gadget (see chapter 5).

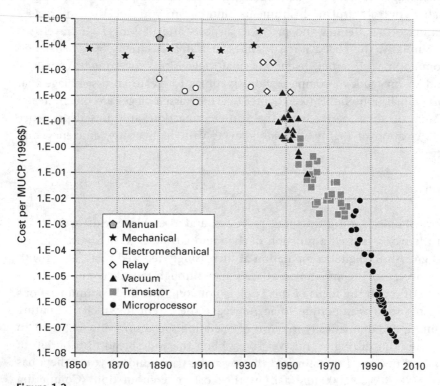

Figure 1.2
Increasing cost efficiencies of computation with a marked step change from mechanical to electronic processing technologies. (Redrawn from Nordhaus 2002, 43)

Communication among computational devices has also become easier, faster, and more widely available. The capability to network devices facilitates all manner of social and economic interactions and transactions and has been underpinned by the rapid development of the Internet over the past two decades. According to George Gilder's "law of telecosm," the "world's total supply of bandwidth will double roughly every four months—or more than four times faster than the rate of advances in computer horsepower [Moore's law]" (Rivlin 2002). In other words, network capacity is growing faster than demand even with increasingly information-rich applications. Network bandwidth is also becoming progressively more diffused geographically at much lower costs (notwithstanding the ongoing concerns over digital divides and the unevenness of telecommunication pricing and regulation). Many people now expect continuous network access regardless of where they are.

Yet it is not just the raw numbers in terms of CPU clock speeds, gigabytes of disk space, and download speed that matter. Pragmatic issues such as physical design, interface usability, reliability, and real cost for daily use have undergone significant improvements that have made computation attractive in terms of widespread consumer confidence and affordability. As a result, social dispositions toward software-enabled technologies have become favorable, resulting in hundreds of millions of computational devices being distributed, embedded into, and carried around environments; these devices often bear little resemblance to desktop computers, and the work that many of them do is hidden from view. As we discuss in detail in chapter 10, some commentators say that we are entering a new age—Greenfield (2006) refers to this as *everyware*—in which computing becomes pervasive and ubiquitous. In this new era, software mediates almost every aspect of everyday life.

The Power of Code

Taken together, coded objects, infrastructures, processes, and assemblages mediate, supplement, augment, monitor, regulate, facilitate, and ultimately produce collective life. They actively shape people's daily interactions and transactions, and mediate all manner of practices in entertainment, communication, and mobilities. As we explore in chapter 2, software has the power to shape the world in a number of ways. It has dramatically increased the capacity of both people and institutions to process information in terms of volume, speed of processing, and the complexity of operations, and at a very low cost per transaction. It has enabled forms of automation, the monitoring and controlling of systems from a distance, the reconfiguring and rejuvenation of established industries, the development of new forms of labor practices and paid work, the reorganization and recombination of social and economic formations at different scales, and it has produced many innovations. And because software can be programmed to read inputs to a system, and evaluate and react to those assessments, it has a significant degree of autonomy. Consequently, as we argue in chapter 5, most people in Western nations are living in a machine-readable and coded world—that is, a world where information is routinely collected, processed, and acted on by software without human intervention.

In many cases, the power of software is significant but banal—a digital alarm clock that wakes a worker or the ATM that provides her with access to money when banks are not open for business. Here, if the software crashes, then its consequence is typically frustration and localized inconvenience. In other cases, software is the difference between something happening or not, because manual systems have been entirely replaced by digital systems. And when some software systems crash, they can create major incidents with serious economic and political effects, and even life-threatening situations. The crash of the Tokyo Air Traffic Control Center in March 2003 meant the cancellation of over 203 flights (Risks List 2003), and seemingly minor failures in routine monitoring software systems at FirstEnergy in Akron, Ohio, were key contributing factors in the large-scale power outage affecting millions of people in the U.S. Northeast in 2003 (U.S.-Canada Power System Outage Task Force 2004). A great deal of resources are expended to keep digital systems that rely on software in working order; much of this routine maintenance and repair is hidden labor but is nonetheless vital to the information society (Graham and Thrift 2007).

Perhaps the best illustration of the contemporary social and economic importance of software was the widespread concern at the end of 1990s associated with the Y2K millennium bug, which triggered a wholesale overhaul of software systems in many nations. The cost to the U.S. federal government alone was estimated at $8.34 billion, and governments and businesses across the world spent an estimated $200 billion to $600 billion to address the problem (Bennett and Dodd 2000). Such investment, and media hype and speculation, would not have been expended if there had not been genuine worry that services in the public and private sectors would suffer serious disruption and possible collapse. Indeed, such is the reliance by governments and businesses on a raft of office applications and larger software systems that it is now unthinkable to backtrack to a predigital age: the nature of tasks has changed, staff levels have been reduced and deskilled in many cases, and operational networks and transactions have become much more complex and interdependent.

Significantly, software engenders both forces of empowerment and discipline, opportunities and threats. Software is enabling the realization of many new forms of creative technology and novel kinds of art, play, and recreation; it makes social and economic processes more efficient, effective, and productive; and it creates new opportunities and markets. At the same time, software has underpinned the development of a broad range of technologies that more efficiently and successfully represent, collate, sort, categorize, match, profile, and regulate people, processes, and places.

Software is at the heart of new modes of invasive and dynamic surveillance and the creation of systems that never forget (see chapters 5, 10, and 11).

Social analysts have a tendency to focus on the active role of software in regulatory technologies, in processing and analyzing capta about people, and in systems of social control. From this perspective, it is difficult not to become pessimistic about the work software does in the world—its use to determine, discipline, and potentially discriminate. And yet the reason that digital technologies are so popular is that they make societies safer, healthier, and richer overall even as they do the work to regulate societies. (We acknowledge that the beneficial outcomes are not necessarily equitably distributed.) Software development has provided innovations across many fields; led to new job opportunities in cleaner industries; driven fresh rounds of capital investment in new and old business sectors; provided more and wider entertainment and retail choices; automated everyday tasks; increased access to credit; opened up new forms of social communication and driven down their cost; enabled new forms of creativity, knowledge production, and artistic practice; opened up original ludic possibilities and ways of recording personal experiences and memories; led to new media for political organization and oppositional activities; and so on (see chapter 6). In this sense, a key aspect of the power of software lies in how it seduces. In Althusser's (1971) terms, software-driven technologies induce a process of interpellation, wherein people willingly and voluntarily subscribe to and desire their logic, trading potential disciplinary effects against benefits gained. And the benefits are often substantial and, in a very quotidian sense, irresistible. Perhaps rather than trying to determine whether the work software does is good or bad, it is better to see it as productive in the broad sense—it makes things happen. We need to understand how this production unfolds in different social and spatial contexts.

Software, Society, and Space

Until recently software was largely ignored by the social sciences and humanities. Instead, with perhaps the exception of research in computer-mediated communication and computer-supported cooperative work, scholars and commentators tended to focus more broadly on the information and communication technologies (ICTs) that software enables, in particular the Internet, rather than to more specifically consider the role of code in relation to those technologies and wider society. This has led over the past fifteen years or so to a burgeoning set of studies focusing on what Castells (1996) has called the *network society*. The general thesis is that ICTs are transformative technologies that enable a shift from an industrial to a postindustrial society by altering the conditions through which social and economic relations take place. ICTs are reconfiguring the means by which capital is generated by allowing businesses to reorganize their operations advantageously, change working practices, reduce costs, increase productivity, and diversify into new products and markets (Castells 1996; Kitchin 1998). Here, capta generation, processing, and information exchange are key to developing knowledge and extracting value. Similarly, social relations are speeded up and altered through new forms of communication media such as e-mail, Web pages, virtual worlds, chatrooms, and mobile phones that allow experimentation with identity and novel social networks to be developed (Rheingold 1993; Turkle 1995; Wellman and Haythornthwaite 2002).

As analysts such as Foth (2008), Mitchell (1995), Graham and Marvin (1996, 2001), and Townsend (2003) detail, ICTs are also having material effects on how cities and regions are configured, built, and managed with the development of smart buildings, the networking of physical infrastructure, the use of traffic management and other information and control systems, and so on. This is what Batty (1997, 155) has termed the *computable city,* noting that "planners . . . are accustomed to using computers to advance our science and art but it would appear that the city itself is turning into a constellation of computers." Such a city is perhaps best illustrated by the proliferation of windowless, semisecret, and hermetically sealed control rooms, with their banks of screens showing software-generated real-time inscriptions of urban infrastructures and flows (figure 1.3).

Software studies is a fledgling field. Although work within this field predates the new millennium, the first notion of the field itself can be traced to Manovich (2000, 48), who argued that "to understand the logic of new media we need to turn to computer science. It is there that we may expect to find the new terms, categories and operations which characterize media which became programmable. From media studies, we move to something which can be called software studies; from media theory—to software theory." Complementing the work of computer scientists on the mechanics of software development and human computer interaction, and research on digital technologies more generally, social theorists, media critics, and artists have begun to study the social politics of software: how it is written and developed; how software does work in the world to produce new subjects, practices, mobilities, transactions, and interactions; the nature of the software industry; and the social, economic, political, and cultural consequences of code on different domains, such as business, health, education, and entertainment. Manovich (2008, 6) asserts, "I think that software studies has to investigate both the role of software in forming contemporary culture, and cultural, social, and economic forces that are shaping development of software itself." In conjunction, Fuller (2008, 2) argues that the field "proposes that software can be seen as an object of study and an area of practice for the kinds of thinking and areas of work that have not historically 'owned' software, or indeed often had much of use to say about it."

The difference between software studies and those more broadly studying the digital technologies they enable could be characterized as the difference between studying the underlying epidemiology of ill health and the effects of ill health on the world. While one can say a great deal about the relationship between health and society by studying broadly how ill health affects social relations, one can gain further insight by considering the specifics of different diseases, their etiology (causes, origins, evolution, and implications), and how these manifest themselves in shaping social relations.

Software studies focuses on the etiology of code and how code makes digital technologies what they are and shapes what they do. It seeks to open the black box of processors and arcane algorithms to understand how software—its lines and routines of code—does work in the world by instructing various technologies how to act. Important formative works include Galloway's *Protocol* (2004); Fuller's *Behind the Blip* (2003), *Media Ecologies* (2005), and *Software Studies: A Lexicon* (2008); Lessig's *Code and Other Laws of Cyberspace* (1999); Manovich's *The Language of New Media* (2000) and *Software Takes Command* (2008); Hayles's *My Mother Was a Computer* (2005); and Mackenzie's *Cutting Code* (2006).

These studies demonstrate that software is a social-material production with a profound influence on everyday life. All too often, however, they focus on the role of software in social formation, organization, and regulation, as if people and things exist in time only, with space a mere neutral backdrop. What this produces is historically nuanced but largely aspatial accounts of the relationship of software, technology, and society. As geographers and others argue, however, people and things do not operate independent of space. Space is not simply a container in which things happen; rather, spaces are subtly evolving layers of context and practices that fold together people and things and actively shape social relations. Software and the work it does are the products of people and things in time and space, and it has consequences for people and things in time and space. Software is thus bound up in, and contributes to, complex discursive and material practices, relating to both living and nonliving, which work across geographic scales and times to produce complex spatialities. From this perspective, society, space, and time are co-constitutive—processes that are at once social, spatial, and temporal in nature and produce diverse spatialities. Software matters because it alters the conditions through which society, space, and time, and thus spatiality, are produced.

Our principal argument, then, is that an analysis of software requires a thoroughly spatial approach. To date, however, geographers and spatial theorists, like other social scientists, have tended to concentrate their analysis on the technologies that software enables and their effects in the world. This work has examined the effects of ICTs on time-space convergence (acceleration in the time taken to travel or communicate between places) and distanciation (control from a distance); the spatial economics of business and patterns of capital investment and innovations across spatial scales; the ways in which cities and regions are being reconfigured and restructured; and notions

Figure 1.3
Control rooms monitoring the city through code. (*a*) Electricity supply (*Source*: courtesy of Independent Electricity System Operator, Ontario, www.ieso.ca). (*b*) Road traffic (*Source*: courtesy of Midland Expressway Ltd., www.m6toll.co.uk). (*c*) Video surveillance and security for a shopping center (*Source*: courtesy of Arndale, www.manchesterarndale.com). (*d*) Water resources (*Source*: courtesy of Barco, www.barco.com).

Figure 1.3
(continued)

of place, identity, and spatially grounded identities (see Daniels et al. 2006; Dodge and Kitchin 2000; Graham and Marvin 2001; Wheeler, Aoyama, and Warf 2000; Wilson and Corey 2000; Zook 2005). Although there is much to learn from spatial accounts of the nature and effects of ICTs on various sociospatial domains and at different scales, it is imperative, we argue, for spatial theorists to think more specifically about how software underpins the nature of ICT and shapes its functioning and effects, and more broadly about the work software does in the world through the growing array of technologies used in everyday situations.

In this book, we seek to detail and theorize the ways in which software creates new spatialities of everyday life and new modes of governance and creativity (which are themselves inherently spatial), and we provide a set of conceptual tools for analyzing its nature and consequences. In so doing, and outlined more fully in chapters 4 and 5, we develop a distinct understanding of spatiality that conceives the world as ontogenetic in formulation (that is, constantly in a state of becoming) and rethink software-based governance as a system of automated management. Our analysis does not stand alone; it seeks to complement and extend a small but significant line of work by geographers and allied scholars on the task of describing and explaining the geographies of software (Adey 2004; Budd and Adey 2009; Crang and Graham 2007; Graham 2005; Mitchell 2004; McCullough 2004; Thrift and French 2002; Zook and Graham 2007).

Software, we argue, alternatively modulates how space comes into being through a process of transduction (the constant making anew of a domain in reiterative and transformative practices). Space from this perspective is an event or a doing—a set of unfolding practices that lack a secure ontology—rather than a container or a plane or a predetermined social production that is ontologically fixed. In turn, society consists of collectives that are hybrid assemblages of humans and many kinds of nonhumans (Latour 1993), wherein the relationship between people, material technology, time, and space is contingent, relational, productive, and dynamic. Taking the ideas of transduction and automated management together, our central argument is that the spatialities and governance of everyday life unfold in diverse ways through the mutual constitution of software and sociospatial practices. The nature of this mutual constitution is captured in our concept of code/space.

What is Code/Space?

Code/space occurs when software and the spatiality of everyday life become mutually constituted, that is, produced through one another. Here, spatiality is the product of code, and the code exists primarily in order to produce a particular spatiality. In other words, a dyadic relationship exists between code and spatiality. For example, a check-in area at an airport can be described as a code/space. The spatiality of the check-in area is dependent on software. If the software crashes, the area reverts from a space in which to check in to a fairly chaotic waiting room. There is no other way of checking a person onto a flight because manual procedures have been phased out due to security concerns, so the production of space is dependent on code. Another example is a supermarket checkout. All supermarkets and large stores rely on computerized cash registers to process purchases. If the computer or the information system behind it crashes, shoppers cannot purchase goods, and in a functional sense, the space effectively ceases to be a supermarket instead becoming a temporary warehouse until such time as the code becomes (re)activated. The facilities to process payments manually have been discontinued, staff are not trained to process goods manually (they no longer rote-learn the price of goods), and prices are not usually printed on items. In other words, the sociospatial production of the supermarket is functionally dependent on code.

People regularly coproduce code/spaces, even if they are not always aware they are doing so, and as we demonstrate throughout this book, they are increasingly common in a range of everyday contexts. Any space that is dependent on software-driven technologies to function as intended constitutes a code/space: workplaces dependent on office applications such as word processing, spreadsheets, shared calendars, information systems, networked printers, e-mail, and intranets; aspects of the urban environment reliant on building and infrastructural management systems; many forms of transport, including nearly all aspects of air travel and substantial portions of road and rail travel; and large components of the communications, media, finance, and entertainment industries. Many of the rooms that people live in; the offices, shops, and factories they work in; and the vehicles they travel in are code/spaces. It is little wonder that many commentators are speculating that most people in Western society are entering an age of "everyware" (Greenfield 2006, see also chapter 10).

Given that many of these code/spaces are the product of coded infrastructure, their production is stretched out across extended network architectures, making them simultaneously local and global, grounded by spatiality in certain locations, but accessible from anywhere across the network, and linked together into chains that stretch across space and time to connect start and end nodes into complex webs of interactions and transactions. Any space that has the latent capacity to be transduced by code constitutes a code/space at the moment of that transduction. So, for example, spaces that have wireless access to computation and communication are transduced by a mobile device accessing that network; for example, the laptop computer accessing a wireless network transduces the café, the train station, the park bench, and so on into a work space for that person. Code/space is thus both territorialized (in the case of a supermarket) and deterritorialized (in the case of mobile transductions). The transduction of code/spaces then often lacks singular, easily identifiable points of control or measurable extents, and they have a complexity much greater than the sum of their parts.

Of course, not all social interactions with software transduce code/spaces. Although much spatiality is dependent on software, software merely augments its transduction in other cases. We term such cases *coded spaces*—spaces where software makes a difference to the transduction of spatiality but the relationship between code and space is not mutually constituted. For example, a presentation to an audience using Power-Point slides might be considered a coded space. The digital projection of the slides makes a difference to the spatiality of the lecture theater, influencing the performance of the speaker and the ability of the audience to understand the talk. However, if the computer crashes, the speaker can still deliver the rest of the lecture, but perhaps not as efficiently or effectively as when the software worked.

In other words, the distinction between coded space and code/space is not a matter of the amount of code (in terms of the number of lines of code or the density of software systems). Rather a code/space is dependent on the dyadic relationship between code and space. This relationship is so all embracing that if half of the dyad is put out of action, the intended code/space is not produced: the check-in area at the airport does not facilitate travel; the store does not operate as a store. Here, "software quite literally conditions . . . existence" (Thrift and French 2002, 312). In coded space, software matters to the production and functioning of a space, but if the code fails, the space continues to function as intended, although not necessarily as efficiently or cost efficiently, or safely. Here, the role of code is often one of augmentation, facilitation, monitoring, and so on rather than control and regulation.

As we detail in depth in chapter 4, it is important to note that the relationship between software and space is neither deterministic (that is, code determines in absolute, nonnegotiable means the production of space and the sociospatial interactions that occur within them) nor universal (that such determinations occur in all such spaces and at all times in a simple cause-and-effect manner). Rather, how code/space emerges through practice is contingent, relational, and context dependent. Code/space unfolds in multifarious and imperfect ways, embodied through the performance and often unpredictable interactions of the people within the space (between people and between people and code). Code/space is thus inconsistently transduced; it is never manufactured and experienced in the same way.

Discursive Regimes Underpinning Code/Space

The adoption of software and digital technologies, and the systems, networks, and ways of doing they underpin, have been complemented by a broad set of discursive regimes that have sought to justify their development and naturalize their use. For Foucault (1977), a discursive regime is a set of interlocking discourses that sustain and reproduce, through processes of definition and exclusion, intelligibility and legitimacy, a particular set of sociospatial conditions. Such a regime provides the rationale for how sociospatial relations are predominantly produced, legitimating the use of discursive and material practices that shape their production.

As we discuss in chapter 5 and illustrate in subsequent chapters on travel, home, and consumption, the development and employment of different types of software and digital technologies are underpinned by their own particular, distinctive discursive regime. That said, they usually consist of an amalgam of a number of common discourses: safety, security, efficiency, antifraud, empowerment, productivity, reliability, flexibility, economic rationality, and competitive advantage. In other words, they argue that the deployment of software will improve the safety of individuals and society more broadly; make society and travel more secure; make government or business more efficient; make the fight against crime more effective; empower people to be more creative and innovative; and so on. These discourses are often promoted by government in tandem with business, driven by the interests of capitalism and, increasingly, the agenda of neoliberalism focused on the delivery of social services for profit within a target-driven culture.

The constituent elements of a discursive regime work to promote and make commonsense their message, but also to condition and discipline. Their power is persuading people to their logic—to believe and act in relation to this logic. As Foucault (1977, 1978) noted, however, a discursive regime does not operate solely from the top downward, but through diffused microcircuits of power, the outcome of processes of regulation, self-regulation, and localized resistance. As such, people are not simply passive subjects, disciplined and interpellated in linear and unproblematic ways by discursive regimes. Rather, as with the technologies themselves, such discourses are open to rupture: subversion, denial, and transgression by flourishing software hacking communities, anticorporate web sites, online activist networks, legal challenges to security and surveillance, and campaigns concerning privacy and confidentiality, for example. In this sense, power is not captive, purely in the hands of an unseen elite, although the discursive regime operates—in conjunction with the operation of code/space—to try to (re)produce such a hegemonic order. As such, code/spaces and their discursive regimes work to reinforce and deepen their logic and reproduction, at the same time as others seek to undermine, resist, and transform their hegemonic status. Software opens up new spaces as much as it closes existing ones. Accordingly, Amin and Thrift (2002, 128) argue that because "the networks of control that snake their way through cities are necessarily oligoptic, not panoptic: they do not fit together. They will produce various spaces and times, but they cannot fill out the whole space of the city—in part because they cannot reach everywhere, in part because they therefore cannot know all spaces and times, and in part because many new spaces and times remain to be invented."

Interestingly, given the increasing power and role of software, resistance to digital technologies has been remarkably mute despite widespread cynicism over the perceived negative effects of computerization. Thrift and French (2002, 313) note, "Even though software has infused into the very fabric of everyday life—just like the automobile—it brings no such level of questioning in its wake." There seem to be a number of reasons for this: the majority of people have been persuaded to its utility and how it is made rational and natural by discursive regimes; people are empowered and recognize the benefits of software technologies to their everyday lives; people see the changes that are occurring as simply an extension of previous systems to which they are already conditioned; how software is incrementally employed is seen as an inherent aspect of how things are now done and are therefore unchallengeable; the employment of software is seen as largely benign and routine rather than threatening and invasive; and people are worried by the consequences of protest (e.g., denial of services or mistreatment) and so refrain from doing so. Whatever the reason, there has been little scrutiny of the extent to which software has become embedded into everyday life or of the discourses that underpin, and subtly and explicitly promote, their adoption.

The Book

Code/Space is principally a book about the relationship of software, space, and society. Its main focus concerns how software, in its many forms, enables the production of coded objects, infrastructures, processes, and assemblages that do work in the world and produce the code/spaces and coded spaces that increasingly constitute the spatialities of everyday life. The goal "is not therefore to stage some revelation of a supposed hidden truth of software, to unmask its esoteric reality, but to see what it is and what it can be coupled with: a rich seam of paradoxical conjunctions in which the speed and rationality of computation meets its ostensible outside" (Piet Zwart Institute 2006).

In the following chapter, we discuss the nature of software and how it is both a product of the world and a producer of the world. In part II, we theorize how and why software makes a difference to society, providing a set of conceptual ideas and tools to think through how code transforms the nature of objects and infrastructures, transduces space, transforms modes of governmentality and governance, and engenders new forms of creativity and empowerment. In part III, we then employ these concepts to analyze the diverse ways in which the employment of software shapes the spatialities of everyday life, focusing on aspects of travel, home, and consumption. In each of these domains, social activities are now regularly transduced as code/spaces. In part IV, we examine likely future code/spaces and the drive toward everyware, explore the ethical dilemmas of such potentialities, and think about how code/spaces should be researched as the field of software studies develops. Our conclusions offer a provisional manifesto for critical scholarship into code—a new kind of social science focused on explaining the social, economic, and spatial contours of software. The glossary provides succinct definitions of key terms, especially technical terms and neologisms that may not be familiar to some readers.

Software matters in ways that extend well beyond simple functional or instrumental utility. *Code/Space* explains and demonstrates why it matters.

2 The Nature of Software

Code, the language of our time.
Code = Law
Code = Art
Code = Life
—Gerfried Stocker and Christine Schöpf

[Software] is philosophical in the way it represents the world, in the way it creates and manipulates models of reality, of people, of action. Every piece of software reflects an uncountable number of philosophical commitments and perspectives without which it could never be created.
—Paul Dourish

The art of creating software continues to be a dark mystery, even to the experts. Never in history have we depended so completely on a product that so few know how to make well.
—Scott Rosenberg

In this chapter, we explore the variegated nature of software. In particular, we argue that a comprehension of software must appreciate two aspects of code; first, that code is a product of the world and second, that code does work in the world. Software as both product and process, we argue, needs to be understood within a framework that recognizes the contingent, relational, and situated nature of its development and use. Software does not arise from nowhere; code emerges as the product of many minds working within diverse contexts. As Mackenzie (2003, 3) notes, software is created through "complex interactions involving the commodity production, organizational life, technoscientific knowledges and enterprises, the organization of work, manifold identities and geo-political-technological zones of contact." Just as software comes from diverse threads, software's effect in the world is not deterministic or universal. Rather, software as an actant, like people as actors, functions within diversely produced social, cultural, economic, and political contexts. The effects of software unfold in multiple ways in many milieus. Often, this unfolding action is messy, imperfect, and always near the edge of breakdown (as is readily apparent when maintaining a working software setup on desktop PC). Surrounding and coalescing around software are discursive and material assemblages of knowledge (flow diagrams, Gantt charts, experience, manuals, magazines, mailing lists, blogs and forums, scribbled sticky notes), forms of governmentalities (capta standards, file formats, interfaces, conventional statutes, protocols, intellectual property regimes such as copyrights, trademarks, patents), practices (ways of doing, coding cultures, hacker ethos, norms of sharing and stealing code, user upgrading, and patching), subjectivities (relating to coders, sellers, marketers, users), materialities (computer hardware, disks, CDs, desks, offices), organizations (corporations, consultants, manufacturers, retailers, government agencies, universities and conferences, clubs and societies) and the wider marketplace (for code and coders).

Code lacks materiality in itself. It exists in the way that speech or music exist. All three have diverse effects and can be represented and recorded to a media (for example, written as text on paper). Yet software when merely written as lines of code loses its essential essence—its executability. Layers of software are executed on various forms of hardware—CPUs, motherboards, disk drives, network interfaces, graphics and sound cards, display screens, scanners and other devices, network infrastructures, printers and other peripherals, and so on—using various algorithms, languages, capta rules, and communication protocols, thus enabling them to coalesce and function in diverse ways in conjunction with people and things by interfacing the virtual (the world as 0s and 1s) with the material. At the heart of this assemblage is code—the executable pattern of instructions.

Code

What software does and how it performs, circulates, changes and solidifies cannot be understood apart from its constitutions through and through as code. . . . Code cuts across every aspect of what software is and what software does.

—Adrian Mackenzie

Code at its most simplistic definition is a set of unambiguous instructions for the processing of elements of capta in computer memory. Computer code (henceforth code) is essential for the operation of any object or system that utilizes microprocessors. It is constructed through programming—the art and science of putting together algorithms and read/write instructions that process capta (whether that is variables held at specific addresses in memory space, human keystrokes or mouse movements, disk files, or network fields) and output an appropriate response (a series of letters appearing on a screen, the field of view changing in a game, a credit card being verified, an airplane ticket being booked, or MP3 files being transferred from a compact disk, decoded, and played). Coded instructions transduce input; that is, the code changes the input from one state to another, and as a consequence the code performs work. As Berry (2008) details, code "does *something* to *something* . . . it performs functions and processing" (emphasis in the original). The skill of a programmer is to construct a set of coded instructions that a microprocessor can unambiguously interpret and perform in ongoing flows of operations.

There is a large variation in how programming is discursively produced from assembly languages (producing machine code) to scripting and procedural languages (producing source code) that has to be compiled (into executable code that the machine can understand). As a consequence, the nature of programming varies depending on how structured a language is, the scope and scale of action available to the programmer, and the extent to which the language is talking directly (instructing) to the hardware rather than through an interpreter or compiler. All programming languages have formal rules of syntax, grammar, punctuation, and structure. In the case of scripting and procedural languages, the coding is less abstract than that written in assembly languages, and has characteristics more akin to natural languages. In this case, programmers use formalized syntax, usually based around natural language words and abbreviations, along with symbols and punctuation, to construct structured programs made up of statements, loops, and conditional operations (Berry 2004). For example, below is a piece of code that calculates whether a point is inside a polygon (a common evaluative procedure in a geographic information system).

```
procedure point_in_polygon;
var
    i, j : integer;
    slope, inter, yi : real;
begin
    j := 1;
    for i := 2 to npts do begin
        if (data [i].x <> data [i + 1].x) then
            if ( ( (data [i].x - data [1].x) ) * ( (data [1].x - data [i
+ 1].x) ) >= 0)
                then
                    if ( (data [i + 1].x <> data [1].x) or (data [i].x >= data
[1].x) )
                        then
                        begin
                            slope := (data [i + 1].y - data [i].y) / (data [i +
1].x - data [i].x);
                            inter := data [i].y - slope * data [i].x;
                            yi := Inter + slope * data [1].x;
```

```
            if (yi > data [1].y) then
                j := j * ( - 1)
        end;
    end;
    if j = - 1 then
        writeln ('point in polygon')
    else
        writeln ('point not in polygon');
end;
```

As Brown (2006) notes, programming languages "do *double duty* in that they work as an understandable notation for humans, but also as a mechanically executable representation suitable for computers. . . . Computer code *has to be* automatically translatable to a form which can be executed by a machine . . . [they] thus sit in an unusual and interesting place—designed for human reading and use, but bound by what is computationally possible" (emphasis in the original). And just as there are different languages, there are different kinds of programming. Programming extends from the initial production of code, to refactoring (rewriting a piece of code to make it briefer and clearer without changing what it does), to editing and updating (tweaking what the code does), to integrating (taking a piece of code that works by itself and connecting it to other code), testing, and debugging, to wholesale rewriting. The skill to model complex problems in code that is effective, efficient, and above all, elegant, is seen as a marker of genuine programming craft. Some have argued that this acumen is akin to being artistically gifted, such as composing beautiful verse or sculpting apollonian forms: "The programmer, like the poet, works only slightly removed from pure thought-stuff. He builds his castles in the air, from air, creating by exertion of the imagination" (Brooks 1995, 7). Crafting code can itself be a deeply creative act (see chapter 6), although one should be wary of glorifying what is for many programmers a daily grind of just getting things written and working.

Regardless of the nature of programming, the code created is the manifestation of a system of thought—an expression of how the world can be captured, represented, processed, and modeled computationally with the outcome subsequently doing work in the world. Programming then fundamentally seeks to capture and enact knowledge about the world—practices, ideas, measurements, locations, equations, and images—in order to augment, mediate, and regulate people's lives. Software has, at a fundamental level, an ontological power, it is able to realize whole systems of thought (algorithms and capta) with respect to specific domains. For example, consider the influence of formalizing and coding how money is represented and transacted and thus how the banking system is organized and works. Many other examples come to mind, such as how a game should be played, how a car operates and should be driven, how a document is to be written, or how a presentation is to be given (see Fuller's [2003] analysis of the ontological capacity of Microsoft Word and Tufte's [2003] critique of Microsoft PowerPoint) and so on. It does this by formalizing a system into a set of interlinked operations through the creation of itineraries expressed as algorithms, "recipes or sets of steps expressed in flowcharts, code or pseudocode" (Mackenzie 2006, 43). The source code above is an example of a coded instruction expressed as an algorithm to solve a specific problem (calculating whether a point is inside a polygon).

Software thus abstracts the world into defined, stable ontologies of capta and sequences of commands that define relations between capta and details how that capta should be processed. The various structures in which capta is stored ("lists, tuples, queues, sequences, dictionaries, hashtables") can then be worked upon by various algorithms designed to sort, search, swap, increment, group, and match (Mackenzie 2006, 6). Agency is held in these simple algorithms in the sense that they determine, for themselves, what operations do and do not occur. Code performs a set of operations on capta to enact an event, an output of some kind (a value is displayed on screen, the antilock brakes are applied following the driver pressing the pedal, a selected song is played through speakers, writing is saved into a word processor document). Even in everyday software applications, such as a word processor or web browsers, code enacts millions of algorithmic operations to derive an outcome at a scale of operation so small and fast as to be beyond direct human sensing (see figure 2.1). Indeed, we only sense the nature of these processes when the response of a software application slows to such an extent it makes us wait. (Research in human-computer interactions, HCI, demonstrates that the necessary response time for interactive use of software to be about 0.1 sec. for people to feel they are in charge. Delays of 1 sec. in response are noticeable but tolerable; and longer delays will lead to user frustration and distraction from a task; Miller 1968).

As Mackenzie (2006, 43) notes "algorithms carry, fold, frame and redistribute actions into different environments." Fuller (2003, 19) thus argues that software can be understood as "a form of digital subjectivity—that software constructs sensoriums, that each piece of software constructs ways of seeing, knowing, and doing in the world that at once contain a model of that part of the world it ostensibly pertains to and that also shape it every time it is used." This digital subjectivity is "an ensemble of pre-formatted, automated, contingent, and 'live' action, schemas, and decisions performed by software, languages and designers. . . . [It] is also productive of further sequences of seeing, knowing and doing" (Fuller 2003, 54). In this sense, "code is saturated with, and indivisible from social phenomena," in the sense that how we come to know the world is always social (Rooksby and Martin 2006, 1).

This relationship between code algorithms, capta structures, and the world is well illustrated with respect to weather prediction and global climate change modeling (see Washington, Buja, and Craig 2009 for an overview). Gramelsberger (2006) details how scientific theories about weather systems and empirical observations from across

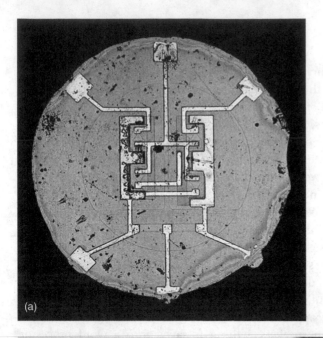

Figure 2.1
Computation microspaces where software works and capta dwells. (*a*) Silicon logic gate (*Source*: www.technologyreview.com/article/21886/). (*b*) Memory cards (*Source*: http://images.suite101 .com/538579_com_ram.jpg). (*c*) Circuit board (*Source*: www.technologyreview.com/article/21886/). (*d*) Hard drive (*Source*: http://commons.wikimedia.org/wiki/File:Hard_disk.jpg).

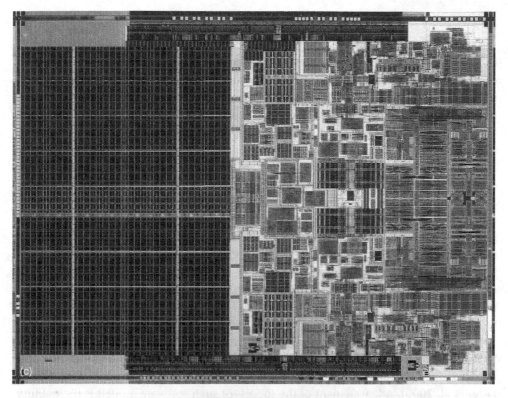

(c)

(d)

Figure 2.1
(continued)

the world are translated into a formal model, which is then translated into mathematical formulae, which is then translated into executable code, which evokes a kind of imagined narrative about future climates. Here, knowledge about the world is translated and formalized into capta structures and algorithms that are then converted into sets of computational instructions that when applied to climate measurements express a particular story. Gramelsberger expresses this as "Theory = Mathematics = Code = Story." Our understanding of weather forecasting and climate models are almost entirely driven by these computational models, which have been refined over time in a recursive fashion in response to how these models have performed, and which are used to theorize, simulate and predict weather patterns (indeed, meteorologists and geophysists are major users of supercomputers, TOP500 2009). In turn, the models underpin policy arguments concerning climate change and have real effects concerning individual and institutional responses to measured and predicted change. The models are coded theory and they create an experimental system for performing theory (Gramelsberger 2006); or, put another way, the models analyze the world and the world responds to the models.

Such simulation models of complex physical systems are now common in the "hard" sciences such as earth sciences, physics, astronomy, and bioinformatics, and may become more significant in social sciences in the coming years (Lane et al. 2006; Lazer et al. 2009). A key element of the success of such software models is their ability to generate (spatial) capta that can be visualized to create compelling inscriptions; figure 2.2 shows an example from climate change modeling. For businesses managing complex distributed operations, with multiple risks and dynamic flows, software models that can anticipate problems before they occur are also becoming important (see Budd and Adey 2009 for a discussion of software models that keep air travel moving). In the realm of international finance, predictive software models of market trading conditions are responsible for millions of automatic transactions worth billions of dollars and the decisions that algorithms autonomously undertake affect the fluctuation in prices (see D. MacKenzie's 2006 work on how complex mathematical equations in financial models translate into operative trading software models that then drive the markets that they purportedly represent). Indeed, the ease with which software models enabled mortgage risks to be manipulated has been blamed for contributing to the recent "credit crunch" (Osinski 2009).

David Berry (2008) suggests that the "properties of code can be understood as operating according to a grammar reflected in its materialisation and operation," detailing seven ideal types through which code is manifested. The *digital data structure* is a static form of data representation, wherein data are held digitally as binary 0s and 1s. The *digital stream* is the flow of digital data structures through a program and across media (for example, from CD to hard disk or across a network). *Delegated code* is human-readable source code that is editable. *Commentary code* is the textual area in

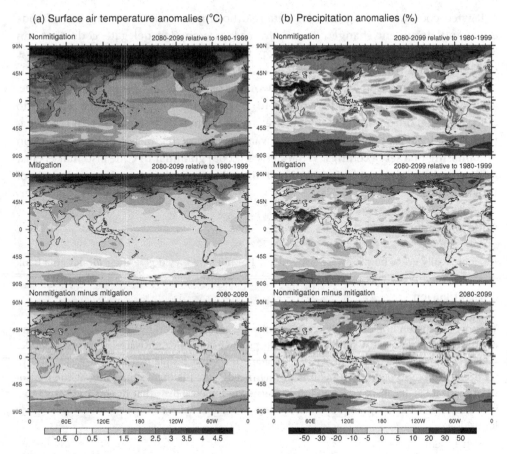

Figure 2.2

Comparative mapping of predictions of (*a*) surface temperature and (*b*) precipitation at the end of the twenty-first century from global climate change model made possible by software. (*Source*: Washington et al. 2009, 3.)

delegated code where programmers detail authorship, describe what a piece of code does, and document changes. *Prescriptive code* is compiled delegate code that can be read and processed by microprocessors to do work on the digital data structure. *Code objects* are the everyday objects that are represented within the delegate code and which the prescriptive code seeks to work on or for (e.g., a car, a washing machine, a PDA). *Critical code* is code written to reverse engineer prescriptive code into delegate code, or to read/hack digital streams and digital data structures. In combination, these ideal types illustrate how software development consists of the production and phasing of a set of codings. What Berry's (2008) grammar of code also makes clear is that code is a product—it is brought into the world by the labor and skills of programmers.

Code as Product

If people really knew how software got written, I'm not sure they'd give their money to a bank or get on an airplane ever again
—Ellen Ullmann

We now depend on unfathomably complex software to run our world. Why, after a half century of study and practice, is it still so difficult to produce computer software on time and under budget? To make it reliable and secure? To shape it so that people can learn it easily, and to render it flexible so people can bend it to their needs? . . . [I]s there something at the root of what software is, its abstractness and intricateness and malleability, that dooms its makers to a world of intractable delays and ineradicable bugs—some instability or fickleness that will always let us down?
—Scott Rosenberg

In reference to the last quote above, Rosenberg (2007) seeks to answer his questions through an in-depth ethnographic study undertaken over a three-year period of one company's attempt to produce a new application. What his study highlights is that producing software is a complex and contingent process. It has these qualities because code is produced by people who vary in their abilities and worldviews and are situated in social, political, and economic contexts. While the activity of programming is often undertaken individually—a single person sitting in front of a computer writing the code—this occurs within a collaborative framework, with individuals performing as part of a team working toward a larger, common goal. Team members interact when needed to tackle problems, find solutions, react to feedback, discuss progress, and define next steps and roles. Often several teams will work on different aspects of the same program that are stitched together later. These teams produce programs often consisting of thousands of routines, interlinked in complex ways, that work together to undertake particular functions. Teams may well be using different coding languages or drawing on existing codebases (either within a company from previous projects or open source), have different visions about what they are trying to achieve, and have different skill levels to tackle the job at hand. Indeed, it is fair to say that individual programmers diverge in coding abilities, experience, motivation, and productivity, which leads to a varying quality and quantity of work. The result is often a project so complex that no single programmer can know everything about it, particularly at a fine scale. Indeed, the sheer scale of labor expended to create code can be immense. Starting from humble origins in the late 1940s, today's software applications often consist of millions of lines of code. For example, it is estimated that the first version of Microsoft Word, released in 1983, consisted of around 27,000 lines of code but had grown to about 2 million by 1995 as more functions and tools were added (Nathan Myhrvold cited in Brand 1995). Operating systems, the guts of mass market computing, consist of enormous sets of code (table 2.1), which in part is responsible for their unreliability and also their susceptibility to malicious hacking and viruses.

Even if a programmer is working on his or her own, the program is implicitly the result of a collective endeavor—the programmer uses a formalized coding language, proprietary coding packages (and their inherent facilities and defaults), and employs established disciplinary regimes of programming—ways of knowing and doing regarding coding practices and styles, annotation, elegance, robustness, extendibility, and so on (as formalized through manuals, instruction, conventions, peer evaluation, and industry standards). Coding then is always a collaborative manufacture with code being a social object among programmers (Martin and Rooksby 2006). Knowledge of the code and its history (its iterations, its idiosyncrasies, its weaknesses, and its inconsistencies) is shared and distributed among the group, although it is possible for other coders to work through, understand, and modify the code by reading and playing with it (Martin and Rooksby 2006).

Table 2.1

Growth in size of Microsoft operating system that is used by a large proportion of the world's PCs.

Year	Operating system	SLOC (Million) [source lines of code]
1993	Windows NT 3.1	4–5
1994	Windows NT 3.5	7–8
1996	Windows NT 4.0	11–12
2000	Windows 2000	More than 29
2001	Windows XP	40
2003	Windows Server 2003	50

Source: www.knowing.net

Ullman's (1997, 14–15) self-ethnography, *Close to the Machine*, illustrates this collective manufacture in detail, highlighting how groups of programmers work together in various (dys)functional ways to produce code. Sometimes this is as individuals working mostly alone but within teams, and sometimes as a group. For example, in relation to the latter, she writes:

We have entered the code zone. Here thought is telegraphic and exquisitely precise. I feel no need to slow myself down. On the contrary, the faster the better. Joel runs off a stream of detail, and halfway through the sentence, Mark, the database programmer, completes the thought. I mention a screen element, and Danny, who programs the desktop software, thinks of two elements I've forgotten. Mark will later say all bugs are Danny's fault, but, for now, they work together like cheerful little parallel-processing machines, breaking the problem into pieces that they attack simultaneously.

"Should we modify the call to AddUser—"
"—to check for UserType—"
"Or should we add a new procedure call—"
"—something like ModifyPermissions."

"But won't that add a new set of data elements that repeat—"

Programming as a creative endeavor means there is inherent unpredictability in its production. There is no single solution to most coding problems and the style of the solution is often seen as important. Many programmers are said to exhibit a hacker ethic, a desire to craft inventive, elegant solutions, deploying algorithms and capta structures that one might view as having aspect beauty. The accounts of Ullman and Rosenberg also reveal the negotiated and contingent processes through which code unfolds; how programming labor is performative in nature (Mackenzie 2006). Code is developed through collective cycles of editing, compiling, and testing, undertaken within diverse, historically-framed, social contexts. It is citational, we would argue, consisting of embedded, embodied, and discursive practices. This type of practice "that echoes prior actions, and accumulates the force of authority through the repetition or citation of a prior and authorative set of practices . . . [and] it draws on and covers over the constitutive conventions by which it is mobilized" (Butler 1990, 51). Software products are inherently partial solutions and imperfect; their code is mutable and contingent—scripted, rewritten, updated, patched, refined; "code . . . slips into tangles of competing idioms, practices, techniques and patterns of circulation . . . there is no 'program' as such, only programmings or codings" (Mackenzie 2006, 5).

Given its citational qualities, once a design approach and programming language are chosen and a certain amount of progress made, a contingent pathway is created that is difficult to diverge from to any great degree without going back to the beginning and starting again. This is especially true because software consists of layers of abstraction. Significantly altering one layer has knock-on consequences for all component layers. And yet as Rosenberg (2007) notes, the choice of programming language often comes down to the arbitrary or ineffable (matter of taste or gut sense) or simply previous experience, rather than being a rational choice informed by reflection and research. (There are quasi tribal loyalties exhibited by some programmers to their favored languages and a dismissal of those who write in so-called inferior ones.) As such, arbitrary choices and contingent progress push projects more or less in a particular direction that then limit future decisions and outcomes.

Adopting the most appropriate approach given the present computational landscape is not straightforward. As Mackenzie (2006) notes, because of ongoing innovations in software languages, code libraries, and development environments, programmers are always trying to keep abreast of the latest developments. For example, Ullman (1997, 100–101) details that in a twenty-year period she had taught herself, "six higher-level programming languages, three assemblers, two data-retrieval languages, eight job-processing languages, seventeen scripting languages, ten types of macro, two object-definition languages, sixty eight program-library interfaces, five varieties of networks, and eight operating environments." This is an enormous sum of learning and adaptation, yet paradoxically, as Joel Spolsky (cited in Rosenberg 2007, 274) states, "most programmers don't read much about their discipline. That leaves them trapped in infinite loops of self-ignorance." Similarly, Ullman (1997, 110) argues that "the corollary of constant change is ignorance. This is not often talked about: we computer experts barely know what we are doing. We're good at fussing and figuring out. We function in a sea of unknowns. . . . Over the years, the horrifying knowledge of ignorant expertise became normal, a kind of background level of anxiety." In other words, programming takes place in an environment that it is changing so quickly that it is often difficult to keep up with new developments, and with such diversity, programmers can differ markedly in their ability to write good code and in how they think a system should be coded. Ignorance is often compounded because programmers can adopt a silo mentality and start a project afresh, producing new code rather than using the vast amounts of code that has already been produced (for example, Sourceforge is an open-source warehouse of code for over 230,000 projects as of February 2009; www.sourceforge.net). In part this is due to the hacker ethos of believing that it is possible and desirable to start afresh in order to produce a new and better solution to a given problem.

The coding itself can be a complex and difficult task, especially when trying to address new problems for which solutions have not been established. As a result, there are various competing schools of thought with regard to how software development should take place, much of it focusing on project management rather than the practice of writing code. For example, the structured programming approach aims to limit the creation of spaghetti code by composing the program of subunits with single exit and entry points. Disciplined project management focuses on advance planning and making sure that a clear and defined route from start to end is plotted before coding takes place. The capability maturity model seeks to move coding organizations up a ladder of management practices. Pattern models divide up projects into orderly and iterative sequences; while rapid application development relies on quick prototyping and shorter iterative phases to scope out ways forward. Another approach, agile software development, that also prioritizes speed, uses experimentation and innovation to find the best ways forward and to be responsive to change (Rosenberg 2007).

However, even when a particular approach has been adopted, the challenges of creating new code and entwining different elements and algorithms together can produce problems that are intellectually demanding and difficult to solve. Abstracting the world and working on and communicating those abstractions (from programmer to machine, programmer to programmer, and program to user) in the desired way can be vexing tasks, often without correct solutions. Consequently, software is inherently partial and provisional, and often seen to be buggy—containing code that does not work in all cases, or only works periodically, or stops working if new code is added or modified. Rosenberg (2007) describes several of what his participants called "black holes"—a coding problem of "indeterminate and perhaps unknowable dimensions" that could take weeks or months to address and sometimes led to whole areas of an intended application to be abandoned. So-called snakes are a significant class of black holes where there is no consensus within a team about how they could and should be tackled, producing internal conflict and disharmony among members that jeopardizes progress and sometimes entire projects. As Mackenzie (2006, 5) notes, code "is permeated by all the forms of contestation, feeling, identification, intensity, contextualization and decontextualizations, signification, power relations, imaginings and embodiments that compromise any cultural object." Indeed, the project Rosenberg (2007) tracked had several high profile programmers working for it, and yet their collective skills and knowledge were severely tested by the challenges they faced. At the time he completed his book, they still only had a limited, beta application that was missing many of its desired components.

Unlike other kinds of product development, adding additional coders to a project to try and resolve problems, somewhat paradoxically, rarely helps. Indeed, a well established maxim in programming—Brook's Law—states that "adding manpower to a late software project makes it later" (cited in Rosenberg 2007, 17); new workers absorb veterans' time, have to learn the complexities and history of the project, bring additional ideas that enhance the potential for further disagreement, and add confusion through a lack of familiarity with key issues. One solution has been to release software through a series of evolving versions and to periodically release updates and patches to fix problems discovered in an existing version. This has also led to software enjoying some unusual legal qualities, with its liabilities for failure being limited to a significant degree. In other words, purchasers willingly accept an imperfect product while abrogating the supplier from responsibility for any damage caused through its use. These imperfections in terms of bugs, glitches, and crashes are at once notorious and yet also largely accepted as a routine dimension of computation. The imperfections also provide instrumental evidence that software is difficult to produce (Charette 2005). These imperfections matter because as well as causing particular problems, they also facilitate new kinds of criminal activity, along with petty digital vandalism. Illegal hacking, software viruses, and network attacks have become an ever present threat in recent years. The scale of corrupted code and deliberate virus infections is hard to gauge with any reliability, but Markoff (2007) reports that some 11 percent of computers on the Internet are infected. Software to secure other software is now itself a significant business opportunity!

Bugs, black holes, and snakes in code have pragmatic implications and can lead to serious slippage in project delivery dates and often a redefinition of intended goals. Of course, slippage can also occur because the client alters the project specification. Such changes highlight that the production of code does not take place in a vacuum. It is embedded within workplace or hacker cultures, personal interactions and office politics, relationships with customers/users, and the wider political and cultural economy. Ullman (1997) and Rosenberg's (2007) ethnographies graphically reveal the different group dynamics within and between teams in a company, and how the development of code takes place in an environment that has frequent staff changes, downsizing and expansion, mergers and takeovers, reprioritization of policy and development, and investor confidence (also explored in Coupland's novels, *Microserfs* (1995) and *JPod* (2006) on the fictional lives of programmers and software designers). These negotiations and contestations between individuals and teams are set in the wider political economy of finance and capital investment, market conditions, political/ideological decisions, and also the role of governments and the military-industrial complex in promoting the knowledge society, innovation culture, and underwriting significant amounts of development and training. For example, the ideology underlying the production and distribution of software varies between projects, as a comparison in the ethos, discourses, and practices of propriety software (executable code sold under license; source code not distributed), free software (code is a collective good; source code distributed), and open-source software (code is property of an individual who has the right to control and develop it; source code distributed) demonstrate (Berry 2004).

Software then is not an immaterial, stable, and neutral product. Rather, it is a complex, multifaceted, mutable set of relations created through diverse sets of discursive, economic, and material practices. The result of all of this contingency is that software development has high failure rates—either projects are never completed, do

not do what they were intended to do, or they are excessively error prone or unreli-
able in operation (hence the wide prevalence of beta releases, patches, and updates).
A comparison of U.S. Federal Government software spending over a fifteen-year period
demonstrated no improvement in the reliability or effectiveness of code delivered, "In
1979, 47 percent of federal software was delivered but never used due to performance
problems, 29 percent was paid for but never delivered, 19 percent were used but
extensively reworked, 3 percent was used after changes, and only a miniscule 2 percent
was used as delivered. In 1995 in the same categories, the statistics were 46 percent,
29 percent, 20 percent, 3 percent and 2 percent" (Lillington 2008, 6). The Standish
Group surveyed 365 information technology managers and reported in 1995 that only
16 percent of their projects were successful (delivered on time and budget and to the
specification requested), 31 percent were canceled, and 53 percent were considered
"project challenged" (over budget, late, failed to deliver on specification). By 2004,
the figures were 29 percent successful, 18 percent canceled, and 53 percent "project
challenged" (Rosenberg 2007). In both cases, over two-thirds of projects failed to
deliver on their initial objectives.

Given those statistics, it is no surprise that the software landscape is littered with
high profile, massively expensive, failed projects and there is even literature detailing
these disasters (see, for example, Britcher 1999; Glass 1998; Yourdon 1997). Brief
examples illustrate this point. The U.S. Internal Revenue Service's overhaul of its
systems was canceled in 1995 after ten years at a cost of $2 billion. The U.S. Federal
Aviation Administration canceled a new air traffic control system in 1994 after 13
years and billions of dollars (at its peak the project was costing $1 million a day). In
1996, a $500 million European Space Agency rocket exploded 40 seconds after takeoff
because of a bug in the guidance system software (Rosenberg 2007). In 2004, UK
supermarket chain Sainsbury wrote off a store inventory system at a cost of $526
million (Lillington 2008). A study by the U.S. National Institute of Standards and
Technology published in 2002 details that software errors cost the U.S. economy about
$59.5 billion annually in 2001 (Rosenberg 2007). It should come as no surprise that
the failure of software systems is now routinely blamed for operating problems within
a government agency or company.

It seems then that workable software that is effective and usable is all too often the
exception rather than the rule. Even successful software has bugs and loopholes that
mean its use is always porous and open to rupture in some unanticipated way. Setting
and maintaining a home PC in working order, for example, takes continual digital
housework (see chapter 8). Code is contingent and unstable—constantly on the verge
of collapse as it deals with new data, scenarios, bugs, viruses, communication and
hardware platforms and configurations, and users intent on pushing it to its limits.
As a result, software is always open to new possibilities and gives rise to diverse
realities.

Code as Process

Software forges modalities of experience—sensoriums through which the world is made and known
—Matthew Fuller

Once software has been written and compiled, it is made to do work in the wider world; it not only represents the world but participates in it (Dourish 2001). Programs are run in order to read capta, process commands, and execute routines—to compile, synthesize, analyze, and execute. In common with earlier technological enhancement like mechanical tools or electrically-powered motors, software enjoys all the usual machine-over-man advantages in terms of speed of operation, repeatability, and accuracy of operation over extended durations, cost efficiencies, and ability to be replicated exactly in multiple places. Software thus quantitatively extends the processing capacity of electromechanical technologies, but importantly it also qualitatively differs in its capacity to handle complex scenarios (evaluating capta, judging options), taking variable actions, and having a degree of adaptability. Adaptability can be in terms of flexibility (making internal choices) but also degrees of plasticity (responding to external change). Software can also deal with feedback, or being able to adjust future conduct on the basis of past performance. In terms of adaptability, resistance to entropy, and response to feedback, it is clear that software truly makes the "universal machine," in Turing's famous phrase.

As Mackenzie (2006) notes, software is often regarded as possessing secondary agency—that is, its supports or extends the agency of others such as programmers, individual users, corporations, and governments; it enables the desires and designs of absent actors for the benefit of other parties. It does more than that though, in that software, like many other technologies, engenders direct effects in the world in ways never envisaged or expected by their creators and in ways beyond their control or intervention. Code also extends the agency of other machines, technical systems, and infrastructures. This is the case even if these effects are largely invisible from those affected, or where an effect is clear but not the executive role of software behind it. For example, code makes a difference to water supply infrastructure, being used to monitor demand quality and actively regulate flow rates to ensure acceptable pressure in the pipes. Turning the tap therefore indirectly but ineluctably engages with software, though the infrastructure appears dumb to the consumer who simply sees flowing water. In other cases, the elevator arrives, the car drives, the mail is delivered, the plane lands, the supermarket shelves are replenished, and so on. Software divulges and affords agency, opens up domains to new possibilities and determinations. In other words, in Latour's (1993) terms, *software is an actant in the world*; it possesses agency, explicitly shaping to varying degrees how people live their lives.

Drawing on Ullman's ethnographic work, Fuller (2003, 31) makes the case that code enacts its agency through the production of events—blips—some outcome or action in an assemblage that the software contributes to, "the interpretative and reductive operations carried out on lived processes." To use Ullman's (1997) example further, in the context of being paid, the transfer of money from employer to employee is a blip in the relation between a company's payroll application and a bank's current accounts' software system. Here, a blip is not a signifier of an event, it is part of the event; the electronic transfer of funds that is then concretely expressed on the employee's bank balance. Fuller (2003, 32) argues that "these blips, these events in software, these processes and regimes that data are subject to and manufactured by, provide flashpoints at which these interrelations, collaborations and conflicts [between various agencies and actors such as employer, bank, tax agency, employee, etc.] can be picked out and analyzed for their valences of power, for their manifold capacities of control and production, disturbance and invention." In other words, for Fuller, we can start to chart the various ways in which software makes a difference to everyday life by studying where these blips occur—how capta is worked upon and made to do work in the world in various ways; to make visible the "dynamics, structures, regimes, and drives of each little event . . . to look behind the blip" (2003, 32). Moreover, these blips are contextual and signifiers of other relations—for example, a person's bank balance is an instantiation of class relations—and they themselves can be worked upon and reinterpreted by code to invent a sequence of new blips (Fuller 2003). Of course, this is not always easy, especially as software is designed to run silently in the background; to be inscrutable; and its use and conventions to appear rational, logical, and commonsensical. It seeks to slide beneath the surface because designers aim for people to be interfacing with a task, not with a computer (see figure 2.3).

As Fuller notes, implicit in the notion of software as actant is power—the power to shape the world in some way. For us, this power needs to be understood as relational. Power is not held and wielded by software; rather, power arises out of interrelationships and interactions between code and the world. From this perspective, code is afforded power by a network of contingencies, but in and of itself does not possess power (Allen 2004). In this sense, Lessig's (1999) assertion that "code is law" is only partially correct. Code might well follow certain definable architectures, defaults, and parameters within the orbit of the code itself—how the 1s and 0s are parsed and processed—but their work in the world is not deterministic as we discuss at length in chapter 5. In other words, code is permitted to express certain forms of power (to dictate certain outcomes) through the channels, structures, networks, and institutions of societies and permissiveness of those on whom it seeks to work, in the same way that an individual does not hold and wield power but is afforded it by other people, communal norms, and social structures. Of course, it should be acknowledged that people are worked upon by expressions of power not of their

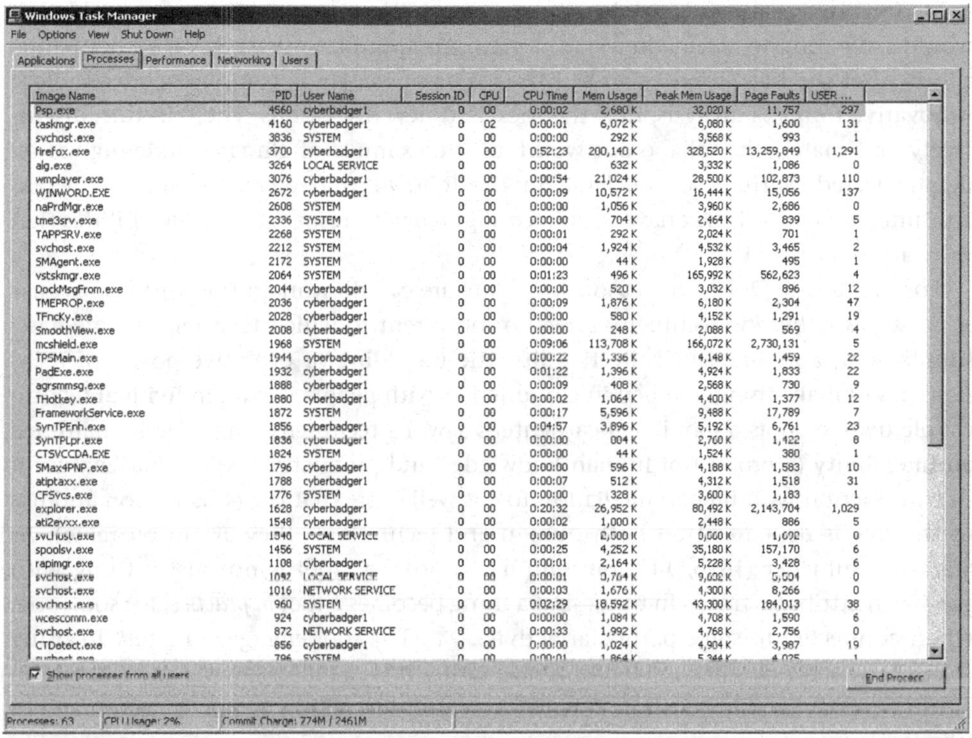

Image Name	PID	User Name	Session ID	CPU	CPU Time	Mem Usage	Peak Mem Usage	Page Faults	USER ...
Psp.exe	4560	cyberbadger1	0	00	0:00:02	2,680 K	32,020 K	11,757	297
taskmgr.exe	4160	cyberbadger1	0	02	0:00:01	6,072 K	6,080 K	1,600	131
svchost.exe	3836	SYSTEM	0	00	0:00:00	292 K	3,568 K	993	1
firefox.exe	3700	cyberbadger1	0	00	0:52:23	200,140 K	328,520 K	13,259,849	1,291
alg.exe	3264	LOCAL SERVICE	0	00	0:00:00	632 K	3,332 K	1,086	0
wmplayer.exe	3076	cyberbadger1	0	00	0:00:54	21,024 K	28,500 K	102,873	110
WINWORD.EXE	2672	cyberbadger1	0	00	0:00:09	10,572 K	16,444 K	15,056	137
naPrdMgr.exe	2608	SYSTEM	0	00	0:00:00	1,056 K	3,960 K	2,686	0
tme3srv.exe	2336	SYSTEM	0	00	0:00:00	704 K	2,464 K	839	5
TAPPSRV.exe	2268	SYSTEM	0	00	0:00:01	292 K	2,024 K	701	1
svchost.exe	2212	SYSTEM	0	00	0:00:04	1,924 K	4,532 K	3,465	2
SMAgent.exe	2172	SYSTEM	0	00	0:00:00	44 K	1,928 K	495	1
vstskmgr.exe	2064	SYSTEM	0	00	0:01:23	496 K	165,992 K	562,623	4
DockMsgFrom.exe	2044	cyberbadger1	0	00	0:00:00	520 K	3,032 K	896	12
TMEPROP.exe	2036	cyberbadger1	0	00	0:00:09	1,876 K	6,180 K	2,304	47
TFncKy.exe	2028	cyberbadger1	0	00	0:00:00	580 K	4,152 K	1,291	19
SmoothView.exe	2008	cyberbadger1	0	00	0:00:00	248 K	2,088 K	569	4
mcshield.exe	1968	SYSTEM	0	00	0:09:06	113,708 K	166,072 K	2,730,131	5
TPSMain.exe	1944	cyberbadger1	0	00	0:00:22	1,336 K	4,148 K	1,459	22
PadExe.exe	1932	cyberbadger1	0	00	0:01:22	1,396 K	4,924 K	1,859	22
agrsmmsg.exe	1888	cyberbadger1	0	00	0:00:09	408 K	2,568 K	730	9
THotkey.exe	1880	cyberbadger1	0	00	0:00:02	1,064 K	4,400 K	1,377	12
FrameworkService.exe	1872	SYSTEM	0	00	0:00:17	5,596 K	9,488 K	17,789	7
SynTPEnh.exe	1856	cyberbadger1	0	00	0:04:57	3,896 K	5,192 K	6,761	23
SynTPLpr.exe	1836	cyberbadger1	0	00	0:00:00	004 K	2,760 K	1,422	8
CTSVCCDA.EXE	1824	SYSTEM	0	00	0:00:00	44 K	1,524 K	380	1
SMax4PNP.exe	1796	cyberbadger1	0	00	0:00:00	596 K	4,188 K	1,583	10
atiptaxx.exe	1788	cyberbadger1	0	00	0:00:07	512 K	4,312 K	1,518	31
CFSvcs.exe	1776	cyberbadger1	0	00	0:00:00	328 K	3,600 K	1,183	1
explorer.exe	1628	cyberbadger1	0	00	0:20:32	26,952 K	80,492 K	2,143,704	1,029
ati2evxx.exe	1548	cyberbadger1	0	00	0:00:02	1,000 K	2,448 K	886	5
svchost.exe	1540	LOCAL SERVICE	0	00	0:00:00	2,000 K	6,660 K	1,692	0
spoolsv.exe	1456	SYSTEM	0	00	0:00:25	4,252 K	35,180 K	157,170	6
rapimgr.exe	1108	cyberbadger1	0	00	0:00:01	2,164 K	5,228 K	3,428	6
svchost.exe	1092	LOCAL SERVICE	0	00	0:00:01	3,764 K	9,632 K	5,501	0
svchost.exe	1016	NETWORK SERVICE	0	00	0:00:03	1,676 K	4,300 K	8,266	0
svchost.exe	960	SYSTEM	0	00	0:02:29	18,592 K	43,300 K	184,013	38
wcescomm.exe	924	cyberbadger1	0	00	0:00:00	1,084 K	4,708 K	1,590	6
svchost.exe	872	NETWORK SERVICE	0	00	0:00:33	1,992 K	4,768 K	2,756	0
CTDetect.exe	856	cyberbadger1	0	00	0:00:00	1,024 K	4,904 K	3,987	19
svchost.exe	796	SYSTEM	0	00	0:00:01	1,864 K	5,344 K	4,025	1

Processes: 63   CPU Usage: 2%   Commit Charge: 774M / 2461M

Figure 2.3

"You think you know your computer, but really all you know is a surface on your screen" (Annette Schindler quoted in Mirapaul 2003). The numerous software processes running on one of the authors' laptops as he edits this chapter. Most are performing work of unknown importance to the immediate tasks at hand.

choosing or consent, but such power is always relational in nature. What that means for software is, as Mackenzie (2006, 10) notes, "agency distributes itself . . . in kaleidoscopic permutations."

One of the effects of abstracting the world into software algorithms and data models, and rendering aspects of the world as capta, which are then used as the basis for software to do work in the world, is that the world starts to structure itself in the image of the capta and code—a self-fulfilling, recursive relationship develops. As Ullman (1997, 90) notes, "finally we arrive at a tautology: the [cap]ta prove the need for more [cap]ta! We think we are creating the system, but the system is also creating us. We build the system, we live in its midst, and we are changed." For example, because software can undertake billions of calculations in a very short space of time, it can undertake analytical tasks that are too computationally demanding for people to perform manually. In so doing, it can reveal relationships about the world that would have otherwise remained out of view. An apposite case of this is in academia, across both the hard sciences and in the humanities, where computers are enabling innovative forms of analysis, new theories, and new inventions. These in turn discursively and materially reshape our world, as the example of climate modeling earlier demonstrated. Further, as we detail in the following chapters, the way we work, consume, travel, and relax have been reconfigured with respect to the possibilities that software has offered.

For Mackenzie (2002) the reason why software can do work in the world is because it possesses *technicity*. Technicity refers to the extent to which technologies mediate, supplement, and augment collective life; the unfolding or evolutive power of technologies to make things happen in conjunction with people. For an individual technical element such as a tool like a carpenter's saw, its technicity might be its hardness and flexibility (a product of human knowledge and production skills) that enables it in conjunction with human mediation to cut well (note that the constitution and use of the saw is dependent on both human and technology; they are inseparable). As Star and Ruhleder (1996, 112, our emphasis) note, a "tool is not just a thing with pre-given attributes frozen in time—but a thing becomes a tool *in practice*, for someone, when connected to some particular activity. . . . The tool emerges in situ." In other words, a saw is not simply given as a saw, rather it becomes a saw through its use in cutting wood. Similarly, a shop emerges as a shop by selling goods to customers. In large scale ensembles such as a car engine, consisting of many components, technicity is complex and cannot be isolated from the sum of individual components (and their design, manufacture, and assembly), its "associated milieu" (for example, the flow of air, the lubricants, and fuel), and its human operator, "that condition and is conditioned by the working of the engine" (Mackenzie 2002, 12).

Software possesses high technicity; it is an actant able to do work in the world, enabling everyday acts to occur such as watching television, using the Internet, traveling across a city, buying goods, making phone calls, and withdrawing money from an ATM. In these cases, and myriad other everyday tasks, the software acts autonomously, and at various points in the process is able to automatically process inputs and to react accordingly to solve a problem. While some of these practices were possible before the deployment of software, it is now vital to their operation. The technicity of code in such cases is high as they are dependent on software to function with no manual alternatives. As already noted, the technicity of code is not deterministic (for example, code turns everyday practices into absolute, non-negotiable forms) or universal (which is to say, such determinations occur in all places and at all times in a simple cause-and-effect manner). Rather, technicity is contingent, negotiated, and nuanced; realized through its practice by people in relation to historical and geographical context. As such, there is no neat marriage between coded objects, infrastructures, processes, and assemblages and particular effects of code. Instead, technicity varies as a function of the nature of code, people, and context.

For example, technicity varies depending on the autonomy and consequences of software. Autonomy relates to the extent to which code can do its work without direct human oversight or authorization. The degree of autonomy is a function of the amount of input (the system's knowledge of its environment and memory of past events), sophistication of processing, and the range of outputs that code can produce. If code crashes, then the consequences of its failure can range from mild inconvenience (such as travel delays) to serious economic and political impacts (such as the failure of the power grid), to life-threatening situations (when vital medical equipment is unable to function or air traffic control towers are unable to direct planes). All types of software do not have the same social significance. For example, the technicity of the host of codes found in a typical home is radically different from that employed in a hospital intensive care unit.

Further, the technicity of code varies according to the people who are entangled with it. Not all people experience or interact with the same code in the same way. Many factors influence a person's interaction with code, from personality and social characteristics (such as age, gender, class, and ethnicity), to economic or educational status, personal histories and experiences, their intentions, their technical competencies, and even whether they are on their own or in a group. Software and its effects vary across individuals. For example, someone with daily use of a software system may experience it in a more banal and ambivalent way than a person encountering it for the first time. As noted above, the relationship between code and people also varies as a function of wider context, including crucially the places where it is occurring. Interactions with code are historically, geographically, and institutionally embedded, and do not arise out of nowhere. Rather, code works within conventions, standards, representations, habits, routines, practices, economic situations, and discursive formations that position and place how code engages and how code is engaged. The use of code is then always prefaced by, and contingent upon, this wider context.

Conclusion

In this chapter we have detailed how we understand and conceptualize the nature of software. Code is an expression of how computation both capture the world within a system of thought (as algorithms and structures of capta) and a set of instructions that tell digital hardware and communication networks how to act in the world. For us, software needs to be theorized as both a contingent product of the world and a relational producer of the world. Software is written by programmers, individually and in teams, within diverse social, political, and economic contexts. The production of software unfolds—programming is performative and negotiated and code is mutable. Software possesses secondary agency that engenders it with high technicity. As such, software needs to be understood as an actant in the world—it augments, supplements, mediates, and regulates our lives and opens up new possibilities—but not in a deterministic way. Rather, software is afforded power by a network of contingencies that allows it do work in the world. Software transforms and reconfigures the world in relation to its own systems of thought. Thinking about software in these terms allows us to start to critically think through its nature and to consider where and how it works. In part II of the book we expand this analysis to think through the difference that software makes, examining how code alters the nature of objects, affects how space is transduced, changes how societies are governed, and even how software is affording new kinds of creativity and empowerment. What our analysis makes clear is that software as an actant is radically transforming our world, and that software itself, and not simply the technologies it enables, merits significant intellectual attention.

II The Difference Software Makes

3 Remaking Everyday Objects

When it is not only "us" but also our "things" that can upload, download, disseminate and stream meaningful-making stuff, how does the way in which we occupy the physical world become different?

—Julian Bleecker

When each object has a unique identity, objects begin to seem more like individuals, and individual people become susceptible to being constituted as objects.

—N. Katharine Hayles

So far we have contended, in broad terms, that software makes a difference to everyday life because it possesses technicity. In this chapter, we look at how the nature of material objects and the work they do has been transformed by code. Software, as we detail below, is imbuing everyday objects, such as domestic appliances, handheld tools, sporting equipment, medical devices, recreational gadgets, and children's toys, with capacities that allow them to do additional and new types of work. On the one hand, objects are remade and recast through interconnecting circuits of software that makes them uniquely addressable and consistently machine-readable, and thus exposed to external processes of identification and linkage that embeds them in the emerging "Internet of things" (in much the same way that the location of a web site can be looked up through its unique domain name from anywhere on the Internet, it is envisaged that this infrastructure will facilitate the same for any uniquely tagged object; Schoenberger 2002). On the other hand, software is being embedded in material objects, imbuing them with an awareness of their environment, and the calculative capacities to conduct their own work in the world with only intermittent human oversight, to record their own use, and to take over aspects of decision making from people. In so doing, our approach is one of building a taxonomy that classifies new types of coded objects as a way to start to make sense of how objects are becoming addressable, aware, and active.

Making Objects Addressable

Since the late 1970s and the widespread application of bar codes to mass-produced consumer goods, objects have increasingly become machine-readable through rapid and reliable reading of identification numbers placed on them (see figure 3.1). Such identification technologies include a range of different printed bar codes, the growing use of radio frequency ID (RFID) tags, magnetic strips, embedded chips, and transponder units which, when read and combined with appropriate information infrastructure (for identification number allocation and specifying product classification formats), can be consistently matched to information held in an organization's captabase to reveal the identity of the object and other associated properties (such as batch number, date of manufacture, and shipping history). As a result, while different instances of the same class of product would have previously shared the same bar code identifier (say bottles of whiskey), now each and every instance (bottle) is uniquely indexable and can be tracked through time and space in ways that were previously impossible. What this increased granularity of addressing means is a twofold change in the status of objects. First, the ontological status of each object is uniquely indexed. This information is knowable in new ways in terms of what information is attributable to the object, and can be generated with respect to it—ranging from purchasing information through to a detailed usage trail and eventual disposal (so it is not just *a* bottle of whiskey in a household's trash can but *the* bottle of whiskey purchased for $19.99 on 12/10/2009, at 19:54 p.m., in the Whistlestop convenience store, Downtown Crossing, by A. N. Other). Second, individuated identification transforms the epistemological

Figure 3.1
The physical manifestation of identification systems. (*a, b*) Bar codes that can be read visually. (*c, d*) RFID chips that can be queried remotely by radio signals.

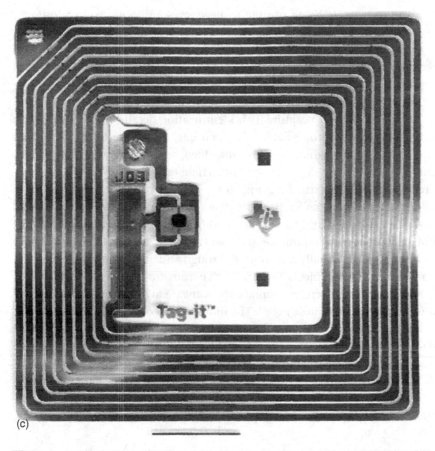

(c)

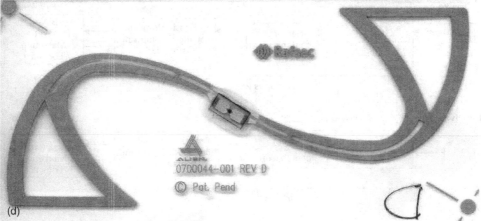

(d)

Figure 3.1
(continued)

status of each object, with it being useable in new ways and able to do additional work in the world and to be worked upon by other entities such as information systems.

There are presently two classes of machine-readable objects: passive and active (see figure 3.2), based on the technicity of the tagging technology that holds the unique identification number. Passive machine-readable objects have to be directly queried (for example, by laser scanner) to capture their identification details. In contrast, active ID tags continually broadcast their details. For example, an active RFID tag consists of a simple digital circuit into which data are embedded, an antenna which broadcasts the information, and a battery to power the unit. These tags can be read at a distance by a radio transponder, rather than having to be passed in line of sight to a laser scanner. In both cases, passive and active, the data read or transmitted is one-dimensional and invariant (typically only a unique identification code number). The object itself does not generate and communicate new capta about its status. However, because the captured information is usually transmitted through and queried across distributed networks, machine-readable objects become active constituent parts of circuits of interchange between objects, sensors, captabases, software algorithms, and work.

Let us consider RFID tags in more detail. The industry aim of RFID tags is to provide a means to automatically identify any object, anywhere. They are presently most widely used in vehicle dashboard tags for automatic toll payment (a widespread system in the United States being E-ZPass) and in livestock to facilitate "farm-to-fork" traceability given growing concerns over food safety (Popper 2007). The main application of RFID tags is likely to be in retail, where they are seen as a major advance in inventory management, the fight against shoplifting, staff pilfering, and in enhancing

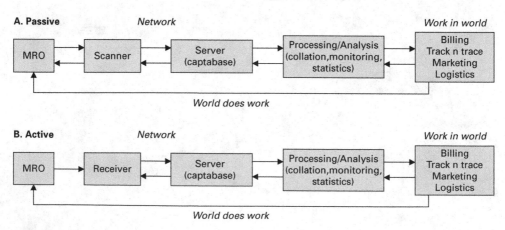

Figure 3.2
Classes of machine-readable objects.

customer profiling (Ferguson 2002) and in surveillance and security (for example, RFID tags are embedded into new passports; see chapter 5).

The leading standard with regard to uniquely coding objects with RFID tags is known as the Electronic Product Code (EPC), developed by the Auto-ID Center, an industry-sponsored R&D lab at MIT, and commercially implemented by EPCglobal Inc. (a joint venture of the Uniform Code Council and EAN International, the main players in UPC bar code management). Through EPCs, RFID tags can be linked together into a global information network—an Internet of things—which provides the means to automatically look up details on any tagged object from any location across distributed networks. Borrowing the domain name schema used on the Internet, the EPC network uses a distributed Object Naming Service (ONS) to link each EPC number to an appropriate naming authority database that provides detailed information. Importantly, the querying of the ONS as RFID tagged products move through supply chains will automatically create richly-detailed audit trails of capta. The result will be a much greater degree of routine machine-to-machine generated knowledge on the status and positioning of many millions of physical objects in time and space.

Evangelists for RFID tagging and the EPC network envision a wide range of innovations in the handling of physical objects arising from these networked capta trails (see Ferguson 2002, for typical speculation). Inside retail stores, a key aim is so-called smart shelving (units that are aware of their own stock levels and the activities of individual customers). In the home, pundits are predicting microwave ovens that check and set the best cooking settings for frozen dinners, washing machines that read the tags of clothing to automatically select the most appropriate wash cycle, and medicine cabinets able to spot out-of-date or recalled pharmaceuticals. There could also be potential for tracking goods at the end of the life cycle, alerting waste disposal collectors to items containing toxic substances, for example. Yet bound up with the promises of greater convenience and more orderly domestic routines, is the capacity to make formally hidden and unrecorded actions newly visible to external organizations and to eliminate anonymity from mass consumption because every time an RFID tag is queried it leaves behind a log. As such, RFID smart tagging raises the specter of a new frontier of potentially invasive surveillance (Albrecht and McIntyre 2005; van Kranenburg 2008; see chapter 5). It also opens up a significant debate about property rights (Hayles 2009) in that a person may legally own a material object but not possess the capta that is generated with respect to it. And such "virtualized [cap]ta about the object has market values that amount to considerable percentages of the value of the material commodities to which the [cap]ta correspond" (Hayles 2009, 54).

Regardless of their wider uses, it is likely that over the next few years RFIDs will replace bar codes on retail packaging and be embedded in all manner of manufactured goods to facilitate asset management and logistics. It is already fair to say, as we explore in chapter 9, that as part of larger infrastructures of identification and addressing, RFID

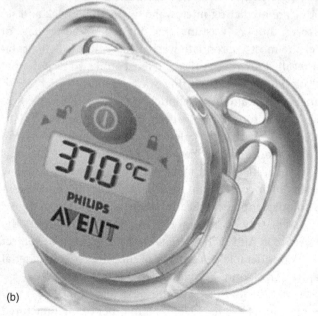

Figure 3.3

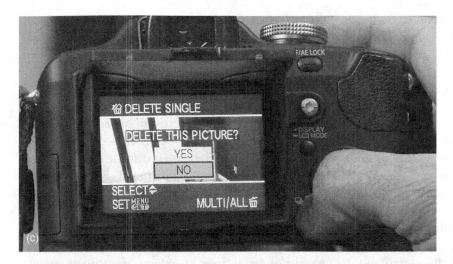

Figure 3.3

A range of coded objects used to solve domestic tasks of heating, health and well-being, capturing photograph memory card data, and cleaning of clothes. The presence of digital display screens is an indicator of the executive presence of software. (*a*) Thermostat (*Source*: www.vaillant.co.uk). (*b*) Pacifier with a built-in thermometer (*Source*: www.p4c.philips.com/files/s/sch540_00/sch540_00_pss_eng.pdf). (*c*) Digital camera interface. (*d*) Washing machine interface.

tagging systems have already started to reshape modes of production and the processes of capital accumulation on a variety of scales. They also pose a significant intellectual and political challenge (see chapter 5).

Coded Objects

In contrast to machine-readable goods and products which simply participate externally in the Internet of things, some objects have code physically embedded into their material form, altering endogenously their ongoing relations with the world. In such objects, software is used on the one hand to enhance the functional capacity of what were previously dumb objects, enabling them to sense something of their environments and to perform different tasks, or the same tasks more efficiently (figure 3.3), or to be plugged into new distributed networks that afford some value-added dimension such as data exchange on how they are used. On the other hand, code is used to underpin the design and deployment of new classes of objects, particularly mobile devices (such as PDAs, MP3 players, and GPS), that in some cases replace analog equivalents (diaries and date books, portable cassette tape and CD players, paper maps and guide books) or undertake entirely new tasks. In either case, the embedding of software significantly increases an object's technicity.

In thinking through the relationship between code and its embedding into objects, we have used the decision-making process detailed in figure 3.4 to subdivide coded objects into two general types based on the level of significance of software to an object's primary function(s). *Peripherally coded objects* are objects in which software has been embedded, but such code is not essential to their use (that is, if the software fails, they still work as intended, but not as efficiently, cost-effectively, or productively). *Codejects* on the other hand are dependent upon code to function—the object and its code are thoroughly interdependent and inseparable (hence our conjoining of the terms code and object to denote this mutual interdependence). Codejects can be further subdivided into three main classes on the basis of the following characteristics: their programmability, interactivity, capacity for remembering, their ability for anticipatory action in the future based on previous use, and relational capacities. In summary, these classes are hard codejects, unitary codejects, and logjects.

Hard codejects   rely on code to function but are not programmable and therefore have low levels of interactivity.
Unitary codejects   are programmable, exhibit some level of interactivity (although this is typically limited and highly scripted), and do not record their work in the world. They can be subdivided into two groups: (a) *closed codejects* and (b) *sensory objects* depending on whether they sense and react to the world around them.
Logjects   are objects that have an awareness of themselves and their relations with the world and which, by default, automatically record aspects of those relations in logs

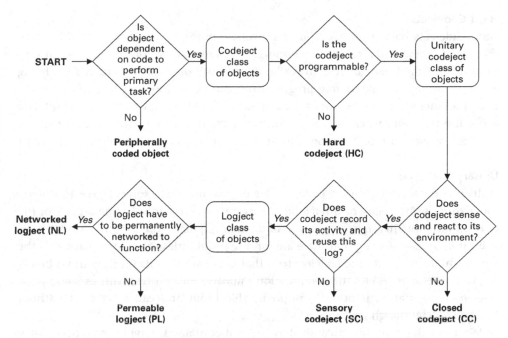

Figure 3.4
A decision tree of the characteristics of different classes of coded objects.

that are stored and reused in the future. Logjects often have high levels of interactivity and multifunctionality. Logjects can also be subdivided into two groups based on their capacity to work independently of wider networks: (a) *permeable logjects* and (b) *networked logjects*.

Peripherally Coded Objects

Peripherally coded objects are objects in which software has been embedded, but where the software is incidental to the primary function of the object. There are relatively few such objects and, in most cases, the code merely augments use, but is by no means essential to its functioning. Often, the presence of code is merely an adornment that serves the purpose of product marketing, to differentiate it from predecessors or acts as a token of added value. For example, an oven might have a digital timer embedded in it, but if this ceases to function, then the appliance will continue to cook food. Similarly, an exercise bike might have a device that digitally displays the speed at which the cyclist is pedaling, but if this ceases to work, the equipment still enables exercise to take place. In both cases, the code does little more than augment the object's use by enabling the chef to know how long a dish has been cooking and the cyclist to know the traveling speed. Both are simply digital replacements for analog technology.

Hard Codejects

Hard codejects have a special kind of software, known as firmware, embedded into them that is essential for their functioning. Firmware consists of a defined set of routines being stored permanently in read-only memory on a device, rather than being enacted through an executable program that can be accessed and interfaced with. Examples include a USB memory stick and basic SCADA (supervisory control and data acquisition) systems wherein code monitors and controls an element of infrastructure, such as a valve. Both rely on code, but its functionality is predetermined and fixed.

Unitary Codejects

Unlike hard codejects, unitary codejects are programmable to some degree and therefore exhibit some degree of interactivity; users are able to control some aspects of the object's functionality, instructing it as and when required. They, along with logjects, exhibit *liveness*—a feeling that there are infinite possibilities to explore; *plasticity*—the person interacting with the codeject feels that they can push its limits without breaking the system; *accretion*—the computation improves and evolves with use; and *interruption*—computation is open to unpredictable input and can react to it without breakdown (Murtaugh 2008).

We term them *unitary* because they are self-contained, having everything they need to function within their material form. In broad terms, unitary codejects can be divided into those that function independent of their surroundings (closed codejects), and those that are equipped with some sensors that enable the object to react meaningfully to particular variables in their immediate environment (sensory codejects).

Closed codejects can include digital clocks, and some audiovisual equipment such as radios, CD players, and DVD players. Code is vital to the functioning and performance of each of these items, but the object executes its task independent of the world around it. Each is programmable to some degree—the time can be adjusted, stopwatch operated, alarm and record times set, the order of tracks selected—but generally they have circumscribed functions and limited latitude to operate automatically.

Sensory codejects have some awareness of their environment and react automatically to defined external stimulus: common domestic examples include a heating/air conditioner control unit; a washing machine that is monitored and controlled by software; and a digital camera and storage card. The heating/air conditioning unit is equipped with a digital thermostat and timer that is aware of the time/date and senses the surrounding temperature. Simple software algorithms react accordingly to temperature measurements in relation to preset requirements. Similarly, software embedded in the washing machine will monitor multiple contextual parameters such as door lock, load weight, and water temperature, necessary for safe and effective operation without human oversight (see table 3.1). The digital camera captures an image of the

Table 3.1
Hotpoint washer-dryer error codes that are displayed by software to the user

Fault codes for LCD EVO1 Washing Machines and Washer Dryers

* F01—Short circuit motor triac—Book a washing machine repair.
* F02—Motor jammed tacho detached—Book a washing machine repair.
* F03—Wash thermistor open/short circuit—Book a washing machine repair.
* F04—Pressure switch jammed on empty—Book a washing machine repair.
* F05—Pressure switch jammed on full—Book a washing machine repair.
* F06—Program selector error—Book a washing machine repair.
* F07—Heater relay stuck—Book a washing machine repair.
* F08—Heater relay cannot be activated—Book a washing machine repair.
* F09—Incompatible eeprom—Book a washing machine repair.
* F10—Pressure switch not sensing correctly—Book a washing machine repair.
* F11—Pump cannot be activated—Book a washing machine repair.
* F12—Communication error—Book a washing machine repair.
* F13—Dryer fan or dryer thermistor faulty—Book a washing machine repair.
* F14—Dryer element faulty—Book a washing machine repair.
* F15—Dryer element relay faulty—Book a washing machine repair.
* H20—Not fillings. Check tap, hose and inlet valves.
* LOCKED—Check interlock—Book a washing machine repair.

Note: These codes give a partial indicator of the range of conditions that the appliance's software monitors.
Source: Hotpoint Service web site "Error Messages and Error Codes," www.hotpointservice.co.uk/hs/pages/content.do?keys=FAQ:ERROR_CODES

world using a CCD sensor and measures light levels to adjust the aperture setting and the lens movement for auto-focusing, as well as monitoring the remaining battery life and available storage space.

Logjects

Logjects differ from unitary objects in that they also record their status and usage, and, importantly, can retain these logs even when deactivated and utilize them when reactivated. In key ways, these logs can have a bearing on the ongoing operation of the object and its relations with people or wider processes. Furthermore, part of their functionality is externalized, lying beyond the immediate material form of the object.

We derive the term *logjects* from Bleecker's (2006) notion of a blogject (where for us a blogject is one type of logject). Bleecker defines a *blogject* as an emerging class of software-enabled objects that generates a kind of blog of its own use and has the capability to automatically initiate exchanges of socially meaningful information—"it is an artifact that can disseminate a record of experience to the web" (Nova and

Bleecker 2006, no pagination). Bleecker (2006, 6, original emphasis) characterizes blogjects as objects that: (1) can "track and trace where they are and where they've been," (2) "have self-contained (embedded) histories of their encounters and experiences" (rather than indexed histories), and (3) "have some form of agency—they can foment action and participate; they have an assertive voice within *the social web.*" Blogjects are things that can do meaningful social acts where their actions shape how people think about and act in the world; they "participat[e] within the Internet of social networks" (Bleecker 2006, 2). Here, Bleecker is very much interested in only a certain kind of software-enabled object, those that produce streams of information very much like a blog written by a person, thus contributing to the "ecology of networked publics—streams, feeds, trackbacks, permalinks, wiki inscriptions and blog posts" (Bleecker 2006, 9). He is very careful to delineate blogjects as political actants that contribute to debates by providing socially meaningful information, rather than being coded objects that log their use and communicate and/or analyze that data across distributed networks.

While Bleecker's notion of a blogject has conceptual utility, for us, it is one form of a logging object in a much larger sociotechnical ecology of logjects. We broadly define a logject as an object with embedded software able to monitor and record, in some fashion, its own operation. More specifically, and expanding on Bleecker, a logject has the following qualities:

• It is uniquely indexable.
• It has awareness of its environment and is able to respond meaningfully to changes in that environment within its functional context.
• It traces and tracks its own usage in time and/or space records that history, and can communicate that history across a network for analysis and use by other agents (objects and people).
• The logject can use the capta it produces to undertake what we have previously termed automated management (Dodge and Kitchin 2007a)—automated, automatic, and autonomous decisions and actions in the world without human oversight and to effect change through the "consequences of their assertions" (Bleecker 2006, 9).
• A logject is programmable and thus mutable to some degree (that is, it is possible to adjust settings, update parameters, and download new firmware).

Logjects then enable the kinds of unobtrusive machine-to-machine, machine-to-person, and person-to-machine exchanges that are a fundamental trait of pervasive computing and are diverse in nature.

Permeable Logjects   Permeable logjects consist of relatively self-contained units such as an MP3 player, a PDA, and a GPS, all of which have the potential to be connected to wider networks. Such devices trace and track their usage by default, recording this capta as an embedded history; are programmable in terms of configurable settings and creating lists (for example, they play lists of songs, keep calendar entries, and provide route itineraries); perform operations in automated, automatic and autonomous ways; and engender socially meaningful acts such as entertaining, remembering an important meeting, and helping an individual to travel between locations. These devices work to relieve the cognitive burden of routine tasks on people who use them, and help to reduce the risks and consequence of unexpected events. Unlike a networked logject, all essential capacities are held locally, and primary functionality does not require a network connection to operate. That said, appropriate capta (such as music, calendar entries, or map files) and software must be downloaded onto the machine at some point; hence they are permeable. These devices can be connected to wider networks in order for information to be uploaded and exchanged with other devices (via Bluetooth wireless transmission, for example) and updates in firmware can be downloaded, though typically this is not automatic and sometimes requires considerable human intervention (what might be classed as digital housework, for example, syncing a PDA or MP3 player). The uploaded information can be processed and analyzed in relation to other usage, thus providing added value. The aggregate social significance of such objects is impossible to estimate, but they are used to solve all manner of domestic problems billions of times a day, often without the active awareness or involvement of people.

Networked Logjects Networked logjects do not function without continuous access to other technologies and networks. In particular, because they need constant two-way data exchanges, they are reliant on access to a distributed communication network to perform their primary function. Such logjects track, trace, and record their usage locally, but because of memory issues, the necessity of service monitoring/billing, and in some cases a user's ability to erase or reprogram such objects, their full histories are also recorded externally to an immediate material form. Some networked logjects are relatively fixed in the environment (satellite/cable television control boxes, home security monitoring systems) and others are inherently mobile (cell phones, vehicles with remote monitoring) that use a range of communication technologies such as GSM, Wi-Fi, and Bluetooth to maintain a network connection. Mobile networked logjects continuously search for connectivity and can respond automatically and autonomously to the network conditions. For example, a cell phone reacts automatically to incoming calls by sounding the ringtone, switches to the answer service if the call is unanswered, and alerts the owner that a call was missed and/or a message is waiting.

Objects Become and Do Other Things

Reflecting on this taxonomy, and the ways in which objects are becoming either externally machine-readable or endogenously coded, it seems to us that the nature of many objects and the material processes that constitute everyday life are being remade in quite radical ways—objects are being alternatively reconfigured and defined, they are gaining additional capacities to do additional work in the world, and the world can do more work on and through them. Individual objects are now knowable in new ways—they are uniquely identifiable and their use and movement is trackable across space and time. They are becoming part of the emerging Internet of things. Objects thus gain capta shadows that can be analyzed for emergent properties, with new knowledge of the life of an object used to refine the system through which it is made, distributed, sold, and potentially used. And importantly, such capta can be processed to anticipate potential future activities.

Let's explore the example of the archetypal machine-readable object: a credit card. A credit card has a machine-readable unique identifier embedded in its chip and/or magnetic strip. Functionally, it is a conveniently-sized material token used to authenticate access to transaction records in financial captabases. The card can be enrolled by software into a secure communications process with the financial captabase through an intranet, which also tracks spending across time and space and is increasingly subjected to real-time analysis for fraud detection. The capta gathered from the card can also be aggregated to provide an individualized spatial history of consumption. In turn, a plethora of other material objects and sociotechnical infrastructures have been built around it (from the design of ATMs and card readers, online baskets, and SSL encryption, through to the mundane shape of wallets). Through its membership of the Internet of things, the credit card does work in the world—enabling the purchasing of goods and services more securely and efficiently than in previous incarnations, and it is also worked upon, with the information concerning usage employed to evaluate credit levels and anticipate future risk; to monitor purchases in real time for potential fraud and regulate the amount of spending for accurate billing; as well as feeding some of the capta into wider marketing profiles and geodemographics models (Burrows and Gane 2006; Leyshon and Thrift 1999; see chapter 9). Importantly, it can legally, and through social convention, now hold a measure of trust that allow actions at a distance that are replacing embodied transactions (Lyon 2002).

Now let us examine the example of a codeject: a cell phone. A cell phone is wholly dependent on software to function; without the ongoing updates of code it cannot work; it is an inert piece of plastic and other materials. Software enables the phone to act as a traditional phone, but to also undertake a range of additional functions such as the sending and receiving of texts, music, and other information; connecting to the Internet; to take and send photos; act as an alarm clock or calendar or a radio or a recorder or a calculator; to play games; to store phone numbers, images, and other files; and so on. It enables the phone to be customizable, selecting ring tones, wallpaper, profiles, and connectivity type. In other words, a cell phone enables its user to do a range of different activities. And fundamentally it allows the user to do all of these things on the move, rather than being tethered by a cable. It has become so ubiquitous and embedded into everyday life for so many people that it is easy to overlook the power of such a spatial reconfiguring in a very short span of time (Rheingold 2002; Townsend 2000; Schwanen and Kwan 2008).

Just as the phone performs work in the world, it is performed upon. Calls, texts, and other information are received, logged, and stored, and capta about usage by the customer is used to monitor service uptake and generate bills and customer profiles. The radio signal also pinpoints the location of phone, which generates spatial capta that can enable all manner of interesting analysis of activity patterns (Ratti et al. 2006) as well as continuous tracking and spatial surveillance (Dobson and Fisher 2003). And like the credit card, a plethora of other physical objects (phone holders, hands-free kits) and infrastructure (such as the tens of thousands of new antennas erected in the last decade) have been built around it, as well as other cultural products and practices such as ringtones, gaming, and web sites for downloads and payments.

Significantly, both the credit card and the cell phone work across a distributed network. If an object is connected into a distributed network, it can be worked on from a distance or it can conduct additional work across the network both in relation to other objects and people. Table 3.2 provides other examples of the changing ways in which objects and people interact and work together at a distance. In all cases, the status and function of an object and the system it resides in has been reconfigured in new ways through the enrollment of software.

Conclusion

In this chapter we have started to document various kinds of coded objects, their emerging characteristics, the work that they do in the world, and how their changing state alters their nature. Machine-readable and coded objects are having a profound effect on sociospatial contours of lives, although often in subtle and banal ways. They augment, supplement, and facilitate people in their daily tasks and routines. They constitute the means by which most people come directly into contact with software. Almost stealthlike, they have seeped into the fabric of social environments and workplaces forming what Thrift (2004b) has termed a "technological unconsciousness." For example, as chapter 8 details, the typical Western household has a growing constellation of coded objects on which it relies for entertainment, communication, and domestic tasks. And yet there has been very little serious academic appraisal of what the creation of the machine-readable and coded object means, both philosophically and practically, for everyday life. As such, we feel that coded objects demand further attention as key, future actants.

Over time, as we become more and more reliant on such objects, there will be a need to more fully examine their nature from an ontological and epistemological

Table 3.2
Coded objects working across distributed networks

Machine to machine	
Cargo monitoring	A telemetric GPS unit on a high-value cargo vehicle communicating its location at regular intervals to a monitoring station
Vending machine	A vending machine communicating its stock levels to a central computer at the end of a day
Health care	Health care monitoring equipment, such as a cardiac monitor or dialysis machine, communicating a patient's status to a medical database
Vehicle services	Automated updating of a vehicle's navigational system to incorporate up-to-date information, such as road construction and weather forecasts

Machine to person	
Remote patient monitoring	A cardiac monitor alerting a physician if the patient's condition suddenly deteriorates, enabling an emergency response
Vending machines	A cellular-enabled vending machine requesting attention from a technician in the case of a technical fault
Driver services	A traffic information system alerting a GPS system that alerts a driver in the event of an accident on the driver's known route
Car rental	A telemetric GPS unit in a rental car alerting the rental company if it was driven outside of its permitted boundary

Person to machine	
Traffic management	Remotely reconfiguring the timing for a traffic signal, allowing traffic patterns to be quickly altered
Vending machines	Changing prices on a vending machine without requiring a site visit
Vehicle services	A key fob remotely unlocking a car door; or turning on the air conditioning in a car before the owner arrives
Maintenance	Conducting remote diagnostics and maintenance on an object, saving the technician a visit to the site

Source: Adapted from Deloitte Research 2002, 7–8

point of view and to tease out the difference they make across a number of domains such as home, work, and public space, and to fundamental spatial processes such as communication and travel. For us, this will need to entail the construction of detailed ethnographies of the development, use and networking of different kinds of coded objects; how they are placed into and become key actants in complex actor-networks; and how they work in diverse conjunctions with people to realize a multiplicity of social processes and spatialities. In the following chapters, we argue that the coding of objects makes a difference in the world because they have additional capacities to modulate the transduction of space and also enable new forms of governance, as well as enabling creativity and empowerment. We provide examples of the difference such objects make in part III, and in chapter 10 we discuss the possibility that a proliferation of such objects will constitute a state of everyware.

4 The Transduction of Space

The modern city exists as a haze of software instructions. Nearly every urban practice is becoming mediated by code.
—Ash Amin and Nigel Thrift

Technicity and transduction account for how things *become* what they are rather than what they are.
—Adrian Mackenzie, our emphasis

In the opening chapter, we proposed that one of the primary reasons why software makes a difference to the world people inhabit is because *it modulates the conditions under which sociospatial processes operate*. We also suggested that software studies to date have largely ignored the role of space as a conceptual and analytical tool for understanding how and why software matters, instead prioritizing the role played by social relations and time. Space has been effectively relegated to the role of mere backdrop or inert stage.

In this chapter, we challenge such a view, arguing that space is a critical component, along with social relations and temporality, in understanding everyday life. Social relations do not operate independently of space or simply at a location, rather space is an *active* constitutive element in the production of social relations, communal formations, political organization, and personal regulation. In other words, the social is inherently temporal *and* spatial. Indeed, one only has to think of everyday living to realize how space provides a defining context in which relations unfold, and which in turn produce space. For example, people's labor is performed in particular workplaces, consumption unfolds in specific retail and leisure spaces, domestic life takes place within individual homes and distinctive neighborhoods, travel consists of journeys through and between localities, and communication is embedded within particular domains or links together geographically separated places. In all these cases, the spatial context is not incidental or inert, it is constitutive and productive—the *where* makes a difference to the *what* that unfolds. Space is a lively participant in the making of meanings and memories. From this perspective, the work that software does is profoundly shaped by the co-constitutive relationships between software, social relations, space, and time; and in turn software matters because it alters the conditions through which society, space, and time are formed.

To commence the discussion we detail a brief genealogy of spatial thinking, summarizing how social scientists' understanding of the ontology of space has evolved. We do this in order to contextualize the recent development of an ontogenetic conception of space, and its utility in illustrating the productive relationship between society and space. In so doing, we make it clear how this new conceptualization differs from more traditional philosophies of space. Starting with implicit and absolute notions of space, we then outline relational conceptions of space, finishing with more recent ontogenetic understandings of space that argue for a shift in focus from questions concerned with "what is space?" to "how does space become?" (for a more detailed discussion, see Kitchin 2009). Developing the latter, we argue that code/spaces are best understood as ontogenetic in nature, bought into being through the technicity of software to invoke processes of transduction. Throughout the discussion we clearly privilege the spatial, but for good reason—to highlight how the social is thoroughly spatialized and to thus illustrate the relevance and potency of sociospatial approaches in understanding how and why software matters to everyday life; how it trasduces diverse spatialities.

A Genealogy of Space

Spatial thinking has developed apace in the last forty years, so much so that commentators now talk of a spatial turn within the social sciences. Prior to the 1950s, however, it is fair to say that beyond physics and theology, little conceptual work had been undertaken on the ontology of space. For social scientists, space was an *implicit* container or backdrop in which things happened. Even geographers—whose primary focus is the spatial—were more interested in describing the uniqueness of places and plotting spatial patterns across regions and within particular landscapes, rather than exploring the nature of space itself. Here, space was loosely understood in absolute terms, as having fixed dimensions across which objects of study could be measured and mapped. While not formally recognized as such by those working at the time, conceptually, space was natural, given, and essential, and spatial processes were teleological and predictable. Epistemologically empiricist, wherein facts spoke for themselves, research was largely analytically naïve, consisting of the accumulation of facts as evidence for generalist theories (Hartshorne 1959).

In the late 1950s and into the 1960s this implicit notion of space was rearticulated as an *absolute* ontology of space wherein space was understood as a geometric system of organization, "a kind of . . . grid, within which objects are located and events occur"

(Curry 1995, 5). Such a formulation, implicit previously, was now explicitly stated and was accompanied by an epistemology that saw geographical scholarship seek to reinvent itself as a "spatial science," transforming itself from an ideographic (fact gathering) to a nomothetic (law producing) discipline focused on locational arrangement, geographical patterns, and processes (see Schaefer 1953; Burton 1963; Harvey 1969). Here, space was defined and understood primarily through Euclidean geometry (with x, y, and z dimensions). The phenomena operating within a given space could be determined objectively and measured scientifically, then analyzed using spatial statistics and modeled quantitatively. Deeply essentialist in formulation, space is effectively reduced to the essence of locational geometry, its properties natural and given. For converts to this new way of researching the world, spatial thought became the science of spatial laws wherein observed geographic distributions and patterns could be explained through functional equations and modeled. Although few of these converts refer to the philosophy of positivism in their work, it is clear that many of spatial science's central tenets are drawn loosely from this school of thought (Kitchin 2009).

Developing from the 1970s onward, as a more explicit counter to the scientific ontology of absolute space, were calls for relational ontologies (see Crang and Thrift 2000). The concept of *relational* space was first articulated overtly within radical approaches within human geography (for example, Marxist and feminist geographies) that developed in opposition to the dominant methods and ideology underpinning spatial science. These theorists argued that spatial science was highly reductionist and by treating space as absolute in nature, phenomena were evacuated of social meaning and political purpose. Space, it was argued, was not a neutral and passive geometry, essentialist and teleological in nature. Instead, space was conceived as relational, contingent, and active, as something that is produced or constructed; "constituted through social relations and material social practices" (Massey 1994, 254). Space was not an absolute geometric container in which social and economic life took place; rather, it was constitutive of such relations.

In such relational thinking it was recognized that the spaces people inhabit—the built environment, transport systems, the countryside—do not simply exist, preformed and awaiting meaning. Instead, these landscapes, and the spatial relations they engender, are produced, they are made, shaped, managed, and given meaning by people; they are the products of diverse material and discursive practices that in turn actively shape social relations. Conceived of in these terms, an everyday space like a football stadium can be seen to be both a physical form constructed by certain agents and institutions for particular ends as well as a space given meaning through the daily labor of staff, the behavior and language of visitors, and the rituals and memories of fans: its use and occupation is shaped both by its material form and the immaterial meanings that coalesce around it (Hubbard et al. 2002). Epistemologically, what this relational conception of space meant was a significant shift from seeking spatial laws to a focus on how space is produced and managed in contingent and relational ways by people to create certain sociospatial relations and not others.

In the last decade, a small cluster of scholars have begun to challenge absolute and relational conceptions of space, seeking to develop new understandings of space based on ontogenetic ideas. In so doing, they change the central question of inquiry from "what space is" to "*how space becomes.*" Space (and everything else in the world), they argue, is not ontologically secure, it is not a fixable, definable, knowable, predetermined entity. Rather, space is always in the process of becoming; it is always in the process of taking place. Space, in these terms, is a practice, a doing, an event, a becoming—a material and social reality forever (re)created in the moment. At a fundamental level space achieves its form, function, and meaning through practice. Space *emerges* as a process of ontogenesis. As Doel (1999) has pointed out, from this perspective space can be understood as a verb rather than a noun, and he suggests that term space might better be replaced by "spacing" to better capture its perpetual production.

The ongoing practice of space can be illustrated in many ways. With respect to geographical form it is clear that the world is never static and fixed. Instead, the material landscape is constantly being altered, updated, demolished, and constructed through the interplay of complex sociospatial relations in ways that continuously moderate, in often subtle and banal ways, the spaces people inhabit. At a macroscale there are new local, regional, and national development schemes that are enacted daily to transform and regenerate built environments, transport infrastructures, and natural landscapes. For example, road layouts are modified, new buildings are designed, bus routes across the city are reorganized, new planning zones for industrial development are drawn up, land management schemes for drainage are devised, and so on, that adjust and revise the physical landscape and space-time relations of places. Locally, streets and buildings are always in a process of being refashioned and remodeled and spatial layouts rejigged. Roads are trenched for cabling, storefronts are updated, shop interiors are redesigned and maintained, trees are planted, grass is mowed, and litter is dropped and cleaned up. In other words, the material fabric and social relations of places are constantly created and recreated through spatial practices that vary in their pacing, so some changes are more immediately noticeable than others. As processes of erosion and entropy at abandoned buildings demonstrate, all places are in the course of change, slowly mutating from one state to another.

Similarly, the function of space is not static but alters with time (whether seasonally, as for tourist destinations, or daily, as for business venues and nighttime establishments) and the use of space is negotiated and contested between individuals and groups. Spaces have multiple functions and through the daily flux of interactions, transactions, and mobilities are always in the process of being made differently. For example, Trafalgar Square in London functions as somewhere to meet, to have lunch, to chat, to visit museums, to gather for protests, to party, to take tourist photos, to travel across, to feed pigeons, to work on a food stall, to steal, to catch a bus or a subway train, to sunbathe, and to people watch. It is always in process, constantly being created in the moment as a collective manufacture composed of hundreds of recursive, interconnected relationships between people and place. Trafalgar Square does not simply exist, fully formed; a still landscape. It is endlessly remade, never the same, ceaselessly reterritorialized. As the Greek philosopher Heraclitus observed, "you cannot step twice into the same river, for fresh waters are ever flowing in upon you" (Russell 2004, 52).

Likewise, the meanings associated with spaces shift, ever changing with mood, action, memory, and events. Again in relation to Trafalgar Square, the meanings inscribed upon that location vary as a function of how the space is being used (as a tourist, or as a Londoner), how the viewer interprets Nelson's Column and the surrounding buildings (as visually stimulating scenery or an imperialist celebration), the social background and attitudes of a person, that person's memories and understandings of the Square, and so on. Similarly, meanings attached to home, workplace, particular buildings, and familiar journeys metamorphose with the passage of time. How space is related to, and the spatiality that engenders, can never be static, but emerges, varying over time, and across people and context.

The spatiality of Trafalgar Square (and indeed the notion of what Trafalgar Square is) is always in the process of taking place—its form, function and meaning is ever-shifting across people, time, and context. Its reproduction as Trafalgar Square *appears* to be relatively stable because it is maintained as such through a diverse set of discursive and material practices, including street cleaning, pavement repairs, policing, social norms, embodied conventions of behavior, history lessons, reading guide books, viewing postcards, sitting on steps, splashing in fountains, and many more. In other words, Trafalgar Square is constantly remade through consistently repeated, iterative practices enacted by people and things. These practices are citational in Butler's (1990) terms in that they endlessly, but imperfectly, cite the previous moment and thus give the appearance of coherence and continuity. Taken as a whole, it is important to realize these sets of practices are not planned or coordinated, nor necessarily conscious; they simply proceed. Moreover, many practices are easily forgotten or so ephemeral as to not be remembered, or are actively precluded and hidden to give impression of complete, fixed, and final existence. They are so banal that they are largely ignored, others are culturally invisible, and increasingly others happen automatically through the employment of technology. For example, this printed book consciously denies the evidence of the writing practices that brought it into being—the multiple versions, edits, revisions, and corrections made to sentences, sections, and chapters using word processors, pen and paper, and lengthy conversations. As such, Trafalgar Square is something that happens rather than something that is. Space emerges, ceaselessly citing earlier spatial practices in a never ending, but always changing, cycle.

A number of spatial theorists have recently started to construct ontogenetic understandings of lived experience that seek to think through how space emerges in process, notably de Certeau, Rose, Doel, Thrift, and their respective collaborators. They have been joined by a growing number of others who have also extended such ideas to other core concepts underpinning spatial thought such as scale, place, nature, representation, and landscape, recasting each within an ontogenetic framework (challenging the ontological security of the concept itself, and rethinking each as emergent in nature).

De Certeau (1984) in *The Practice of Everyday Life* sought to move beyond theories centered on representation and observed behavior to consider the more subtle practices that are constitutive of both. In particular, de Certeau (drawing on Foucault) was interested in how people live within, negotiate, and subtly challenge circuits of power and the "proper" order of space as reproduced by dominant elites, such as states and corporations. For de Certeau (1984, 29), space is the outcome of the complex interplay between discursive and material strategies that seek to reproduce "places in conformity with abstract models" of scientific rationality and political economy, through persuasion, seduction, coercion, intimidation, and violence, and resistive tactics that seek to undermine such citational practices by "manipulat[ing] events in order to turn them into opportunities" (p. xix); such tactics could be overt like boycotts or organizing protests, or more covert such as transgressing social norms, ridiculing authority figures, lying on official forms, or ignoring the lawbreaking of others. De Certeau understood these tactics as performative, as often emerging unconsciously within context, so that as individuals "move about, their trajectories form unforeseeable sentences, partly unreadable paths across a space" (1984, xviii), where a trajectory *"comes into being*, the product of a process of deviation from rule governed . . . practices" (p. 5, original emphasis). Individuals actualize spatial possibilities, making space exist as well as emerge (p. 98); they invent and transform space. De Certeau (1984, 117, original emphasis) explains:

Space occurs as the effect produced by the operations that orient it, situate it, temporalize it, and make it function in a polyvalent unity of conflictual programs or contractual proximities. On this view, in relation to place, space is like the word when it is spoken, that is when it is caught in the ambiguity of an actualisation, transformed into a term dependent upon many conventions, situated as the act of a present (or of a time), and modified by the transformations caused by successive contexts. . . . In short, *space is a practiced place*. Thus the street geometrically defined by urban planning is transformed into space by walkers.

From a related perspective, Rose (1999, 248) draws on Butler's theory of performativity to argue that:

Space is a doing, that does not pre-exist its doing, and that its doing is the articulation of relational performances . . . space then is not an anterior actant to be filled or spanned or constructed
. . . [i]nstead, space is practised, a matrix of play, dynamic and iterative, its forms and shapes
produced through the citational performance of self-other relations.

For Rose, space itself, and thus its production, is brought into being through performativity—through the unfolding actions of people. She argues that this produces a
"radically unstable notion of spatiality" that allows for a critical analysis of space as
"extraordinarily convoluted, multiply overlaid, paradoxical, pleated, folded, broken
and, perhaps, sometimes absent" (1999, 247). In other words, she suggests that a
performative understanding of space allows for a nuanced analysis that appreciates
individual differences across place, time, and context, and the paradoxical, contradictory, and complex nature of sociospatial relations as lived and experienced by people.

Drawing on the ideas of Butler, Latour, and Deleuze, among others, Nigel Thrift
has developed the notion of nonrepresentational theory. Thrift suggests the world
emerges through spatial practices that are often unreflective and habitual, that are not
easily represented and captured because they are unconscious and instinctive; they
are performed without cognitive and rational thought (Thrift 2007). These human
practices are complemented by other actants—animals, objects, machines, circuits,
networks—that do diverse work in the world. In particular, Thrift is interested in how
new sentient technologies automatically produce space; that is, they bring space into
being without human interference. As such, he has examined the automatic production of space by software embedded into everyday objects and environment enabled
devices (Thrift 2003, 2004a, 2004b; Thrift and French 2002).

While de Certeau, Rose, Doel, Thrift, and others have undoubtedly influenced our
thinking, in the rest of this chapter we detail our own take on the ontogenesis of
space. What we are particularly interested in, like Thrift and French (2002) and Crang
and Graham (2007), is the process by which software automatically produces space.
We theorize this process using the concepts of technicity and transduction, drawing
on the work of Mackenzie (2002, 2003) and Simondon (1989a, 1989b, 1992, 1995) to
argue that *space is constantly bought into being as an incomplete solution to an ongoing
relational problem.*

The Transduction of Code/Space

From an ontogenetic perspective, code/space, like all space, is beckoned into being
through various practices and processes. What makes code/space a unique spatial
formation, however, is that it is profoundly shaped by software. Code/space is quite
literally constituted through software-mediated practices, wherein code is essential to
the form, function, and meaning of space. Software acts as the catalyst to shift space

from an uncoded state to code/space, and works to maintain that transformation through an ongoing set of contigent and relational processes.

The reason why software can modulate the perpetual production of space is because it possesses significant degrees of technicity. This technicity is realized through the process of *transduction*. For Mackenzie (2003, 10, original emphasis), "transduction is a kind of operation, in which a particular domain undergoes a certain kind of onto-genetic modulation. Through this modulation *in-formation* or individuation occurs. That is, transduction involves a domain taking-on-form, sometimes repeatedly." Transduction is a process of ontogenesis, the making anew of a domain in reiterative and transformative individuations—it is the process by which things transfer from one state to another. According to Simondon (1992, 313), "the simplest image of the transductive process is furnished if one thinks of a crystal, beginning as a tiny seed, which grows and extends itself in all directions in its mother-water. Each layer of molecules that has already been constituted serves as the structuring basis for the layer that is being formed next, and the result is amplify-ing reticular structure."

Mackenzie (2003, 10) explains that "through transduction, a domain structures itself as a partial, always incomplete solution to a relational problem." From this per-spective, everyday life is seen as a stream of never-ending relational problems; for example, in writing, how to spell the next word, finish the sentence, structure the paragraph, and make a convincing argument. These problems are provisionally solved by some action consisting of individuations (looking in a dictionary, typing, editing, thinking, refining), thus transferring the situation from one state to another, yet also immediately creating a new problem to be solved (the next sentence). To take another prosaic example, a person traveling through a city constantly changes their relation to their milieu, thus posing a continuous supply of new problems, such as maintain-ing bearings, avoiding obstacles and other people, and reacting to situations such as the changing of traffic lights, the instructions of signs, requests for tickets, and so on, that have to be provisionally solved to make progress.

Individuations are the small incremental steps that constitute a transduction. They can consist of speech acts, physical movement, mental occurrences, memories, psy-chological perceptions, and physiological sensations, with the process of individuation resulting in a modulation in conditions of the person and their milieu. Most individu-ations are ordinary—routine, habitual, banal, beyond conscious thought, and reiterate previous individuations (walking by placing one foot in front of the other). In this sense, they are citational in that they imperfectly cite previous individuations, as with a layer of molecules in the growing crystal taking a similar form to the previous layer, or a step following a step. Others individuations are singular and can result in radical transformation (starting and stopping walking, changing direction, tripping).

Software solves relational problems by acting as a catalyst for transductions to occur and sustaining individuations within a modulation. Code thus transduces everyday life, alternatively modulating sociospatial relations. From this perspective, *space is transduced*—bought into being—as a part of a provisional solution to an ongoing set of relational problems. Coded space and code/space occurs where the transduction of space is mediated by or is dependent on software. For example, using a checkout computer in a store to calculate the cost of goods and process a payment transduces its spatiality by modulating it into a state of code/space. Similarly, as we detail in chapters 7 through 9, software is increasingly providing the solution to relational problems, such as checking in for a flight (the space of an airport), cooking a dinner using a microwave (the space of the kitchen), playing a computer game (the space of a living room), and tracking goods from factory to shop (the spaces of logistics). In these cases, people's lives unfold in the moment as conjunctions between themselves, space, and coded objects (for example, bank cards), infrastructures (for example, cell phone networks), processes (for example, electronic fund transfer for direct debit payments), and assemblages (for example, the airport), in each case temporarily solving (or not) a relational problem by beckoning into being code/space. Thinking about how the transduction of space proceeds, and in particular the nature of code/space, raises a number of related issues. Here, we focus on four of them: the specter of determinism, the collectivized unfolding of space, the issue of scale, and the nature of structural power.

The Specter of Determinism

While the essential role of software in the transduction of code/space implies a certain technological determinism, the relationship is in fact contingent and relational. It is the case that the nature and meaning of space is dyadically produced through code, so that this mutual constitution makes a difference to the transduction of space, defining the practice and experience of that space. This is most obvious in spaces where code is used to regulate access and what is permissible and required behavior within those arenas (with associated penalties such as warnings, expulsion, fines, and imprisonment). Here, the mutual constitution of code and space is pervasive, consistent, routinized, effective (action is consistently instigated if the "rules" of code/space are violated) and determinate (but only in the sense that, as noted, failure of either code or space means that code/space fails and the intended transduction of space is not transduced).

Code does not determine in absolute, nonnegotiable means the transduction of space. Nor it is universal—that such determinations occur in all such spaces and at all times in a simple cause-and-effect manner. Rather, how code/space emerges, operates, and is experienced *is* open to rupture: code/space is embodied through the performances and interactions of the people within the space (between people, and between people and code). In this sense, code/space is not consistently produced, not always manufactured and experienced identically. Instead, code/space is constantly in a state of becoming, produced through individual performance and social interactions that are mediated, consciously or unconsciously, in relation to the mutual constitution of code/space. As such, code/spaces should be understood and conceptualized as relational and emergent spaces in which software frames the unfolding but does not determine it. This can be illustrated in a number of ways.

First, the extent to which space and code are mutually constituted and their effects explicitly invasive—where code/space is visible and explicit in its consequences—alters as one passes through coded assemblages. For example, within transition zones in airports, characterized by the intersection of flow and security (check-in, security checkpoints, boarding, customs, immigration), the visible transduction of code/space is magnified, so that a highly particularized transduction of space is relatively consistently produced through the explicit scrutiny of *every* inhabitant (passenger or worker). In contrast, in the check-in area, or the departure lounge, or airport shopping mall, or the walkway from lounge to gate, or in the air, or baggage claim area, the mutual constitution of code and space is backgrounded and less invasive unless provoked. For the most part then, except for the small proportion of time spent in these transition zones, the vast bulk of time in code/space—either in the airport or in the air—is largely banal: spaces of chatting, waiting, shopping, fidgeting, reading, staring, and eating, (see Gottdiener 2001). The space may well be dependent on code to function as intended, but the work that software does fades into the background, allowing other social relations to dominate.

Second, even within the more overt and invasive code/spaces, spatiality is still a *negotiated* production. To continue with the air travel example, which is elaborated in detail in chapter 7, while the processing of passengers is verified and approved by code, the decision to allow onward passage through the assemblages is often mediated by an airport or airline employee (for example, the check-in agent, airline supervisor, security guard, flight attendant, or immigration official). These individuals are often vested with degrees of power to disregard and override the system, for example, allowing passage without full documentation or passage through security after setting off alarms. (Other times the staff can also choose to *not* override the software decisions and defaults for professional, commercial, or even personal reasons.)

Third, it is clear from observation that code/space is experienced differentially—not everyone experiences the work of software in the same way (and not simply on the basis of privilege). For example, while we would argue that an airplane is a code/space, it is experienced by crew and passengers very differently (as is every assemblage), but not in a binary way (all passengers and all crew have the same experience). Rather, code/spaces are *peopled* and despite the belief that airports and air travel are devoid of culture and meaning (so-called non-places, Augé 1995) the identity politics that sustain divisions in labor and between passengers still operate (factors such as age, class, gender, and race still shape social interactions) (Crang 2002). Code/spaces are always diversely peopled and the meanings and experiences of code/spaces differ precisely because of how they are peopled.

Fourth, the relationship between code and people varies as a function of wider *context*. Mobilities, transactions, and interactions that involve code are historically, geographically, and institutionally embedded and do not arise from nowhere. Rather, code works within conventions, standards, representations, habits, routines, rules of thumb, and unofficial kludges, economic climates, and discursive formations, that position how code engages and is engaged with. The use of code is then always prefaced by, and *contingent* upon, this wider context.

Fifth, it is important to note that assemblages of code/spaces have accreted over time with technological advances and political and economic decisions to employ digital technologies. As such, they have not been planned in a comprehensive manner, but rather have *evolved*, often in an ad hoc manner and in response to specific needs. For example, new software versions and new technologies are always being sought to increase efficiencies and productivity, how different systems work together is constantly evolving, and the legal and economic frameworks underpinning code/space is negotiated and subject to periodic change (such as new licenses and changed pricing structures). The production of code/spaces is constantly evolving with these changes.

Finally, code/spaces are open to subversion. Here, the intended purpose of the code/space—productivity, security, safety, efficiency—is subverted through the system being duped. For example, people presenting false details to avoid being placed onto junk mailing lists, or stealing a person's identity for criminal gain. In this sense, while the system strives for perfection in terms of regulating and producing code/ space, it continues to have cracks that allow unintentional sociospatial relations and formations.

The nature and transduction of code/space is then never fixed, shifting with place, time, and context (social, political, and economic relations and situations). Code/ spaces are relational, emergent, and peopled.

Code/Space as a Collaborative Manufacture

Their swarming mass [people traversing a city] is an innumerable collection of singularities. Their intertwined paths give their shape to spaces. They weave places together. . . . They are not localized; it is rather that they spatialize.
—Michel de Certeau

The transduction of space is rarely, if ever, a singular occurrence. Instead, space and social life is beckoned into being through multiple, collectivized practices undertaken by many actants (including people, technologies, capta, nature, animals, and the weather) working in conjunction with each other and addressing multiple relational problems. Sociospatial relations are embedded in and emerge from a complex and diverse matrix of social relations, with the interplay between actants shaping how space is beckoned into existence. To take a busy street as an example—it is full of actants (drivers, cars, traffic management systems, pedestrians, signs, workmen) that are all seeking to resolve particular relational problems (how to get from A to B; how to augment the driving experience for the driver and passengers; how to manage the road network to maximize throughput and safety; how to repair the road so that it meets certain criteria and standards). They do not seek to resolve these problems in isolation from each other. Rather they are solved relationally, taking account of shifting contexts and situations. For example, the drivers are moving their cars about in relation to other cars, traffic signals, and disciplining devices such as speed cameras; the multiple onboard systems are monitoring driver behavior and reaction and are shaping how the car is driven; and the traffic management system is monitoring road usage and reacting appropriately by changing the phasing of the lights.

Each of these actants has a degree of autonomy to do work in the world, but none can work in total isolation. The street emerges as a *collaborative manufacture* (Crang 1994, 686)—as a collective, heterogeneous series of transductions, the outcome of multiple complementary, competing, and sometimes contradictory, practices enacted by many actants. What this means is spaces emerge in a polyvalent manner, bought into being simultaneously by many actants, who do not contribute to the manufacture in the same way or in equal degree. They experience the resultant space from different perspectives and in diverse ways. Indeed, a pedestrian and a car driver both contribute to the spatiality of the road in varying ways and the road shapes their respective unfolding, sociospatial relations differently. Space is transduced as more than the sum of its parts.

Even when coded objects and infrastructures seem relatively localized, they can transduce spatiality in different ways. For example, a person talking loudly on a cell phone in a subway car reshapes its spatiality for other travelers, even if they only get to hear one side of the conversation. In this case, all travelers are modulated into the code/space of the cell phone user, although its effects are uneven and unequal, dissipating with distance from the phone or countered by other coded objects such as an MP3 player that blocks out the conversation (but which might also be affecting nearby passengers through noise pollution). Here, code is making a difference to the unfolding spatiality but in multifarious ways.

Scaling Code/Space

Once there was a time and place for everything; today, things are increasingly smeared across multiple sites and moments in complex and often indeterminate ways.
—William J. Mitchell

Just as there has been a rethinking of space, a similar reconceptualization has occurred with respect to the concept of scale. Initially, scale was implicitly taken for granted as a "nested hierarchy of bounded spaces of differing size, such as the local, regional, national, and global" (Delaney and Leitner 1997, 93). Scale was treated simply as different levels of detail and modes of analysis. With the quantitative revolution in geographical analysis in the 1960s, scale took on more formal geometric properties, as an objective set of definable measurements useful for making relative comparisons. Recent research, however, has challenged scale as "unproblematic, pre-given and fixed hierarchy of bounded spaces," with theorists suggesting instead that scale be "conceptualized as socially constructed rather than ontologically pre-given, and that the geographic scales constructed are themselves implicated in the constitution of social, economic and political processes" (Delaney and Leitner 1997, 93; Jonas 1994; Marston 2000). In short, a number of authors have argued that scale is produced by actors and, therefore, open to transformation. Delaney and Leitner (1997, 95) posit that scale is (re)produced and transformed through the interplay of "context, actors, strategies, maneuvers, stakes, ideologies, and time." For some, such as Leitner (2004), this has meant rethinking scale as networks of relations which span space and cut across hierarchical structures (such as political units) that carve space up into discrete scalar units—in other words, scale works in complex ways both horizontally and vertically.

More recently, Marston, Jones, and Woodward (2005) have forwarded a proposition to eliminate the notion of scale, to be replaced with a flat ontology—one that neither privileges the vertical or horizontal (which tend to also create hierarchies of worth, such as cosmopolitan-parochial, or core-periphery). They understand scale as being epistemologically employed to put a shape on the world, but with no essential ontological foundation. Here, there is no natural scale, only scaling actions applied to the world to try to make sense of it, with this scaling emergent, constructed specifically for an analytic purpose. Consequently, Marston, Jones, and Woodward (2005) argue that spaces are not discretely bound (for example, the body, home, neighborhood, city, region), but are stretched out; the production of the intersections of diverse, spatially dispersed interactions and transactions that emerge through space and time (that is, an individual is simultaneously embedded in, works across, and is worked upon across space-time).

Likewise, we suggest that code/spaces (and indeed all space) are diversely, multiply, and ceaselessly scaled—they emerge as self-organizing systems of relations stretched out across space and time, the product of processes and relations occurring in many locales. For example, coded infrastructures create shifting, scaling networks linking together different actants located at distant sites or even on the move. An ATM may be physically located on Main Street, but it is connected in real time to a bank's server located several hundred miles away. At what scale is the transaction and withdrawal of money occurring? Or not occurring if the request is denied? Locally, nationally, both simultaneously, across a network? Similarly, consider the example of a busy road intersection. At what scale is the road being produced when drivers are using GPS systems to navigate; traffic light phasing is being updated in real time by management systems that are physically located in another part of the city, that base their decisions on data collected from many different sensors dotted around the network; cars are being tracked by cameras that relay license plate details to information systems hundreds of miles away? We would argue that road intersection is being transduced through coded processes scaled across space-time.

Code/space then is *extensible*. It does not consist of solely of localized individuations. Instead, the transduction of space occurs through ongoing individuations across networks (assemblages of relations) of greater or shorter length, so that scales such as local and global become redundant. The ATM and the road intersection exhibit, to paraphrase Massey's (1994) phrase, a progressive sense of scale, the product of multiple networks working across time and space. And each network is just one of a multitude of networks, creating multiple, simultaneous but partial spatial-time configurations that are at once local and beyond.

Such configurations induce a constant, emergent mode of time-space distanciation (decisions and actions in one locale have an effect in another), although they do not necessarily mean that decisions or actions at one location produce material outcomes at another. For example, the use of an ATM leads to a communication with and updating of a banking captabase located somewhere else in the world, but does not necessarily change the material conditions there (one could be just checking an account balance as opposed to withdrawing money). This is not to deny that for each individual these networks, and the transduction of space they help induce, occur at the site at which they are physically located. Rather, it is to acknowledge that this localized transduction is the grounding of one part of a complex, geographically distributed network, and that this grounding might be just one of a number that are simultaneously happening across the network. Here, the network becomes "a mass of currents rather than a single line of force" (Whatmore and Thorne 1997, 291) and is a "performative ordering (always in the making) rather than a systematic or structural entity (always already constituted)" (p. 289).

Endogenous Structural Forces

It should be noted that our conceptualization of space as an ontogenetic, collaborative manufacture does not deny the salience of structural or institutional expressions of power, variously labeled and analyzed within frameworks such as political economy, corporate capitalism, neoliberalism, or theocratic power, or the processes, practices, or systems of institutionally situated and enacted structures, such as the state and its delegates. Clearly, there are significant institutional actors and systems in the world that do work through various means—they seek to manage and regulate social and economic life, supported by ideologies expressed through discursive regimes, in ways favorable to their interests and ongoing survival. However, an ontogenetic approach recasts them not as monolithic, essential entities but as sets of ongoing, relational, contingent, discursive, and material practices, that are citational and transformative, and which coalesce and interact to produce a particular trajectory of interrelated processes. These practices emerge in context, inducing fresh transductions in collective life. As such, institutions and structural forces do not sit outside of collective life, shaping them from afar, but are (re)made through its performance, providing citational context at the same time that they are perpetuated. The means of production that underpin capitalist societies, and the ideologies that sustain and produce neoliberalism, are things that emerge in space-time through discursive and material practices, not things that are fully formed, preordained, and separate from the societies that they refer to and work upon.

In other words, for us, capitalist and neoliberal structures, and expressions of power, are things that emerge; ceaselessly produced through billions of actants every minute of every day. They appear to have form, substance, and solidity for two reasons. First, the actions performed by different actants generally appear to work toward a common goal (for example, the accumulation of capital) and are citational (they reproduce themselves in their own image, giving the appearance of stability). Second, they are supported by powerful discursive regimes that seek to make them clear and knowable to people; to make them appear commonsensical and rational (accepting economic and social injustice as inevitable and acceptable). Institutions, however, are complex, evolving entities consisting of amalgams of many people with different, competing ideas and interests, agendas, abilities, and ways of doing things, that emerge through processes of contestation and negotiation. Discursive regimes then are always in the process of taking shape, consisting of millions of exchanges, discussion, and documents, all read, interpreted, and acted upon in diverse ways. This is why the modes, of what appear to be coherent, knowable, consistent structural forces, when analyzed in any depth have no solidity; they are constantly in a state of metamorphosis. Indeed, they can never be fixed, as they are continuously in the process of being reproduced in millions of different ways. The work of institutions is then often haphazard, contradictory, and paradoxical.

While institutional forces and ideologies cannot be fixed, they are not without power, but this power is diffuse, contingent, and afforded, rather than held and wielded (see Allen 2004). However, the power is real nonetheless; for example, when expressed as violence with police ordered to raid a house and arrest an individual. The state draws its legitimacy and its power through the apparent solidity and actions of countless employees, and their associated discursive apparatus, that perform "the state" and by those who recognize the state through their interactions with state actors (even if their actions are ones of resistance) and thus afford the state, as a fluid, emergent entity, power. Here, power is conceived as something exercised by everyone and which is productive, complex, messy, and contradictory, bound up in everyday practices of living, consisting of acts of domination countered by acts of resistance (Foucault 1977). Power thus unfolds through the enactment of strategies and tactics between people, rather than being wielded by one actor onto another. In the case of coded assemblages, several different institutions, each composed of many actors, seek to shape the transduction of space. These assemblages have no central control per se and possess a complexity much greater than the sum of the parts. In this sense, they are an assemblage that needs to be analyzed with respect to power, in Deleuze and Guatarri's (1987) terms, as striated—that is, complex, gridded, rule-intensive, regulated; and as complex systems with emergent properties (Holland 1998; Waldrop 1994). We discuss the issue of regulation and governance further in chapter 5 and also provide an illustrative example with respect to air travel in chapter 7.

Conclusion

In this chapter, we have provided a brief genealogy of philosophical of thinking about space, before setting out how our own work seeks to rethink the concept of space from an ontogenetic position. We have then elaborated this conceptualization, detailing how we understand space to be constantly in a state of nondeterministic becoming, operationalized through the process of transduction. Software makes a difference to everyday life, we argue, because it alternatively modulates the conditions through which space is beckoned into being, transducing code/space and coded space. Through their work in the world, coded objects, infrastructures, processes, and assemblages bring forth new possibilities and augment, mediate, supplement, and regulate spatial formation. This transduction of space is contingent, relational, scaled, and context-dependent, emerging through the discursive and material practices of a collaborative manufacture that is diversely and ceaselessly scaled. In part III we illustrate our arguments through three extended empirical examples—traveling by air, making homes, and practicing consumption. We highlight the transduction of various kinds of code/ spaces and coded spaces, and how software is transducing new forms of spatiality and sociospatial governance that is profoundly changing how we partially solve the relational problems we encounter in our everyday lives.

5 Automated Management

We live life in real space, subject to the effects of code. We live ordinary lives, subject to the effects of code. We live social and political lives, subject to the effects of code. Code regulates all these aspects of our lives, more pervasively over time than any other regulator in our life.
—Lawrence Lessig

By code, we refer to a system of regulation, a regime, which is both structured and structuring . . . the primary function of code is normative.
—Douglas Thomas

In this chapter we turn our attention to how software is transforming the means by which individuals and societies are governed. Every society is organized and managed through a system of governance based upon a particular mode of governmentality—the interlocking rationale, apparatus, institutions, roles, and procedures of governance. The general system of governance in operation in most Western countries at the present has its roots in the Enlightenment era and the shift from a feudal to a modern society. At this time, Foucault (1977, 1978) among other theorists, argues a new ethos and form of governance was developed that on the one hand provided a much more systematic means of managing and governing populations, and on the other created the institutional mechanisms to impose a uniformity of social services across whole populations (for example, law enforcement, public health and sanitation reform, compulsory elementary education, civil service bureaucracies). Such changes, it can be argued, originated in the need to more effectively and productively propagate and sustain the emerging capitalist system and its associated processes of industrialization, urbanization, and colonization, and to maintain order and discipline among a rapidly growing population and facilitate a dramatic adjustment in socioeconomic relations. The sociotechnical ability to maintain centralized control was seen as vital, given the potential of social revolution to threaten the power of the capitalist class.

From Foucault's perspective, the new mode of governmentality introduced at this time relied on a biopolitics that viewed people as components in larger systems as labor commodities, as problems to be solved (ill-health, criminality, illiteracy), and as citizens with rights and obligations to the state. To make the modern system of governance work required a new apparatus of surveillance and policing that captured, cataloged, and classified people, and facilitated the imposition of uniform and universal regulations that instilled forms of self-discipline (people regulated their behavior for fear of discipline and punishment). As such, new systems and technologies of regulation and management were devised to provide a detailed knowledge of a population and to render people calculable in a formal sense, making it possible to govern according to norms defined and legitimated by science with its rationality, logic, and objectivity. This provided new professional elites (civil servants, teachers, doctors, police officers, health inspectors, sanitary engineers, welfare officers) who took their authority by grounding their actions in scientific and objective ways of knowing and doing (Rose 1996). To make people calculable required the quantification of society; the creation of universal and accurate means of social measurement and human identification (Barnes and Hannah 2001; Crampton 2004; Desrosières 1998; Thrift 2004b). Such means included censuses, records relating to health, school attendance, housing standards, crime rates, insobriety and prostitution, the comprehensive civil registration of births, deaths, and marriages, and also the representation of populations in new kinds of statistical graphs and thematic maps (see figure 5.1).

This multitude of new statistical information was collected, collated, and analyzed by institutions in order to monitor and regulate society as a whole and to also mete out punishment to particular people who did not comply with regulations and required criteria of behavior. These institutions also made it readily apparent to all people that they were open to surveillance in its various guises and would be judged against known criteria and, as such, the mode of governmentality not only disciplined but worked to self-discipline. That is, people were compelled to modify their own behavior to conform to expectations and rules or face punishment, and were thus were rendered, in Foucault's (1978) term, "docile bodies"; bodies that are orderly, noncomplaining, and compliant. As such, a key element in the new system of governance—the attempt to create an objectifying panoptic ("all-seeing") gaze—produced a particular form of rational subjectivity designed to ensure good government through a more efficient and systematic legal and social field (McNay 1994).

In tandem with the growth in systems designed to manage populations, similar rationalities and technologies and systems of governmentality were applied to businesses and the practices of factory work, in particular, in order to mobilize and discipline workers to ensure the maximization of profits by increasing efficiency, productivity, and competitive advantage, while also reducing risk, workplace fraud, and crime. Over time, particular organization schemas or workplace apparati of production came to dominate (for example, Taylorism and Fordism in the early twentieth century), which were replaced as new technologies and rationalities emerged.

Figure 5.1
Part of Charles Booth's famous poverty map of London from the 1890s. Streets and houses are classified and the population is rendered visible and knowable. *Source:* British Library, www .bl.uk/learning/artimages/maphist/wealth/boothextract/boothslondonpovertymap.html

In the last two centuries, this form of disciplinary governance has dominated in Western capitalist nations, with its mode of governmentality mutating and evolving, but always seeking to bind individuals into surveillant grids of power/knowledge, where self-disciplining is an integral component. In recent years, Garland (2001, cited in Lyon 2007, 12) argues that the present mode is one of a "culture of control," driven by the desire for "security, orderliness, risk management and the taming of chance." To this end, a range of new technologies have played an important role. The development of unique mechanisms of identification such as fingerprinting and photography, and forms of documentation like passports, driver's licenses, national insurance or social security numbers, created new ways to identify, verify, and process people, forming "tokens of trust" to manage populations that were too large, diverse, and distant to be known through local, subjective knowledge alone (Lyon 2002, 244). Such tokens provided a scientific means of authentication and accreditation, replacing forms of self-authentication and personal vouchsafing. They also provided common units that linked together separate strands of capta within filing systems, enabling associated records to be reliably cross-referenced, queried, and processed, thus converting capta into operative *information* (Checkland and Holwell 1998). When fields of information are combined to create larger, collective structures, they become systems of *knowledge*. Identification codes work to place people accurately into a rhizomic assemblage of capta that make them visible and amenable to modes of governance. Similarly, closed circuit television (CCTV) has had a major impact on regulating streetscapes and spaces of consumption (shops, malls, stations, sports arenas) by providing the ever ready threat that transgressive and criminal behavior will be caught on camera, and penalties and punishment will follow.

These technologies have been employed in an effort to make the systems and apparatus of governance more panoptical in nature—to ensure that citizens are always open to surveillance, regulation, and discipline in order to produce good government, effective administration, profitable business, and sustainable and stable communities. However, despite advances in the surveillance tools and systems of organization, particularly in the last few decades, the disciplinary grid created has remained open to vertical (within an activity) and horizontal (across activities) fragmentation (Hannah 1997). For example, within an activity, observation, judgment, and enforcement has often been undertaken by different agencies who communicated imperfectly; and across activities, different organizations, for legal, institutional, or technical reasons, have not easily been able to exchange or compare information (Hannah 1997). Indeed, the extent of fraud, deviance, and crime throughout contemporary Western societies is clearly indicative of the fragmentary nature of surveillance and self-disciplining. Governance then has consisted of an imperfect panopticon with blind spots and fissures that is best described as an oligopticon—partial vantage points from fixed positions with limited viewsheds; "a series of partial orders, localized totalities, with their ability to gaze in some directions and not others" (Latour cited in Amin and Thrift 2002, 92).

In rest of this chapter, we detail the ways in which software is increasingly being employed to create oligopticons with wider and more dynamic and mobile fields of view; to produce a more panoptic mode of governance that enables more effective regimes of self-disciplining and societal disciplining. We argue that software is ideally suited to monitoring, managing, and processing capta about people, objects, and their interaction, and is leading to a new mode of governmentality that we term automated management.

The Emergence of Automated Management

Put simply, automated management is the regulation of people and objects through processes that are *automated* (technologically enacted), *automatic* (the technology performs the regulation without prompting or direction), and *autonomous* (regulation, discipline, and outcomes are enacted without human oversight) in nature. Here, software is central for the ability of different technologies to perform such as role. Software controls how capta is generated, cataloged, and analyzed, and to make decisions and act on the basis of those decisions. On the one hand, software is being used to create more effective systems of surveillance and, on the other, to create capture systems that actively reshape behavior by altering the performance of a task. Automated management thus works in a different way compared to other modes of governmentality, creating a situation wherein "code is law" (Lessig 1999).

Traditional forms of surveillance, as detailed by Foucault and many others (Lyon 2007), are being transformed by the application of software to their functioning and processing. Consider the example of the monitoring of road traffic for driving offenses. Until relatively recently, the system of traffic governance relied principally on the vision of police officers, who were thinly scattered across the road network; drivers were not aware of where officers might be, so were encouraged to self-discipline their driving in case they encountered one. These were largely replaced by analog video cameras that started the process of automation, and these in turn are being exchanged for networked, digital equivalents that use ANPR (automatic number plate recognition) software to automatically determine if an offense has taken place, to cross-reference to a captabase to determine the offender, and to generate and post notification of a fine or penalty points (Dodge and Kitchin 2007a). Such developments are designed to more effectively enforce a system of regulation and instill a stronger regime of self-discipline, the main premise being that if drivers know they are being monitored more comprehensively, then they will drive more safely, and this in turn will reduce fuel consumption, maintenance, and insurance costs, and people will refrain from illegal activities such as car theft. There are many other automated forms of surveillance, in use or under development, that seek to recognize unique aspects of bodily physiology and activity such as the structure of faces and voices, the manner of walking, idiosyncrasies of typing, and writing a signature.

As noted, records of activities, movements, and transactions have long been generated with respect to people and significant objects (for example, cars). Such capta might well have been generated without surveying the person directly. In recent years, surveillance has become ever more sophisticated with the rise of digital technologies to capture and process different forms of capta relating to individuals, objects, and communication. Further, every action and transaction captured by these systems necessarily generates subsidiary information, such as time and place of capture, which is of potential value and is routinely stored for future analysis (Andrejevic 2007). Unlike traditional forms of surveillance that seek to self-discipline, new forms of surveillance seek to produce objectified individuals where the vast amount of capta harvested about them is used to classify, sort, and differentially treat them, and actively shapes their behavior (Agre 1994; Graham 2005; Lyon 2002). Individuals are often largely unaware that such capta is being generated about their activities and interests, except when it is explicitly revealed to them, for example, as itemized entries on a telephone bill or when a credit application is rejected. Such a form of governance is described by Deleuze (1992) in his notion of "societies of control." Here, expressions of power are not visible and threatening as with sovereign or disciplinary regimes, rather power is exerted subtly through distributed control and protocols that define and regulate access to resources and spaces, without those who are being governed necessarily being aware of such processes. As Graham (2005, 566) notes, "most processes of software-sorting are actually invisible from the point of the users, these prioritizations are often not evident either to the favored groups or places or to the marginalized ones."

Software is a key actant in creating societies of control, as it makes possible a fundamental shift in how information is gathered, by whom, for what purposes, and how it is applied to anticipate individuals' future lives. Software, as noted by Agre (1994), is being used to underpin systems that work to actively discipline (as opposed self-discipline) citizens by altering how tasks are performed, often in very banal, mundane, and subtle ways. Termed the "capture model," Agre notes that the mechanisms by which capta is generated are increasingly an *integral* part of the system that it seeks to monitor and regulate, and that these mechanisms, in turn, redefine and reconfigure that system, quite often in real time.

For example, a computerized register in a store is configured in such a way that the practices of checkout labor are also the mechanisms by which the retail worker is monitored, disciplined, and rewarded. The worker has to log into the register to begin work, and then proceeds to scan items across a laser. The rate of scanning is automatically logged, monitored, and assessed, and linked to the employee's record. In other words, rather than the worker being monitored by an external surveillance system that works to self-discipline, the worker is scrutinized through a wholly internalized process that actively shapes worker performance. Similarly, purchasing a plane ticket can only be achieved via online booking systems (even if purchased through a travel agent, they type this information into the system on our behalf) as certain compulsory fields of information have to be registered at the time of purchase in order to generate a passenger name record (PNR) (see figure 5.2). If requisite capta fields are left empty, then the transaction cannot be completed, as all passengers have to be accompanied by a shadow PNR that can be compared to government captabases for the purposes of security and safety in order to fly. The process of buying an individualized flight ticket, tied to a named person, has become the means by which an individual's credentials are automatically authenticated and risk assessed and commercial worth calculated—it is an integral part of booking the ticket (see chapter 7 for further discussion).

The capture model, outlined by Agre (1994), differs in several important respects from traditional surveillance-based, self-disciplining forms of governmentality (see table 5.1). As noted, capture is an inherent part of a system's architecture—it is inescapable and exhaustive, exerting direct regulation over what the user of the system (in this case a worker) can and cannot do. Its work is often hidden or backgrounded so that those it disciplines might not be aware of how the software is working to reshape their activity. It works across distributed systems and regulates in real time. Whereas capta generated by traditional surveillance technologies are principally for the purpose of regulation (for reasons of safety, law enforcement, security, or revenue recovery), capture technologies generate capta for a much wider purpose and broader constituency. Some of these reasons might include anticipating new markets, creating a competitive advantage, increasing efficiency and productivity, reducing employee crime, mitigating potential future risks, and providing value-added services. As such, the capture model is often championed by consumption-driven corporations who want to know more about customers to influence and channel and create behaviors that maximize revenues. The call-center architecture that is dependent on software and captabases, is in some sense the idealized environment for the capture model.

Agre (1994) argues that the capture model has been made possible because a *grammar of action* has been imposed on a system. A grammar of action is a highly formalized set of rules that ensures that a particular task is undertaken in a particular way, given certain criteria and inputs. It involves a systematic means of representing aspects of the world (a formalized ontology) and an organized language for processing those representations. As Galloway (2004) notes, the organized language consists of protocols that govern the set of possible behaviors within a contingent system. Sequences of protocols—proscriptions for structure (Galloway 2004)—constitute the grammar of action. In the case of the retail store, the worker is represented by an employer ID, the goods by bar codes and RFIDs, and the work rate by units of time.

Sample PNR (Passenger Name Record)

```
1.1HASBROUCK/EDWARD MR   2.1FOO/BAR MR
 1 CO1234Q 12APR 6 SFOLHR HK2   1630   1030    1350
            /ABCO*123ABC /E
OPERATED BY VIRGIN ATLANTIC
 2 CO4321Q 21APR 1 LHRSFO HK2   1100   1350
/ABCO*123ABC /E
OPERATED BY VIRGIN ATLANTIC
TKT/TIME LIMIT
   1.T-13FEB-1B2D*A69
PHONES
   1.SFO415-365-1698-A AIRTREKS
   2.SFO415-365-1645-A FAX
INVOICED
ADDRESS
     AIRTREKS.COM
     442 POST STREET 4TH FLOOR
     SAN FRANCISCO CA 94102 USA
FARE - PRICE RETAINED/HISTORY
GENERAL FACTS
   1.SSR TKNA CO HK1 SFOLHR1234Q12APR/00512345678901
   2.SSR TKNA CO HK1 LHRSFO4321Q21APR/00512345678901
   3.SSR TKNA CO HK1 SFOLHR1234Q12APR/00512345678914
   4.SSR TKNA CO HK1 LHRSFO4321Q21APR/00512345678914
REMARKS
   1./AIRTREKS.COM
   2./442 POST STREET 4TH FLOOR
   3./SAN FRANCISCO CA 94102 USA
   4.-*CC1234567890123456+12/06
   5.H-XXAUTH/012345/CC1234567890123456/CO/
     USD902.40/13FEB/M
ACCOUNTING DATA
   1.   CO+1234567890/     .00/     356.00/      95.20/
        ONE/CCVI1234567890123456
        1.1HASBROUCK EDWARD MR/1/F
   2.   CO+1234567891/     .00/     356.00/      95.20/
        ONE/CCVI1234567890123456
        2.1FOO BAR MR/1/F
RECEIVED FROM - EH
1B2D.1B2D*A69 1824/29JAN03 ZXYVUT H
```

Figure 5.2
The extensive fields of a PNR (passenger name record) created for individuals on each flight. The PNRs are processed by code in various situations, institutions, and places unknown to the individual represented by the capta. (Redrawn from Edward Hasbrouck, The Practical Nomad, www.hasbrouck.org/cfp2003/PNR.html)

Table 5.1
Comparing surveillance and capture models of governmentality

Parameters	Surveillance model	Capture model
Concept	Vision	Linguistic
Site	Collection of information external to a system	Capture of information inherent to a system
Extent	Selective, but threatens exhaustive	Exhaustive (within its frame of reference)
Mechanism	Disciplines through self-disciplining	Manages by modulating experience and disciplining
Visibility	Always visible	Often hidden, sometimes deliberately secret
Capta	Collected information is representation	Captured information is representation and product
Agency	People operated (somebody watches the camera or reads the file); increasingly automated	Software operated (automated)
Viewfield	Static (at fixed points with fixed views)	Typically distributed and increasingly mobile
Temporality	Partially dynamic, usually employed retrospectively	Dynamic—updates and potentially regulates in real time
Organization	Centrally organized and structured	Diverse, locally organized, institutionally structured
Predictability	Nonpredictive	Sometimes predictive, facilitates anticipatory governance

Source: Adapted from Agre 1994

The organized language is the protocols for processing capta to derive certain results, in this case the sale of goods, ensuring correct monies are collected, an updating of the store's stock inventory, and efficient workers. In purchasing a plane ticket, the passenger and the travel itinerary is represented by key capta such as name, address, passport number, flight number, credit card number (as in figure 5.2 above). These capta, along with the specifically structured language, are the protocols for checking, authenticating, and verifying those capta with respect to payment and security. Capta is thus recorded in sequence and processed with respect to the governing protocols. If the recording is not in sequence or the capta does not meet the required protocols, then the system disciplines the worker (making the worker perform the task again) or the passenger (denying permission to take the next stage in the journey)—they fail to successfully write their way through the grammar of action. Behavior is therefore necessarily reshaped to make it more amenable to capture in order to fulfill the essential requirements that make a system work (Wardrip-Fruin 2003).

As Agre (1994, 752) notes, while grammars of action necessarily structure activity, there is always some flexibility: "people engaged in captured activity can engage in an infinite variety of sequences of action, provided these sequences are composed of the unitary elements and means of combination are prescribed by the grammar of action." It is this contingency that makes a system, such as the Internet, appear to be very open and democratic. Nonetheless, they are highly regulated at one level, only allowing actions that protocols enable. In this sense, the Internet is distributed but not decentralized. It is this paradoxical relationship—of freedom and fluidity versus control and rigidity—that makes automated management such a powerful form of governmentality. As we explore in chapter 6, it enables creativity, choice, and expression, at the same time that it monitors, regulates, and structures. In this sense, "societies of control" are seductive to participants—in Althusser's (1971) terms, the systems they employ interpellate by enticing people to desire them and willingly and voluntarily participate in their ideology and practice (rather than simply disciplining them into docile bodies).

Moreover, it should be noted that increasingly automated surveillance and capture systems are also being engineered into close combination, working to the same objective. Much of the capta generated by external surveillance systems are translated into a form suitable for processing by capture models, though their effect is one of self-discipline. For example, capta from a digital traffic camera are translated into a form—a license plate registration—amenable to grammars of action through ANPR software.

The Capta Shadow

The capta from surveillance and capture systems provide a means of linking entities and processes together across domains and systems in complex ways to form dense rhizomic assemblages of power/knowledge. This assemblage constitutes what might be termed a capta shadow (capta that uniquely represents and records people and their lives) and associated capta trails (records of the locational positions of interactions and transactions) across space-time. This idea of an individual having a capta shadow residing in information systems has been conceptualized by a number of scholars—"shadow order" (Bogard 1996), "digital persona" (Clarke 1994a), "dividuals" (Deleuze 1992), and "data doubles" (Lyon 2003). We prefer the term *capta shadow*, as the metaphor of the shadow usefully conveys the idea that it is something you can never be rid of. The effect of the capta shadow is that more and more aspects of everyday life are transformed into a legible landscape—into "simple and visible forms of order" (Curry, Philips, and Regan 2004, 359)—for those seeking to enact and regulate systems. In short, software thus provides the means to collect, structure, and process capta and to more effectively identify, monitor, and track subjects, objects, and transactions.

This capta shadow is available to institutions—states and the companies that generate it—but, unlike traditional forms of disciplinary surveillance, also to other individuals, institutions, and companies (sometimes freely, other times traded for a fee). As Andrejevic (2007) notes, although small scale communities always had an ability to monitor individual behavior through embodied observation ("snooping") and tightly connected social networks ("gossiping"), widespread, cheap digital capta recording devices such as miniature cameras and microphones, spying software such as keystroke programs, the construction of large captabases, and the ability to search them online, has meant an explosion in peer-to-peer surveillance. It is relatively easy to check the call log of a mobile phone, look up recent computer use (web site history, documents last opened), browse playlists on an MP3 player, consult the previous destinations set on the car GPS, and more broadly to pinpoint the information that people are willing to share through personal web pages, blogs, and social networking sites. It is possible to track down other reports relating to a person, for example, in a newspaper, to look through public records and do background checks; and to set up covert surveillance systems such as nanny-cams that allow one to view via a computer or mobile phone how a child is being cared for, or to use GPS tracking to monitor the location of children. Much of this can be undertaken in relation to people we have never met, making it possible to profile and "get to know" individuals before encountering them. For example, online commercial services such as Abika.com and US SEARCH.com allow customers to check the histories of individuals (whether they be acquaintances, family, potential dates, or prospective employees) with respect to issues such as marital status, solvency, property ownership, employment history, tax status, criminal record, sexual or domestic abuse allegations, or educational background. Despite the vast scale of captabases, it is surprisingly easily to exactly pinpoint a single person with only a few of their characteristics. Online mapping tools also provide free access to detailed overhead imagery and street-level views for many cities, which mean homes can also be studied. Never before has it been so quick and affordable to find out information about our peers, without their knowledge or permission. Interestingly, the act of searching and querying is itself captured, and gives quite a distinctive capta footprint.

Automated Capta

With respect to both automated surveillance and capture, the automatic generation and analysis of capta is vital. There have been several key developments, all underpinned by code, that have made such automatic capture possible. First, there have been significant advances in the tagging of people, objects, information, transactions, and territories to make them more amenable to capture by making them machine-readable and to increase the granularity of capture (discussed in chapter 3). Second, the technologies to record capta have been significantly improved, with increases in accuracy, sophistication, distribution, and form (for example, always on and mobile). Third, there have been enhancement in the virtual and physical storage of capta, along with decline in size and cost overheads. Fourth, there has been progress in the ability to make sense of the capta and its analysis, and to enact appropriate responses without human oversight.

Identifying Capta

Over the past thirty years or so, with the advent of new technologies and more and more sophisticated and distributed information systems, there has been a marked increase in the ability to label and identify people, objects, information, transactions, and territories. Indeed, there has been a huge proliferation of identification codes, accompanied by an increased granularity (uniqueness) in identification. These codes are increasingly machine-readable—that is, they can be automatically read by hardware and can be verified, processed, analyzed, stored, and shared by a variety of different systems.

So, for example, with respect to people, individuals are now uniquely identified through identification codes in a plethora of ways that can be classified into three general types: (1) something you have (a physical token like a passport, store and loyalty cards, credit cards), (2) something you know (a username, password, or PIN), and (3) something you are (biometric characteristics, particularly fingerprints, irises, DNA, face) (Clarke 1994b). These can be combined for purposes of authentication, such as providing both a credit card and a PIN; or a passport and a fingerprint scan. Present trends are to move from the first and second types to third type, especially for higher order transactions such as accessing high-value areas within a company building or entering a country, although fingerprint scanners are now being increasingly embedded into more mundane objects such as laptops to increase capta security.

At present, there is an emphasis on trying to increase the accuracy of identification. For example, personal identification in the form of a passport has traditionally consisted of printed matter—text and a photograph. This has meant it has been open to forgery or doctoring. Consequently, traditional forms of personal identification, like a passport, are being replaced by biometric capta that are much more difficult to fake. Biometric identification systems seek to render people machine readable, and by "fusing together flesh and machine" (Davies 1994) they enforce the supposedly infallible linkages of individuals to their digital records—it reduces individuals to "quantifiable, recordable, enumerable, and encodable characteristics" (Galloway 2004, 113). At present, the most well-known biometric techniques concentrate on the distinctive physiological patterns of the fingers-tips and the eyeball, while the ultimate biometric is the patterning of human DNA. The fingers, eyes, and genes become the physical media of identity (the loops, arches, and whorls of skin on the fingertip) that are scanned in some form to produce digitized capta suitable for storage and processing by software. These biometric forms of identification seek to fulfill Clarke's (1994b) list of desirable characteristics for effective human identification codes:

- Universality of coverage (everyone should have one)
- Uniqueness (each person should have only one, and no two people should have the same one)
- Permanence (should not change, nor be changeable)
- Indispensability (a natural characteristic that cannot be removed)
- Collectibility
- Storability
- Exclusivity
- Precision
- Simplicity
- Costand convenience
- Acceptability.

Similarly, as discussed in chapter 3, material objects are increasingly assigned unique identifiers that allow them to be processed, tracked, and traced through complex logistical networks (manufacturer serial numbers, UPC bar codes, order numbers, shipping waybills, vehicle license plates). Here, the granularity of the capta has increased markedly. For example, the granularity of a twelve digit UPC bar code is coarse, with all objects of the same product type assigned the same bar code, meaning that they cannot be discriminated. Replaced with a 2D bar code or an RFID, the object becomes uniquely labeled, meaning that each and every entity can be identified and its movement and use tracked and traced.

Likewise, information and transactions are being assigned ever more unique identifiers for purposes of supporting intellectual property rights (digital object identifiers) or monitoring communication and interactions for the purposes of billing, dealing with queries by customers, and deriving knowledge from them (for example, codes to support electronic data interchange, EDI, networks and electronic funds transfer, ETF, networks). All e-mail communications, for example, have unique identifying codes, as do all financial transactions, so they can be logged and traced. In many capta processing systems, billions of transactions can be logged each day as they happen, each transaction encoded with unique identifiers that usually include the time stamp and location details of the transaction (examples of such transactions are banking and stock market trades, as well as air traffic control). Something of the extent and utility of these codes is revealed through a telephone query to a customer service center where calls most often begin with a reference number handshake (the quoting of an account number or reference code to establish authenticity and retrieve records from a captabase). For some interactions, especially financial ones, this often involves a lengthy series of identification codes and security phrases.

More and more frequently, the identification codes of people, objects, information, and transactions are being tied to spatial referents (grid references, latitude and longitude, postal codes, administrative districts, and geodemographic area types). Moreover, the increased granularity with respect to other codes are mirrored with respect to territorial units, with capta being tied to finer spatial resolutions (individual households and land parcels as opposed to neighborhoods, or the routine use of submeter coordinates from GPS). What this means is that entities can be located in, and tracked through, space and time in ways that were previously impossible to achieve.

This proliferation of ID codes has led to a widening and deepening of capta shadows and trails. With respect to individuals, it is fair to say that each of us is now accompanied by an extensive capta shadow that includes many thousands of records concerning personal and family history, finances, housing, tax payments, spending patterns, welfare, health, education, communications history (e-mail, phone records), international travel, criminal activity, and so on, referenced across time and space. Indeed, the agencies and companies that generate such capta know more about more individuals than at any point in history. Much will likely never be deleted, and records that would once have faded and been lost will be recallable well into the future (see discussion in chapters 10 and 11). While much capta about people is undoubtedly left unexamined, an increasing amount of personal information is employed by a large number of institutions and corporations to monitor, profile, and regulate, using various software systems to process and analyze it in sophisticated ways and with multiple consequences for the people represented.

Recording Capta

The essential quality of tokens of identification that make them amenable to supporting a condition of automated management, is that they are either generated within a software system (transaction codes), entered into a system (usernames and passwords), or that they are machine-readable (2D bar codes, RFIDs). They are, therefore, open to being recorded in scripted, consistent, and automatic ways. There have been a number of developments that have made the recording of such capta more effective and efficient.

A number of new technologies for capturing digital capta, that include scanning and sensing devices and digital forms, have been developed.

Systems are being designed so that the surrender of capta is a default element to receive services or that users have to opt out, rather than opt in.

Systems are designed to be excessive in nature, seeking to obtain as much capta as possible.

More and more of what were previously "dumb" technologies are being imbued with degrees of awareness and are thus able to measure elements of the world around them. The means of measurement is shifting from intermittent to continuous.

The capture of capta has become mobile, both in the sense of being able to track people and things as they move through space and time, and also the means of measurement is mobile and not from fixed points.
The systems of capture are networked and distributed.

We will explore each of these features in turn.

Advances in Sensing and Scanning Technologies Along with advances in unique identification tagging has been the development of sensing and scanning technologies used to automatically machine-read them (see figure 5.3). Typically, scanning devices use visual light, laser, or radio waves to sense tags. For example, surveillance cameras operated using ANPR software are programmed to accurately recognize lettering and to then match the license plate details to a vehicle captabase. Iris or fingerprint scanners capture biometrics as a way of uniquely identifying a person. Laser scanners in supermarket checkouts read bar codes, and credit card readers query the magnetic strip on the back or the embedded EMV chip on the front. Transponders in ticket barriers search for the RFID tag in a smart ticket and deduct the correct fare. As noted above, in capture systems operated by a person, such as scanning bar codes at a store checkout, the sensing process also becomes the means of monitoring the performance of the retail worker at the same time as tallying the purchases of the shopper.

In addition, there have been significant advances in other forms of capta generation. For example, there are now a plethora of sensing technologies that measure aspects of the world around them. A wide range of batch fabricated, inexpensive, micro-electromechanical systems (MEMS) have been developed that can automatically monitor different kinds of information such as light, temperature, motion, and pressure, transduce them into digital capta, and communicate this capta to other devices. Air-conditioning units utilize humidity and temperature sensors; vacuum cleaners and washing machines use pressure sensors; motion of all kinds can be tracked by accelerometers and orientation, inclination, and vibrations sensors (Mitchell 2004). MEMS also enable the capture of haptic information and are being used to transform computer interfaces. For example, video game controllers utilize tilting and pressure capta generated by a player's action to direct the action on the screen. Some capta generated by sensors are processed in the moment (for example, in moving vehicles, capta are transmitted in real time from brake pedal to ECU), while others are stored as logs and are transmittable to third parties for later analysis and use (especially through wireless technologies such as Bluetooth).

Existing forms of manual capta generation are also being digitized. For example, Internet inferfaces often ask users to upload capta through filling in capta fields. More traditional forms of records can also be scanned and automatically matched against an individual identifier. For example, widely deployed official forms, such as those in government censuses, while filled out by hand, are typically scanned by machine

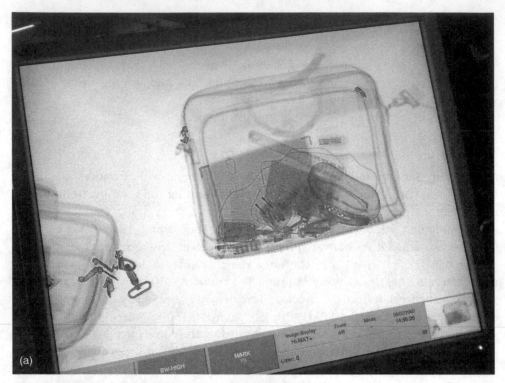

Figure 5.3

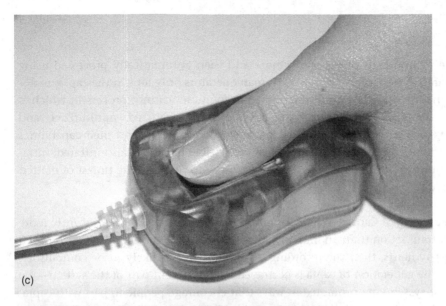

Figure 5.3
Sensing and scanning equipment is increasingly common in everyday practice. (*a*) X-ray bag scanner. (*b*) Kinetic sensing in video game controllers. (*c*) Portable fingerprint scanner for local authentication. (*d*) RFID transponder in the ticket barrier of the London Underground reading Oyster smartcard ticket.

at the rate of hundreds of pages a minute and then automatically processed using optical character recognition software. Human operators only look at the capta manually if the handwriting is so indistinct that the computer cannot process it, which is relatively rare. Other analog technologies are being digitized, miniturized, and networked, such as microphones, cameras, and video cameras, and their capabilities are being extended (cameras are able to capture visible light, but also infrared, ultraviolet, and low-intensity light, and to be able to record in detail the tiniest of matter; Mitchell 2004).

Default Recording of Capta Where a controlling organization has significantly more power in a transaction than an individual, for example in a monopoly situation such as welfare payments, then the recording of certain capta is likely to be compulsory. Otherwise, the generation of capta is portrayed as an inherent part of the system—the way it is—or systems are promoted in ways that encourage people to part with capta, with penalties such as degrading of service, or additional costs (in time or money), or service denial. Often, the default settings are rigged so that people have to consciously choose to opt out. Web browsing patterns can be recorded in great detail—so called clickstream surveillance—using cookies and other transaction identification codes (see Bennett 2001). Turning off cookies (and their surveillance) seriously degrades the functionality of a large part of the Web and, in effect, they constitute a form of casual surveillance which largely goes unnoticed and unchallenged. In many ways, the compulsory nature of surveillance is rarely an issue—people voluntarily provide huge amounts of capta about themselves through their interactions with organizations and businesses. In this sense, "we are not simply subject *to* surveillance, but we are subjects *of* surveillance" (Lyon 2007, 7, original emphasis). Often surveillance is something that people willingly take part in, and we sometimes desire (for example, CCTV is often called for, rather than something forced onto a community). Indeed, many people invest in technologies that enable them to undertake their own surveillance (baby monitors, children trackers, home security cameras, fitness equipment, health monitoring—see chapter 10 concerning so-called sousveillance, or surveillance of oneself).

Excessive in Nature Contemporary systems are often set to gather excessive amounts of capta—that which is actually necessary to undertake a transaction, along with additional capta deemed of potential interest or likely utility (sometimes this is revealed in the design of online forms that distinguish between compulsory and optional fields). The tendency to excess is driven by two concerns. First, there is simple expediency, a philosophy of "get it if we can as the capta might be useful." Here, capta is generated that is not needed for a task at hand, such as purchasing goods online (for which name, credit card, and address details are needed) but will be useful for building a personal profile of that customer (for example, asking about the purchaser's lifestyle and buying habits). Second, the cost of generating and storing additional capta are marginal, especially as storage costs continue to decline. In addition, there is an abundance of programs designed to make sense and add value to such capta (see next sections).

From "Dumb" to "Smart"   As detailed in chapter 3, many of the material objects and environments used in everyday life are shifting from being "dumb" to "smart" in nature, and in the process are becoming capable of creating significant new streams of uniquely identifiable capta. In this context, smart means programmed awareness of use, rather than intelligence. So household appliances (televisions, washing machines, cameras), cars, and everyday spaces are, through the application of sensors and software, being made aware of how they are being used (time, location) and, crucially, which people use them. This awareness of usage is easily captured as logs and transmittable to third parties. The car is prime example of an assemblage that is rapidly shifting from inert machine to aware object. As Thrift (2004c, 50) notes, "almost every element of the modern automobile is either shadowed by software or software has become . . . the pivotal component." While the car still appears the same, and drives in the same fashion, its systems are increasingly aware of their performance through onboard diagnostics, its location through GPS, and the actions of the driver. The result is that cars are now rich capta generators, that store information in event data recorders that are hidden from view but recallable (Dodge and Kitchin 2007a).

Continuous Monitoring   Conventionally, a capta shadow consisted of a sporadic and partial record revealing the actions of a person or object only at particular known times. In most cases, capta generation was triggered by an overt transaction of some kind (e.g., swiping of a credit card, entry of a PIN to open a door). Increasingly, however, the ability to continuously generate capta about people and objects in real time is being realized. Here, capta generation is always on; always part of the system. For example, the performance of a worker in a supermarket checkout is continuously recorded in order to monitor their performance. Clearly, this has the effect of extending the temporal regime of surveillance and capture, meaning that a worker finds it increasingly difficult to escape automated management.

Mobile   In conventional captabases, only a rudimentary capta trail can be constructed for a person or object by mapping the time, date, and location of each transaction. However, movement in between the point of direct identifiable contact remains unknown. These spatial gaps are in the process of being filled in through the employment of measurement technologies that can track machine-readable tokens of identification (stored via RFIDs, 2D bar codes, or license plates) across time and space. In the case of wireless information and communication technologies, particularly cell phones, the location of devices can be much more continuously monitored using triangulation from masts to a relatively fine spatial resolution by network companies, even if the device itself is inactive from the user's point of view. Here, capture becomes mobile with a complete, location-enriched capta trail of the device and person revealed (as shown in figure 5.4). It is probable that such continuous spatial tracking of a large proportion of the population will become commonplace in next few years, encouraged in large part by the commercial development of novel location-based services (LBSs). In essence, LBSs consist of creating individualized information to people that is contextually relevant to their present geographic location. It is likely that such capta related to LBS will be automatically logged and be folded into the growing capta shadow of consumers.

Networked   The development of the Internet, in harness with meshes of telematic and wireless networks across cities, has redefined the scaling, spacing, and timing of capta generation. Capta is now seamlessly and rapidly distributed across communication networks that stretch out across space. Moreover, the cost of distribution across digital networks is fast approaching zero in some contexts. As a consequence, capta can be captured at a distance and can be easily circulated within and between organizations and states. What this means is that the space-time distanciation of surveil-

Figure 5.4
Visualization of cell phone SMS activity across Amsterdam on New Year's Eve, 2007. *Source*: courtesy of Filippo Dal Fiore and Aaron Koblin, Currentcity project, www.currentcity.org

lance and control has been markedly shrunk. Capta generated in Dallas can be controlled and monitored in real time from New York and appropriate actions taken automatically.

Storing Capta

In the era of paper records, storing vast quantities of capta was an expensive and labor intensive business involving large warehousing operations. Capta that once would have filled thousands of yards of shelving can now be housed digitally on a single disk. Developments in hard disks technologies, in particular, have relentlessly pushed up the capacity, and thus driven down the cost per megabyte, of data storage, making it considerably cheaper than paper or film (Grochowski and Halem 2003; see figure 5.5). The growth in storage density, as measured in bits per inch on magnetic disks,

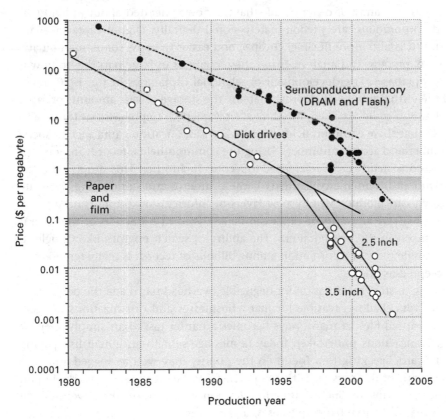

Figure 5.5
Step decline in storage cost over recent decades. (Redrawn from Grochowski and Halem 2003, 341)

has even outpaced the curve of Moore's Law, and shows little sign of slowing down in the near future. Storage capacity has been further enhanced by compression algorithms that enable the rapid encoding, decoding and streaming of capta. Codecs (coder-decoders) compress capta such as images, video, speech, and music, making the transmission and processing of vast quantities of capta across networks possible (Mackenzie 2008, 48). The technical nature of codecs is esoteric, but their application is felt in everyday contexts. For example, codecs underpin the whole cultural shift to digital music with the rise of the MP3 (which is an acronym for a codec: Moving Picture Experts Group-1 Audio Layer 3).

This is not to say that secure, long-term storage of paper records has become a thing of the past. Digital supplements do not necessarily supersede printed documentation such as deeds, wills, or contracts—in short, pretty much anything legally binding relating to money or property that required a signature. Capta relating to these documents, plus the vast array of other details that are now generated about individuals, groups, and corporations, are predominately stored digitally. Digital capta takes up less space, but it is also more flexible, cheaper, and easier to copy, share, manipulate, cross-reference, process, and analyze. It has these qualities in large part due to how it is stored in captabases. The development of relational captabases in the 1970s revolutionized the virtual storage of records, enabling the storage of vast amounts of capta in a form that was easily accessed, interlinked, and queried. Captabases store capta in related tables that share common fields (usually key identification capta such as social security number and account number). Using the common fields, records in one captabase can be consistently cross-referenced to records in another. This simple function has a powerful utility in many contexts because linking and connecting disparate pieces of capta can produce wholly new layers of information. Capta can be easily retrieved and massive amounts of capta can be analyzed in a fraction of the time it would have taken in the predigital era. The ability of search engines like Google to zero in on a single piece of information among billions of records is really remarkable, but now accepted as normal.

The capacity to store information for negligible overhead has made the permanent archiving of capta shadows feasible for many businesses and organizations. Indeed, removing unwanted files in many ways becomes a harder task than simply keeping everything. Transactions undertaken today (a message sent to an e-mail list, paying with a credit card, speaking to a friend on the phone) may well be logged and kept beyond the death of the person, with the potential to be recalled and worked-upon at any point in the future. Such long-term retention is driven, on the governmental side for security and surveillance purposes, and on the business side for its present commercial value, or likely future potential value. It should be acknowledged, however, that there are real difficulties in maintaining digital storage over time in a usable form given the rapid changes and redundancy in capta and file formats.

Making Sense and Acting on Capta

Given advances in capture and storage technologies, enormous amounts of capta are being recorded daily by an array of organizations. For the capta to gain utility and value, however, it needs to be processed and analyzed to create information. Software enables the structuring, organizing, and storing of enormous volumes of capta and a sophisticated means of representing, collating, sorting, filtering, linking, and matching capta; of generating information, knowledge, and control through processes of abstraction, correlation, classification, pattern recognition, profiling, modeling, and visualization. Moreover, it can perform these processes on huge amounts of records incredibly quickly, processing millions of operations per second (or even more in optimized systems, like handling thousands of concurrent search engine queries). In so doing, it allows those managing capta to undertake tasks and forms of analysis that would never be attempted if the capta were stored as paper records.

Crucially, software systems enable capta to be queried interactively and processed in near real time; to be run through sophisticated algorithms that can enhance the capta (for example, clean or rectify it), identify patterns and trends, and use the capta to profile, model, predict, and simulate people and situations. The results of this analysis can be further refined using complex statistics and forms of visualization. These forms of analysis create new knowledge and generate potentially significant value for their analysts. Not surprisingly, such analysis has become commercially profitable, leading to new software sectors such as data mining or knowledge discovery from databases (KDD), geodemographics, and visual analytics consultancies. KDD consists of a set of exploratory analytical techniques (see table 5.2) designed to better understand peoples' behaviors through an analysis of what they do and is used extensively by commercial organizations, particularly retail, fraud detection in financial services, and also in policing. Geodemographics links social and territorial capta to produce segmented categories of space in order to label the kinds of people who live in particular places, and their propensity to consume particular goods and services (see chapter 9). Capta, although inextricably tied to an individual, is thus made to work in new ways independent of the original person.

With respect to surveillance and governance, a range of commercial capta aggregators/resellers such as US Search and ChoicePoint specialize in enabling consumers (individuals, companies, states) to pull together vast amounts of capta from related captabases to profile individuals. The variety of captabases include social security, health, education, court, criminal, and property records. Reasons for consumers to use this service include screening contractors, nannies, neighbors, and so on; see figure 5.6. The three major U.S.-based credit reference agencies, Equifax, Experian, and Trans-Union, have also been joined by a number of other lower profile data consolidators, such as Acxiom and Innovis, that are especially involved in developing predictive models of consumers.

Table 5.2
Key data-mining techniques

Data-mining task	Description	Techniques
Segmentation	Clustering: determining a finite set of implicit classes that describes the data Classification: mapping data items into predefined classes	Cluster analysis Bayesian classification Decision or classification trees Artificial neural networks
Dependency analysis	Finding rules to predict the value of some attribute based on the value of other attributes	Bayesian networks Association rules
Deviation and outlier analysis	Finding data items that exhibit unusual deviations from expectations	Cluster and other data-mining methods Outlier detection
Trend detection	Lines and curves summarizing the database, often over time	Regression Sequential pattern extraction
Generalization and characterization	Compact descriptions of the data	Summary rules Attribute-oriented induction

Source: Miller and Han 2001, 8

The aim of such an analysis is to socially sort people—by calculating and enforcing differential access—and to evaluate perceived worth and risk through activities such as customer, credit, and crime profiling (Leyshon and Thrift 1999; Lyon 2003; Graham 2005). Such sorting is undertaken to search, sift, differentiate, and regulate citizens and customers—to filter and channel particular goods, services, information, opportunities, and life chances to some people and not others—in order to reduce risk (whether that be issues of security and safety or capital return), to target markets, and to provide a competitive advantage. Individuals rated as a low risk are offered preferential treatment such as individualized goods and enhanced services or speed of passage. In contrast, those rated as a high risk are excluded from certain forms of credit, opportunities, and services, and are discriminated against by adverse pricing models. Social sorting thus underpins discriminatory practices such as the redlining of communities deemed unprofitable or high risk by insurers and banks (Danna and Gandy 2002, Graham 2005). Stalder (2002, 120) notes that our capta shadow "does more than follow us. It has also begun to precede us. Before we arrive somewhere, we have already been measured and classified. Thus, upon arrival, we're treated according to whatever criteria has been connected to the profile that represents us." These acts of algorithmic classification and sorting are moral in nature because they assign values that confer differing status (Lyon 2007). Code is used to judge people's worth, eligibility, levels of access, and ease of mobility—to reinforce social and economic

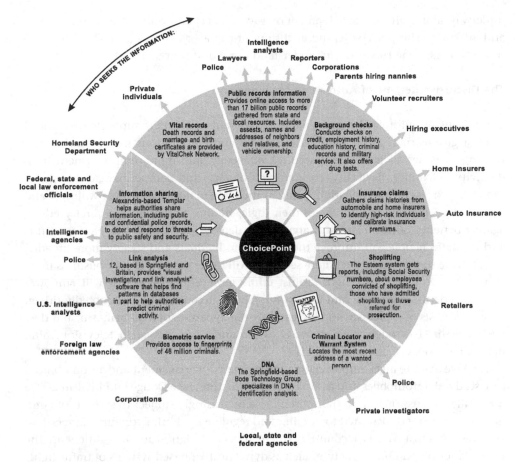

Figure 5.6
The scope of ChoicePoint's activities as a so-called one-stop-shop for personal information in 2005. (Redrawn from the *Washington Post*, January 19, 2005)

inequalities with little democratic accountability, scrutiny, or right of redress (Graham 2005).

Beyond governance, software processing has fundamentally reshaped just about all academic disciplines and how professions from architects to zoologists make sense of and use capta. In addition to providing access to massive amounts of capta from around the world, and new kinds of capta via MEMS and other software-enabled technologies (face, voice, and handwriting recognition), software has enabled new modes and methods of analysis not previously possible, such as the running of new complex algorithms, pattern recognition, simulation, and sophisticated forms of inter-active visualization. Even in the humanities, sizable digital archiving projects are underway, along with the development of novel ways of analyzing archival documents and artworks. The processing and analyzing of capta has thus significantly changed how scholars come to know and understand our world (Borgman 2007).

The Discursive Regime of Automated Management

The rollout of automated management in different contexts is supported by vested interest groups such as the state bureaucracies and corporations that use discourses relating to issues such as safety, security, efficiency, anti-fraud, empowerment, productivity, reliability, flexibility, economic rationality, and competitive advantage, to induce a process of interpellation, wherein the large majority of people willingly and voluntarily subscribe to and desire their logic, trading potential disciplinary effects against benefits gained. Here, it is argued, the deployment of software that monitors and regulates people will improve the safety of individuals and society more broadly; it will make society and travel more secure; it will make government or business more efficient; it will make the fight against crime more effective; and it will empower people to be more creative and innovative. These discourses are undoubtedly driven by the interests of capitalism and increasingly the dynamics of neoliberalism, and they are normalized through their everyday and mundane portrayal in television, film, newspapers, novels, and other media.

Here we explore an example relating to automated management and automobilities (the study of automobiles and associated infrastructure) (see Dodge and Kitchin 2007a for a fuller discussion). Road transportation is increasingly subject to systems of automated management designed to monitor and regulate road infrastructure, drivers, and vehicles. In most Western countries, there has been significant investment in the surveillance of road infrastructure, such as dynamically phased systems of traffic lights with monitoring cameras designed to manage congestion. Other surveillance examples include automated toll booths on highways, networked speed, red light, and bus-lane cameras, intended to continuously discipline driver behavior (from not driving too fast, not running red lights, and not occupying bus lanes), ANPR cameras that scan license plates to ensure compliance of payments for congestion or other charges, and even transponder networks to monitor the location of buses and update bus stops of wait time.

To be a legal and legitimate car driver in developed countries means enrolling in a raft of interlocking information systems of authorization and ongoing validation. Typically, drivers are fixed within a five-point control grid: a valid license, insurance coverage, registration of the vehicle, road taxation, and a vehicle roadworthiness test (the last two common in many countries). This interlocking information system covers the world in which the vehicle travels. Within the vehicle itself, there is more software that assists drivers.

Drivers are subject to software-enabled regulation through driver assistance systems embedded entirely in the vehicle. These systems consist of two broad classes: those aimed at increasing driver safety and those aimed at enhancing convenience. In both cases they are enabled by using software to:

• Reduce the cognitive burden on drivers (turn-by-turn voice navigation instructions)
• Reduce the level of kinesthetic and spatio-perceptive skills required (distance detection parking aids)
• Reduce the physical strength/endurance needed to drive (for example, active steering, active cruise control)
• Sense environmental conditions beyond normal human senses (black ice detector)

Vehicles are now, in many cases, a collection of computers on wheels, with ECUs that not only monitor how a car is performing and being driven, but mediate and augment the driving experience.

The arguments for such systems are driven by both state agencies and corporate interests. States want to reduce congestion, improve driver safety, ensure law enforcement, tackle fraud (untaxed cars and unlicensed drivers), and generate revenue. Business interests, such as vehicle manufacturers, insurers, rental car companies, repair shops, mechanics, and other third parties such as transportation planners and road safety campaigners, argue that software-enabled technologies provide value-added services, reliable journeys, cost-effectiveness, enhanced driver experience, and risk reduction. These systems also of course produce huge amounts of capta. Companies can use this capta to refine their products, protect their self-interest (for example, using the capta to assess warranty validity), and undertake effective target marketing.

The vested interests constructing such a discursive regime are powerful and able to access a range of resources to promulgate their message. And, of course, the discourses themselves are potent in their constitutive logic. It is quite difficult to argue that one wants to be less safe, less secure, less competitive, less productive, or less empowered. Nonetheless, there are a number of negative outcomes and ethical questions related to technologies that are "all-knowing," having complete histories of people and things, and which are explicitly designed to regulate society and potentially treat people in a discriminatory fashion based on automated profiles. However, in arenas where nascent forms of automated management have become routine, such as in air travel or highway driving, to date there has been remarkably little mass organized resistance by either individuals or interest groups. The resistance that has occurred is either expressed in disquiet, in individual resistance such as vandalism of speed cameras or boycotts of travel to particular destinations, or legal challenges to government policy by groups such as the American Civil Liberties Union and Electronic Frontier Foundation in the United States. As we noted in chapter 1, this lack of mass resistance seems to occur for five reasons that raise interesting questions about how automated management technologies seep into everyday life and become hegemonic in nature, reinforcing the logic of the discursive regime.

First, people have been persuaded by the new emerging logic either through discipline or seduction. In other words, people seemingly accept, often subconsciously, the arguments that are being put to them that automated management is necessary to ensure safety and security in an unstable world, particularly in relation to the so-called war on terror. Other arguments people seem to have embraced are to combat the problems of illegal immigrants and asylum seekers, to reduce costs, and to increase economic competitiveness and productivity in a globalized marketplace infused with the specter of job insecurity.

Second, people see the changes that are occurring as simply an extension of previous systems, which they are already inured to. For example, many people do not interpret the introduction of biometrics as a step change in the levels and sophistication of surveillance, particularly in an environment that has long been subject to levels of surveillance in excess of nearly any other space (airport immigration). Rather, new technologies and systems are seen as the outcome of an inevitable progression as new developments occur.

Third, given this progression, how contemporary surveillance technologies and practices are structured and used is seen as an inherent, and therefore unchallengeable, aspect of different assemblages. That is, systems are seen as necessarily built in a certain way, with certain parameters and defaults, thus the grammars of action employed are hard-coded into the makeup of the system in a natural and neutral way ("that's the way it had to be" to fulfill certain requirements such as safety and security targets), rather than the system and its architecture being seen as something that is relational and contingent in their formulation, design, and implementation. For example, Graham (2002) has made the case that the way CCTV systems are being deployed throughout city spaces has many characteristics of existing invisible infrastructures like water and electricity.

Fourth, the point of contact with automated management is typically designed to appear relatively painless and where possible empowering. For example, the mechanics of flow make passing through airport security and immigration checkpoint relatively banal—a few security questions, placing items on an x-ray scanner, a swipe of a passport, a finger on a scanner plate—with the bulk of the screening process taking place in the background, using software algorithms. In this sense, while being subject to new modes of surveillance, this exposure is seemingly benign and routine rather than invasive (and broadly socially beneficial—nobody wants to be the victim of a terrorist attack).

Fifth, and perhaps most troubling, it seems to us that many people do not openly question new forms of intensive surveillance and software sorting because they are worried of the consequences of protest. The fear in these cases is one of discrimination and mistreatment when traveling (such as names being placed on a secret watch list, extra security checks and delays) or being barred from certain forms of travel altogether (for example, being denied entry to a country). Here, the nature of automated management works to instill a deep level of reflexive self-disciplining. That is, people are instinctively wary of new systems fearing potential misuse and abuse, but feel powerless to openly challenge the system for fear of inciting those potential misuses and abuses. Such fears, and how people react to them, raise serious ethical concerns and political questions of equity pertaining to the development and widespread role of surveillance systems that have the capacity to capture details about people's lives in great detail.

As we examine in chapter 10, while resistance is presently not well coordinated, it certainly exists in various spheres, with individuals and campaign groups adopting a range of tactics to combat and subvert forms of surveillance. Furthermore, the extent of recorded criminality in all parts of Western societies also demonstrates the degree to which surveillance and automated management is disregarded on a daily basis.

Conclusion

In this chapter we have detailed the ways in which software is reshaping the technologies, ideologies, and systems of governance. We have argued that a significant new mode of governance is being introduced through the employment of software—automated management has the capacity to reshape and reorder important aspects everyday life in time and space. The grammars of action of code increases the power of traditional of surveillance and also actively reshapes behavior, creating automated capture systems in which software algorithms work automatically and autonomously.

Automated management has become a reality for four dominant reasons. First, we now live in a world where information can be collected, processed, and acted upon by software algorithms without human intervention or authorization. Second, software is routinely becoming embedded in existing systems and labor practices, and an integral part of how work in the world is both conducted and surveyed—the means by which a task is conducted, is also the means by which it is measured. Third, the rationale for automated management and its discursive regime has quickly become hegemonic in status, becoming accepted as the natural and dominant order—desirable, inevitable, taken-for-granted, and commonsense—underpinning practices of governance with respect to significant domains of everyday living (policing, work, travel, consumption, and communication). Fourth, the developments in software have been complemented by major developments in theoretical and conceptual ideas (e.g., new methods of classification, and algorithms for simulation), in hardware and digital technologies (CPU, materials, sensors, networking, devices, design, and manufacture), and by broader changes in the nature of governance—with new standards, legislation, and ways of doing things shaping what software and technology can do, and how it can do it. The work that software does then, while central, is not independent of technological contexts, political economy, and social relations. Taken together, the result is that many aspects of social and economic life are now captured, processed, and governed to a significant degree by software (on behalf of state agencies, companies, and also individuals themselves).

In part III, we examine more fully how automated management is having a number of profound effects on the ways in which everyday domains and tasks take place. Using detailed empirical material, we illustrate how software, by introducing a new mode of governmentality, has reconfigured the code/spaces of travel, domestic living, and consumption, producing automated, automatic, and autonomous systems of regulation that more effectively self-discipline and actively discipline. In part IV we examine how forms of automated management are developing within a framework of everyware, exploring some of the future implications of surveillance and sousveillance.

6 Software, Creativity, and Empowerment

Programming is a poetry for our time
It's a poetry for our time

I wonder would Wordsworth have written in Perl?
Would Keats have used Notepad for HTML?
I reckon Byron would see
The irony
Of writing words to change the world that we
Can't live without but no-one ever sees

Programming is a poetry for our time
It's a poetry for our time

—MJ Hibbett

While software underpins new forms of governance, it is important to recognize it as productive in the widest possible sense. So, while code is used as a key actant in regulating society, it also fosters new forms of creativity and empowerment. For example, the technicity of software means it is increasingly a pivotal element in the creative practices of many professions and opens up creative opportunities for people to enact novel solutions to problems of entertainment and play. In often small, mundane, but valuable ways, code empowers people to make domestic and work tasks easier to solve, enables a multitude of low-cost and flexible means of personal communication and information distribution, and provides enhanced power in consumption activities. We discuss many of the broader issues of empowerment in part III. In this chapter, we examine the ways in which code opens up new possibilities for creativity for ordinary citizens and those working in knowledge intensive professions. We explore coding itself as a creative process, then how software facilitates new forms of knowledge production, artistic practice, and processes of innovative design, such as "mashups" (ad-hoc combination and hybrid reuse), "modding" (informal user modifications to improve performance), and "remixability" that make new and unexpected forms of expression and play possible. Lastly, we discuss how the technicity of software to produce new media is opening up an exciting array of opportunities for personal empowerment through self-authorship and sharing, as well as offering novel channels for political organization, engagement, and dissent that can jump scale barriers at low cost.

Our aim is to illustrate how software often works as a progressive force for personal and social change and to counter some of the more doom laden commentaries, as detailed in the previous chapter, which casts the work that software does in an almost universally negative light. While we, like other commentators, are cautious about the potential harmful and corrosive effects of a society infused by software, we also recognize that the technicity of code is undoubtedly opening up new creative and innovative possibilities and empowers individuals and society more broadly. This is perhaps no surprise. As with any tool or technology, how it is conceived and enrolled in daily practice is crucial. Further, as we detail in chapters 5 and 11, narrowly conceived notions of everyware as the building block of a future Big Brother society fail to account for the myriad ways in which software is resisted, reworked and reappropriated in everyday life. Not least of these reworkings are the raft of new criminal opportunities opening up through the creative, yet malicious, manipulation of code.

Software, we argue, needs to be interpreted as a special kind of media. Unlike other conventional creative products such as novels, films, or a piece of music, which undoubtedly do discursive work in the world, much of the output of coding can itself be used to foster creative acts; software is itself a medium for intellectual work and invention. Unlike spoken language and conventional writing, software is computational and executable, and can thus create products that themselves afford creativity.

Code and Creative Practice

As noted in chapter 2, writing software can be a deeply creative act; lines of code, algorithms, and capta structures therefore offer a new medium through which fresh ideas can be expressed and executed. While much of the code produced today is derivative and borrowed from programs that have preceded it, and much of it is routine, mediocre, and uninspired, there is a steady stream of new code that continues to push boundaries with respect to software itself, and the work that it does in the world. This code consists of elegant new routines, sophisticated algorithms, efficient and novel designs for applications and protocols, or original ways of collating, analyzing, and presenting capta that are creative because they go beyond simply repeating something. Rather than being citational, imitative, and formulaic, the solutions are innovative and extend how we think and act in the world. The results can be unanticipated, sometimes deeply pleasurable, and have elements of beauty in how it solves a task (Knuth 1974).

It is important to note, however, that the creativity of programmers, software engineers, and systems designers does not arise out of nowhere, some innate embodied talent. Instead, their creativity is a product of their skills and competencies coupled with their embeddedness in networks of people, things (technologies, documentation, resources) and places. These networks profoundly shape coding. Programmers learn the various aspects of how to write effective code—language syntax, capta structure, abstraction, and translation. While some might possess a great competency for programming skills, these supposed gifts are nurtured, shaped, and encouraged by diverse factors such as educational experience, tutoring in literary theory and praxis, mathematical knowledge, exposure to other programmers' work, encouragement, and critical feedback from peers. While some programmers might claim to have had no formal training, their abilities to craft an efficient and elegant software solution have nonetheless been nurtured in informal ways and through hours of intensive practice. Nobody sits down to code for the first time as a fully formed programmer. Similarly, those who enroll code to do creative and innovative work in the world are situated in relational and contingent contexts, often in organizational settings that foster the talent to explore (studios, galleries, labs, and museums).

In contrast to other creative products, such as novels, films, or songs, which certainly do much discursive work in the world—entertaining, inspiring, providing insight—much of the output of coding can itself be used to foster creative practice. Code creates products that themselves afford creativity and some software applications have permeated creative practice so thoroughly (QuarkXPress in publishing, Photoshop in graphic design, After Effects in animation, Maya and 3D Max in solid modeling, and Pro Tools in music mixing) that being proficient in their use has become an essential prerequisite to success in these professions.

Indeed, various computers and their operating systems supporting word processing, image editing, desktop publishing, e-mail and Web browsing, have fostered the creation of this book (table 6.1). Together they have enabled us to compose the text, edit, format and track changes to it, quickly exchange drafts and ideas, efficiently look up factual information in library catalogs, download and read academic papers, easily contact people with research questions, analyze capta, create numerical tables, and capture, alter, and embed images. While all of these research problems and writing tasks could be solved in an analog pen and paper environment, it would be more time consuming, less efficient, more cumbersome, and, most likely, less effective. In addition, it would have involved more people with specialized skills in typing, photography, and drawing. By enrolling a range of software, and concomitant digital capta and

Table 6.1
Personal software audit

Software	Solutions	Frequency of use*
MS Windows XP (SP3)	PC operating system	Continuous
McAfee VirusScan Enterprise (v. 8.5.0i)	Safety, security	Continuous
MS Notepad (v. 5.1)	Taking quick notes; reformatting text	Sporadic
MS Windows Media Play 11 (v. 11.05.5721.5268)	Playing MP3 music, viewing animations, movies	Frequent
MS Word 2000 (v. 9.0.2720)	Word processing	Frequent
MS PowerPoint 2000 (v. 9.0.2716)	Viewing and arranging images, drawing diagrams	Sporadic
MS Excel 2000 (v. 9.0.2720)	Open spreadsheet files, creating numerical tables	Occasional
Paint Shop Pro (v. 6.00)	Viewing and manipulating image files	Sporadic
Adobe Acrobat (v. 7.0.0)	Viewing PDFs	Sporadic
Mozilla Firefox (v. 3.0.4)	Web browsing, platform for online search and communication	Sporadic
MS Internet Explorer (v. 6.0.2900)	Web browsing, platform for online search and communication	Occasional
WinSCP (v. 3.7.6)	File transfer across the Internet	Occasional
Gmail service	Collaborative file store	Occasional
Pine (v. 4.58)	Handling e-mail	Sporadic
Putty (v. 0.58)	Remote access to e-mail	Sporadic

Note: A superficial audit of the range of software enrolled by one of the authors to form the creative environment that supported the writing of this book. It is a unique configuration that has accreted over time and seems to work. Different software was activated to solve a range of tasks as they arose, and some were chained together to tackle particular problems. There is also a hidden labyrinth of executable software, code libraries, and drivers existing beneath the surface of MS Windows XP and a wider, unknown ecology of software and captabases providing online services external to the laptop itself.

*Usage levels: continuous, frequent, sporadic, occasional.

information services, we have been able to write a book together, to undertake tasks previously reserved for specialist workers, bounce ideas off each other, and swap versions of chapters several times a day, despite being located on two different islands. Software has afforded us a suite of tools that has profoundly influenced how the book came into being.

Since the commercial release of the WordStar application for MSDOS in 1982, and the mass market success of WordPerfect in the early 1990s, and the dominance of Microsoft Word from the late 1990s (Bergin 2006), it is clear then that writing practices, through the switch from analog typing onto paper to digital composition on screen, have been transformed. Importantly, the technicity proffered by word processing applications has provided quantitative gains in efficiency, but more significantly much greater flexibility in composition and ease in editing. It also gives authors increasing degrees of automation (deleting mistakes, cutting and pasting text, counting the number of words, automated line wrapping, WYSIWYG formatting and display, page and section numbering, and basic spell-checking). The deeper question though, is the degree to which the essential creative act is altered by the medium that the author is working in. This is not easy to address, because not all aspects of writing are dependent on code. For example, in writing this book, we often wrote out ideas and passages in longhand, or made edits onto hardcopy, and made use of a print dictionary and thesaurus in parallel with the software versions offered in Microsoft Word. Indeed, as in other domains discussed elsewhere in this book, the ways code permeates daily practices and does work in the world is always contingent and often incomplete (see part I).

Drawing on our own wider experience, it is certainly the case that software has radically transformed knowledge-intensive industries such as academia. As Borgman (2007, xvii) has pointed out, "scholars in all fields are taking advantage of the wealth of online information, tools, and services to ask new questions, create new kinds of scholarly products, and reach new audiences." Many research areas are thoroughly entangled with code, with some projects only progressing through the use of analytical applications and captabases, and others depending on software simulations, most particularly in the hard sciences, but not exclusively so, as computational social science and humanities grows in importance (Lazer et al. 2009). Code has enabled the generation of huge amounts of capta that is significantly enhancing scholars' capacity to understand the world. For example, for earth scientists and meteorologists, the software systems controlling the sensors in earth imaging satellites generate terabytes of capta daily, mapping out processes of land cover change, ocean temperature variations, and weather patterns, and feeding into increasingly sophisticated and comprehensive models of natural systems. Software systems in astronomical observatories across the world make it possible to automatically gather, process, and distribute masses of capta concerning the history and structure of the universe. Some scientific disciplines, such as molecular biology and particle physics, are dependent on software-controlled instrumentation because the phenomena they seek to understand operate at scales impossible to perceive by human senses alone. One can argue that CERN's Large Hadron Collider experiment, for example, is as much a software project as it is a physical machine for smashing atoms (figure 6.1). In the social sciences, a new deluge of detailed individual level capta on movements and transactions generated by every-day interactions of millions of people, offers great opportunities for novel, algorithmic modeling of human behavior and societal processes, but also poses significant practical and ethical challenges for academics (see Savage and Burrows 2007 in relation to the transformation of research methods in sociology).

Capta generation and analysis on these scales was nigh on impossible before computing. It was simply too labor intensive and complex to attempt. In addition, the lifeblood of academia in terms of journal publishing is now thoroughly software-mediated, from electronic documents, to manuscript review, and distribution as e-journals. It is undoubtedly much easier to search and retrieve material from digital

Figure 6.1
Scientists and engineers are smashing atoms via software. The operation of the LHC being observed via banks of display screens in the CERN control center, September 10, 2008. *Source*: http://cdsweb.cern.ch, image id. 0809002_35.jpg

rather than physical journals, although improved access does not necessarily translate to enhanced creativity. (It should also be acknowledged that the digital production and distribution of knowledge is driven as much by economic efficiency of large commercial publishers as it by some Athenian notion of scholarship!).

The result is that the humanities and social sciences, through to engineering, natural sciences, and medicine, have been transformed by the application of computing to their disciplines. Practically every office and lab in a university operates as code/space. Such a transformation clearly changes how scientific research is being conducted and, ultimately, the types of discoveries and innovations that come into being. Academics, therefore, are very much software workers, like many other occupations and professions, even though most do not write code, and probably could not do so even if they desired. That said, one must be wary of deterministic hyperbole—the application of sophisticated software and petabytes of capta does not necessarily equate to better science. While software is often a prerequisite for creative scientific practice, it is not a determinant of scientific discoveries.

The same is true for many workplaces, including the sites of much media production and creative industries, including artists' workshops, design studios, theaters, publishers, and photography, television, and film studios. Much creative practice at these sites now takes place in front of computer screens, manipulating digital objects.

For example, in the music industry, the technicity of software has been widely enrolled to distribute creative practice both through time and across space, enabling the required consistency and repeatability at much lower costs (that is, professional quality sound recording) (figure 6.2). Within recoding studios, the engineer's control consoles for mixing and recording sound are crucial sites of creative work. As Leyshon (2009, 1324) notes, by "integrating software and memory into the operating of desks, producers and engineers were able to easily re-establish the settings between recording sessions." Leyshon's work highlights the degree to which code can automate some aspects of the embodied and tacit knowledge held by specialist sound engineers, although it is not able to replicate the emotional labor of studio staff who are able to formulate the sense of congeniality deemed significant for the highest caliber of creative musicianship. One can also make a case for code changing not only the epistemic culture of music-making, but also the dominant kind of sound. Correlated with the rise of greater access to audio editing software, and its technical capacities, was a growing fashion for sampling and remixing songs in the 1990s. Some musicians and DJs/producers, particularly in dance and rap music, enjoyed great success through this technique, although it clearly poses a challenge to notions of originality of authorship and what counts as creative (Marontate 2005).

Similarly, the creative impact of code is changing the nature of visual images in all kinds of media. The art of photography has undergone a profound change in the last decade, with the rise to complete dominance of digital camera technology and

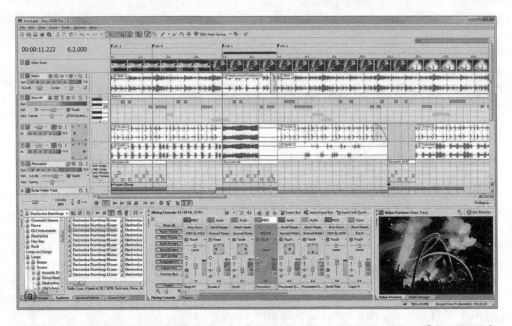

Figure 6.2

Example interfaces of four of the leading digital audio workstation applications for recording, editing, and mixing professional quality music. From these images it is apparent that they are complex applications that offer a panoply of functions and are likely to take a significant investment in time to master. They render musical sequences visible and workable as digital objects and often employ graphical simulations of physical controls (sliders and knobs) to facilitate user interaction. (*a*) Sony ACID Pro (*Source*: www.sonycreativesoftware.com/acidpro). (*b*) Digidesign Pro Tools (*Source*: www.soundonsound.com/sos/jan09/articles/protools8pt1.htm). (*c*) Cakewalk SONAR (*Source*: www.cakewalk.com/Products/sonar/). (*d*) Image-Line Software's FL Studio (*Source*: http://forum.image-line.com/files/fl85screenshot_104.jpg).

Figure 6.2
(continued)

software-based practices for processing digital images rather than print film. There has been, according to Wells (1997, 252), a significant shift in the "mode and location of photographic production from the chemical darkroom to an electronic darkroom of computer software." The taking of a photograph has also become a software task, with the nature of an image determined to an important degree by code operating automatically within the camera, that evaluates the conditions and even the context of the image (for example, using face recognition algorithms) and automatically determining the optimal focus, shutter speed, flash, and other settings to ensure clear, crisp pictures. Indeed, contemporary compact digital cameras are packed with features, including basic editing software, designed to make it easy for unskilled photographers to take professional quality photos, regardless of conditions. Via an LCD screen, the photographer can also make an instant assessment and evaluation of the image, offering the chance to correct mistakes and make alternative compositions. As such, much of the creative craft of photography is delegated to code, although the essential decision of *what* to photograph remains with the photographer. In addition, the per image costs are vastly cheaper in comparison to print film, meaning that many more images can be taken for effectively zero additional cost, adding greater flexibility and opportunities for creative experimentation.

The resultant photographs, as digital entities, enjoy almost endless possibilities for editing and manipulation by software tools. Of course, the image has always been open to manipulation in darkroom operations, but software has made image manipulation much easier and more widespread, and offers up a hugely increased palette of possible ways to revise and rework. The market leader in image manipulation software over the last twenty years has been Adobe Photoshop, which has had a significant impact on visual culture with many millions of images seen daily having retouched in various ways by its filtering algorithms and erasing tools (Manovich 2008). Photoshopping images can be playful, and it can also skillfully change, in often subtle ways, how people consume an image and perceive "reality." The depth of digital manipulation now completely corrupts any vestigial belief in the maxim that the camera never lies:

Photoshop . . . has become so ubiquitous that most of us gaze at faces, bodies and landscapes, not even registering that wrinkles have been diminished, legs lengthened and the sky honed to a dream-like shade of blue. And, unlike its predecessor, airbrushing, anyone can use it. . . . But Photoshop's popularity has proven to be divisive. While some laud it for its ability to allow people—and things—to look their best in a photograph, others see it as a vehicle for feeding our culture's desire for uber-perfection. (Stein 2009)

Beyond sound and vision, the creative impact of code is changing the landscapes in which people live. In terms of architectural practice and construction industries, the rise of end-to-end digital building design using CAD software has enhanced and extended creative opportunities by supporting the conception and realization of radically elaborate spaces, curving voids and irregular envelopes. Antić and Fuller (2006) assert that software works "as 'a material' for sculpturing buildings." Buildings are being constructed that simply could not have been brought into being without software, as their complex and potentially unstable structural geometries can now be robustly calculated and rigorously tested in simulations before construction starts. Calculations from virtual architectural models can also feed into evaluations of energy requirements and projected running costs of the building. The models can also be rendered and animated to provide photo-realistic views and virtual walk-throughs, that can assist in terms of convincing clients, in planning reviews, for public communication, and evaluating the visual impact of the building on the surrounding urban fabric. The model can also be easily updated to accommodate the changing demands of clients or planners. Lastly, it can generate realistic engineering schematics, quantitative surveys of materials, and construction schedules, meaning that the building can be constructed more safely, on-time, and within budget.

The rise of affordable desktop software to create and manipulate music, large scientific data sets, graphic designs, photographic images, and architectural models has been particularly significant in terms of widening access to creative activities and opportunities. For many decades, these creative practices have largely been confined to specialized places, often tied to expensive bespoke equipment, and a skilled cadre of technicians and engineers. Creativity could only take place in professional recording studios, large architectural workshops, staffed laboratories, drawing offices, and specially equipped darkrooms, which were usually controlled by large institutions and all too often driven by narrow commercial imperatives. Since the late 1980s, increasingly capable software applications, running on off-the-shelf PCs, have enabled many more people to become involved, and also opened up spaces for outsiders to experiment, and for new start-ups and freelance outfits to compete. There has been a marked decline in the barriers to entry into professional quality music recording; as Leyshon (2009, 1309) puts it, there has been a "democratisation of technology." Since the 1990s, software has contributed to a burgeoning of "back bedroom" creativity through desktop design, improvised studios, home recording setups, and self-publishing. This, when combined with standardized formats for exchanging capta, and the Internet as a means to communicate and promote the work, has clearly had an impact on established monopolies for creating innovative media products. Although the competition from cheaper bedroom facilities has denuded the exclusive preserve of purpose-built studios, it has also contributed to deteriorating employment conditions and salaries for many skilled engineers and practitioners.

Of course, the enrolment of software in workflow does not guarantee creative results. While proficiency with software tools may be a requirement in certain creative industries, their use does not mean creativity will happen. Much of the output of even the most sophisticated software is often ordinary and derivative. Word processors can as easily produce works of little worth as a pen and paper, although it may superficially appear professionally formatted, with adequate grammar and some spelling errors automatically corrected by algorithms. Moreover, in some respects, it can be argued that the reliance on software can actually stifle creativity. Software applications like Microsoft Word or Adobe Photoshop are flexible and open-ended tools, but they come loaded up with structures, templates, defaults settings, algorithmic normalities, and path-dependences that often subtly but necessarily direct users to certain solutions. Some have argued that the ways in which the design of software structures human cognitive processes can have a detrimental effect on performance. For example, criticism has been directed at the way Microsoft's successful PowerPoint application has shaped the rules of giving presentations (figure 6.3), encouraging a dull linearity of bullet-pointed text over deeper, more discursive talks; the software overtly focuses the audience on the presentation format and not its content (Tufte 2003). PowerPoint's operative logic is imbued with the "corporate sales pitch," but too easily this ethos

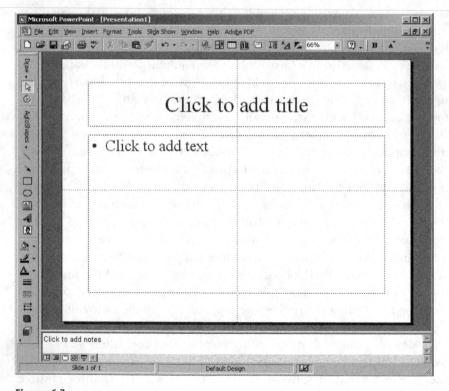

Figure 6.3
The curse of creativity? The default slide in Microsoft PowerPoint encourages people to reduce their ideas to short bullet points of text.

travels when it is applied in other contexts (for example, teaching; Adams 2006). The nature of word processors, like Microsoft Word, particularly their automated features that "correct" writing, and wizards that impose styles, have also been criticized for affecting not just how writing happens, but also what gets written (Fuller 2003). In terms of scholarship, critics have often argued that the available functions in core analytical software applications can all too easily determine research questions. For example, it has been suggested that empirical sociology is being driven by what SPSS can enable (Uprichard, Burrows, and Byrne 2008). This kind of algorithmic determinism is antithetical to truly original and creative research.

Sophisticated applications have hundreds of functions and tools, most of which come with default settings that provide "acceptable" or "appropriate" results, from the perspective of the software designers and corporate vendors. Many users never change the defaults; some are little aware of the degree to which what they create is shaped by these defaults. The result is that the products of certain software applications can often have a look that is identifiably shaped by the default settings. From this perspective, one might argue, software is a powerful force for homogeneity, rather than the diversity that marks creativity. As a consequence, one needs to be wary and alert to the contradictions inherent in the ways software works in the world. Software can constrain creative practice, as well as opening up opportunities for original solutions.

New Media

As Manovich (2000) discusses in detail, software has both redefined cultural forms such as the photographic image and cinematic film and enabled new cultural media such as computer games, web sites, online interactive services, and immersive virtual worlds—software remakes old media anew (switching to computer-mediated forms of production, distribution, and consumption) and facilitates new innovations that together make up "new media." Indeed, Manovich contends, such is the pervasiveness of software in the contemporary production of cultural media that people interact less with a computer per se, but rather culture encoded in digital form (a jpeg picture, an mpeg movie file, a PDF document, and an MP3 song). The interfaces of keyboard, mouse, icons, graphic boxes, pull down menus, have begun to form a new cultural language, a new unconscious layer for manipulating digital realities (just like a multitude of switches and dials mediate our tactile engagement with the electromechanical).

Manovich (2000) defines the unique character of new media in terms of five dimensions, each of which is made possible by the technicity of software: numeric representation, modularity, automation, variability, and transcoding. The effect of these five trends is, he argues, the creation of media that are interactive, programmable, and mutable; media that provide distinct and novel ways for people to express emotion and ideas, to record their thoughts and experience, and to engage in new kinds of social activities, exchange, and communication.

Numerical representation   New media are composed of digital capta, which means they can be consistently described mathematically and they are open to algorithmic manipulation (they are, in a fundamental sense, programmable entities). Converting capta into binary code consists of the processes of sampling reality into discrete capta (dividing up a continuous picture into a known grid of pixels) and quantization (assigning the pixel a value[s] that represents its color).

Modularity   New media are composed of elements (pixels, polygons, characters, layers, sound channels) that have a modular structure that is scaleable—they can be assembled into larger objects, while continuing to retain their individual identities. As a result, individual pixels can be edited without the whole picture having to be redrawn, and individual frames from a movie can be altered without having to reshoot a whole sequence.

Automation   Numerical representation and modularity enable the many operations involved in the capture, editing, manipulation, and use of new media to be automated. For example, image correction to improve contrast and remove noise is undertaken automatically by the software in a camera once the person activates the shutter control button.

Variability   New media can exist in multiple exact copies or in an almost infinite number of variations; they are variable and mutable in ways that old media, as analog cultural objects, could never be. As a consequence, new media are qualitatively easier to manipulate, and capta can be customized to meet the requirements of creators and users without damaging the original or requiring highly specialized knowledge or expensive resources (for example, the degree to which typical camera user can crop, enlarge, and print a digital photograph, compared to undertaking the same operations with 35 mm film negatives).

Transcoding   To transcode is to translate meaning and function from one media to another. The technicity of code enables the translation of important aspects of culture into a framework defined by the software ontology, epistemology, and pragmatics, in so doing meaning and language become translated into code or transcoded, with the resulting shift having an effect on how people understand and act in the world. Consequently, as "we work with software and use the operations embedded in it, these operations become part of how we understand ourselves, others, and the world. Strategies of working with computer data become our general cognitive strategies" (Manovich 2000, 118). The result of transcoding, as Manovich (2000) notes, is that common operations in software, such as selection, sorting, composition, sampling, and filtering/classification, become common in culture at large.

New media significantly overlaps producers and users of cultural forms. Production and consumption become blurred, with users able to participate in the production of many media, but also to alter the nature of the media itself by reprogramming the underlying software. New media then are an inherently creative media that can significantly empower users through the fostering of creative acts and by enabling new forms of information-seeking, performing work, communicating with others, and participating in entertainment. Nowhere is this more apparent than in the recent growth of Web 2.0 applications.

Software and the Web 1.0 to Web 2.0 Transition

In 2004, a now widely-cited brainstorming session asserted that the dominant operative nature of the Web as a media was in the process of passing from one phase to another (table 6.2) (O'Reilly 2005). Web 1.0 is usually considered the first phase of the commercial, mass-market Internet. In this phase, people were empowered to access a vast collection of information that could be searched, retrieved, and read in new ways. Crucially, the Internet was primarily focused on consumption rather than participation. Only by using proprietary software, and employing a significant degree of technical knowledge, could people and groups create their own home pages and use the Web as a vehicle for self-expression and business transactions. Web 2.0, it is argued, is a new, distinct phase of online production that opens up authorship to allow much greater creative enterprise. Rather than simply browsing information, the Web becomes a media through which users can easily and actively participate in the production of the online world, designing and editing content, and contributing freely to services that share material with others. Web 2.0 is a read/write media, in which people add value to sites as they use them.

Table 6.2
Contrasting the operative dynamics of Web 1.0 and Web 2.0

Dimensions of difference	Web 1.0 (1993–2003)	Web 2.0 (2004–beyond)
Mode	Read	Write, contribute, and participate
Primary unit of content	Page	Post/record
State	Static	Dynamic
Viewed through	Web browser	Anything
Content created by	Specialists	Everyone
Domain of	Web designers and geeks	A new culture of public research?; citizen scientists?

Source: Adapted from Beer and Burrows 2007

Web 2.0 sites and services tend to focus on many-to-many publishing, social communication, and providing richer, contextualized information. Examples include social networking services, photo and video sharing sites, wikis (open, collectively authored web sites), blogging, and mashups (open application programming interfaces, APIs, allowing the merging of capta from different sources to create new applications). A key feature of these diverse online services is their very low barrier to entry (typically they are free, work in a Web browser, and have straightforward interfaces) to galvanize mass participation. For success in Web 2.0, it is essential to: (1) motivate people to work collaboratively and take on shared responsibility for constructing knowledge about themselves, each other, and the world through processes of writing, editing, extending, remixing, posting, sharing, tagging, and communicating (Beer and Burrows 2007); (2) employ well designed software infrastructure that is robust, scalable, and, in some senses, invisible to user experience.

Such has been the rapid rise of Web 2.0 applications that commentators note that they have already become an embedded and routine part of everyday life for many people, especially those under the age of thirty or so (Beer and Burrows 2007). Much of the social life of students seems to be transacted on Facebook; Wikipedia is said to be threatening the viability of for-profit encyclopedias; and user-generated media posted on YouTube is seen as more entertaining than commercial television. That said, one needs to be cautious about whether some of these services and sites will prosper once the initial burst of enthusiastic participation begins to wane. Indeed, much of Web 2.0 is funded through venture capital that is unsustainable in the longer term without viable revenue streams, which remain far from certain. There is also skepticism about the degree of democratic participation evident in Web 2.0 services with the majority of users being free-riders profiting from the work of a few. As such, an argument can be advanced that Wikipedia is no less an elite form of knowledge written by a few than the *Encyclopaedia Britannica*. There is also an element of the emperor's new clothes about some of the grand claims for Web 2.0, as a number of social spaces and self-governing participatory online activities, such as MUDs, mailing lists, bulletin boards, and Usenet newsgroups, existed long before the World Wide Web was invented (Dodge and Kitchin 2000, Turkle 1995).

Nevertheless, Web 2.0 applications do afford their users and creators with enhanced degrees of agency that empower them to participate in the construction of the Web and to solve their relational problems in novel ways. For example, blogging, a popular form of social media, has created new forms of participatory dialog. Blogs are Web media through which people write for online audiences and in which that audience can respond to create a dialog. Key to their success is the software architecture in which the interface for composition and posting lowers the barriers to entry as far as practicable. The ease of posting encourages frequent updates (giving rise to a conversational structure), along with unmediated feelings of informality and immediacy.

Blogs can thus "capture a moment-to-moment picture of people's thoughts and feelings about things happening right now, turning the Web from a collection of static documents into a running conversation" (Tapscott and Williams 2006, 40). New posts can be added from any PC or device that has a Web browser. A professionally looking blog is possible, including the embedding of images and video, without an understanding of html coding and design skills, or the reliance on an administrator to upload content onto a Web site. Blogs and photo/video sharing sites are often syndicated and aggregated, that is, they are designed to be automatically downloaded or streamed to a user's device every time there is new content. The result is that blogging has significantly empowered many people to express their opinions and to engage in constructive dialog with others who would not have been willing or able to do so otherwise.

Similarly, social networking sites, such as MySpace, Facebook, and Bebo, have become enormously popular in recent years, enabling their users to easily build rich profiles of themselves, post information about their lives, their preferences, and their views on different issues, and to contact former and current friends, make connections with other people who might share similar interests and activities, and to easily communicate with each other. Users have control over their page's content, and also who can access and connect to their pages. Importantly, who looks at their profile is recorded. Some sites such as Facebook also allow the use of externally developed applications that enable users to visualize their social network, others have photo-sharing or video-sharing capabilities and/or built-in blogging and instant messaging technology. As Beer and Burrows (2007) note, building the site and making connections "is an act of production as it generates a path with its own history." For example, Facebook provides automated alerts about what a user's friends have been doing, including how their profiles have changed, and who they have made friends with. Individuals such as artists, and groups such as bands, use social networking as a means to interface with their fans and as a way of building up a reputation and following. Other social network sites relate to building business networks, one of the most popular being LinkedIn, which claims that it connects, at the time of writing, over 24 million people across 150 professions.

Mashups harvest the capta of services such as Google, Yahoo!, craigslist, Flickr, open government databases (such as the UK Land Registry) and plug them into other applications and services to create new, innovative ways of accessing, analyzing, and adding value to the capta. For example, Google Maps can be integrated into an individual or company's web site, enabling the mapping of their capta using Google Maps' full set of utilities and extensive base capta. By far the most popular type of mashups are in fact mapmaking, wherein capta from one source, such as Flickr, are fed into another, such as Google Earth, to create a hybrid mapping application. In another example, it is possible to plot the location of available apartments and their price (http://housingmaps.com) or to map the locational hotspots of photographs (Mappr). Other types of mashups relate to photos, shopping, travel, news, sports, messaging, music, real estate, events, visualization, and searching, and hundreds of new mashups are being created each month (see http://programmableweb.com).

Case Study: Mapping and Web 2.0

Since the early 2000s, there has been emergence of the geospatial web with many new ways to access and manipulate spatial capta to solve a wide array of mapping and navigational tasks. Internet mapping portals, in particular, have proved to be key sites of free access to interact with growing volumes of geographic new media, and they have also begun to offer high-resolution aerial photographs and satellite imagery in unprecedented detail to a global audience through straightforward interfaces. The capabilities and technical beauty of Google Earth, in particular, has garnered wide-spread praise, and a rapidly growing online fan-base, since it launched in 2005. More recently, Google's Street View is providing novel ground level views of city streets as new media that can be "walked through," again, in a simple, intuitive interface. Many people also have a dashboard mounted navigation system in their car, whose routing software seeks to reduce the cognitive burden of navigation tasks by rendering spatial decisions into a simple stream of turn-by-turn voice instructions. The way in which digital maps and online geographic imagery can be searched and browsed almost effortlessly, and without the upfront cost of data purchase and specialized software, is clearly opening up sophisticated mapping techniques and capta that only a few years previously had been the preserve of the military, government, academia, and corporations, employing highly skilled staff.

Mapping provides a good exemplar of how the key components of Web 2.0 can be harnessed together for creative action by engaging mass participation (Crampton 2009; Goodchild 2007). Web 1.0 software for online mapping typically consisted of traditional cartography transferred to an Internet environment. A user could access scanned map images and use basic functionality to zoom and pan, and undertake basic queries. Web 2.0 cartography differs radically by enabling the production of user-generated geographic capta, along with the collaborative building of open-source mapping solutions that can be widely shared and reused. As a result, the distinction between map users and map producers has become increasingly blurred.

Open source mapping projects also challenge the restrictive copyright licenses applied to conventionally produced commercial and government mapping (even the free Google Maps service has strictly defined terms and conditions for what users can do with it). One of the most successful open source projects is OpenStreetMap, that has exploited many Web 2.0 software tools and online media, to galvanize volunteer participation in creating what they describe as "a free editable map of the whole world. It is made by people like you" (wwww.openstreetmap.org). A very small group of mapping enthusiasts and software activists initiated the project with minimal financing, free software, old hardware, and borrowed bandwidth. In the space of a few years it has grown to map a significant portion of populated places and continues to expand rapidly.

At its heart, OpenStreetMap is fundamentally Web 2.0 because its licensing is open (a Creative Commons Attribution/ShareAlike license), it exploits a crowd-sourcing model of production (premised on mass participation, distributed voluntary effort, and loose coordination, it stands in contrast to traditional modes of centralized cartographic production undertaken by paid employees of institutions working to predetermined specifications), and its core architecture is wiki based. This has both practical and political consequences; it means anyone who registers with OpenSteetMap can upload their capta and can edit the capta of everyone else.

The central OpenStreetMap captabase also has a freely accessible API that fosters an ecology of different editing tools, auditing services, and all manner of mapping projects. The captabase also holds the full authorship history of each capta object, which can be interrogated and visualized (figures 6.4 and 6.5). The base geometric capta is also tagged to create geographically rich objects that can be rendered into visually meaning maps (for example, a line object is tagged as a river, with a name).

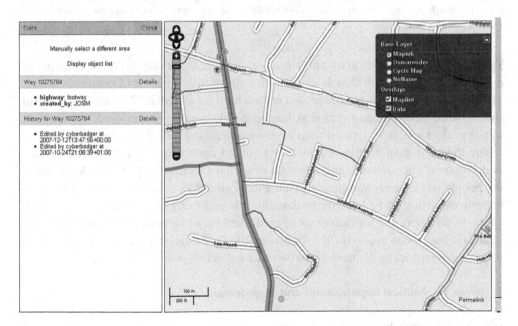

Figure 6.4
The authorship of wiki mapping laid bare. Here an individual element of capta within the OpenStreetMap captabase has been interrogated to reveal who has edited it and when.

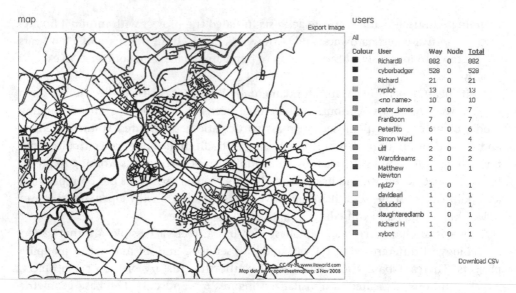

Figure 6.5
At a larger scale one can see how the work of multiple map authors contributing voluntarily to the OpenStreetMap can, over time, build a usable, open-source map of a whole town. The authors created this figure in Glossop using ITO!'s OSM Mapper service, www.itoworld.com/static/osmmapper.

The tagging ontology for geographic features in OpenStreetMap is classic example of a generative folksonomy that emerges from both online debate and pragmatic usage. The main portal web site for the project is itself built on a MediaWiki software platform (http://wiki.openstreetmap.org) that has been collaboratively authored. Participants in the project are also provided with a personal blogging tool (known as User Diaries) where they can share stories of how they go about collecting capta, their future plans and problems encountered, and elements of spatial SNS that helps to provide context for people working on mapping the same local area. RSS feeds are available for contributors wanting to be kept up to date on new additions or changes made to their capta. In addition, old fashioned social media software like mailing lists and IRC chat channels have been successfully enrolled by the OpenStreetMap community to bind people geographically dispersed together in a collective effort.

Software for Political Organization and Engagement

Web 2.0 has often been hailed as a democratizing technology because of the way it seems to directly challenge established interests with radically new modes for authoring, disseminating, and consuming media. As Beer and Burrows (2007) detail, Web

2.0 can be characterized by people increasing their influence over the shape of Internet, taking control of its content and the means of content production, as well as, to an extent, being able to determine its larger organizational logic. In this sense, online software fosters an open culture wherein anyone who is so motivated can become involved in the development of the underlying infrastructures by participating in open-source software initiatives, and everyone has the potential to be seen and heard, and to contribute to collaborative ventures such wikis and folksonomies as the mechanics of authorship become qualitatively easier to exploit. Projects such as Open-StreetMap, discussed above, also allow collectives to challenge the position of established institutions by creating their own capta, with different and more open licenses and copyright terms, that mean it can be more easily shared and productively utilized in any number of applications, without negotiating permissions or paying substantial fees. Web 2.0 software then empowers people in diverse ways—socially, culturally, and politically, it can open opportunities to be creative, to innovate, to gain information, to organize, and to mobilize.

Such political rhetoric has been a feature of the discourse about information and communication technologies for several decades. For example, Web 1.0 attracted similar claims. It was argued that the Internet was instigating a democratic renaissance based on the notion that an abundance of available information from multiple sources is liberating, that it allows greater access to officials, and that it undermines the traditional media bases of democratic institutions such as broadcasters by allowing individuals to be both sender and receiver, and potentially permitting a greater diversity of views be disseminated. In addition, it enabled some limited forms of community-orientated, participatory democracy within city-regions wherein registered users can access city information, complete some transactions, send e-mail to departments and elected officials, and engage in online consultation and virtual public meetings. In this context, Web 1.0 was seen to strengthen the civic, public dimensions of cities and nations by providing a free access, public space for debate and interaction.

The Internet as a social media is now a key battleground for political debate and organizing. Web pages, e-mail, forums, blogs, and social networking sites have been used extensively for orchestrating electoral campaigns by candidates and political parties to try to reach voters through bypassing conventional broadcast media, that are seen as either biased or ineffective. Online media are also enrolled by activists and campaign groups protesting against injustices, seeking to mobilize local, national, and international support. For example, groups such as Tibet Information Network, Greenpeace, and Amnesty International all use web sites to disseminate information and raise political awareness at a variety of scales. Readers are given specific information on how to undertake more effective political action. To varying degrees, they also send out e-newsletters; feed their content to RSS subscribers; promote social bookmarking; host debating forums, blogs, and podcasts; provide interactive games, wallpaper images, and free e-cards; and encourage people to submit information, photographs, and videos that can be used in campaigns. Importantly, a depth of analysis to support campaigns can be made available online for marginal cost (for example, full reports available online as PDFs); previously such information dissemination could only be achieved with the larger resources of the state or corporations.

Political power can also be enacted by software through greater scrutiny of otherwise hidden activities and secret spaces. New software tools and services are providing public access to information that can enable corporations and government to be held to account (audits of human rights, press freedoms, and levels of corruption). Another potent example is access to high-resolution aerial photography and satellite imagery that is facilitating a shift from secrecy in the shadows into the spotlight (Perkins and Dodge 2009). Timely access to high-resolution satellite imagery has helped campaigners and advocacy networks to set the media agenda and overcome scale limitations (such as their small staff and limited budgets) to reach out and connect across the world. While much Internet-based protest is focused on the rapid and uncensored distribution of existing evidence, Aday and Livingston (2009) argue that in the case of satellite imagery there are real opportunities for advocacy organizations to generate new evidence that is, crucially, authoritative and autonomous from the state.

Online software is significant in this shift because of its apparent ability to super-empower individuals and small groups to reach across scales and connect with mass audiences, and as such is playing an important role in the dissemination and sharing of alternative ideas and visual representations, often unmediated by hegemonic forces of the state or large corporations. This democratization of access can impact powerful institutions that prefer to work hidden from public view. The military and state security apparatus, in particular, are struggling to deflect scrutiny from online activism. For example, seeking to counter the activities of satellite watchers who share technical information in online captabases about the orbits of "secret" spy satellites to reveal something of their purpose (Keefe 2006); or the work of plane spotters across the world logging flight patterns on specialist blogs and forums and helping to expose the secret CIA program of extraordinary rendition (Paglen and Thompson 2006). What begins to emerge is a bricolage of counter-mapping of secret state operations based on a collective, crowd-sourced, and amateur gaze.

Lying at the ethical edge of these campaigning and counter-mapping strategies is the quasi-illegal direct action that has been undertaken online to disrupt corporations by virtual sit-ins using software for distributed denial-of-service attacks and by defacing homepages by deliberately hacking into Web server software. This so-called hacktivism that exploits vulnerabilities of software for political advantage, will likely increase in the future as more aspects of daily communication and civic engagement become coded.

Similarly, mobile phone technology is being used to organize political campaigning and protest. In August 2008, Barack Obama announced Joe Biden as his Vice Presidential running mate in the U.S. Presidential election via SMS direct to individual supporters, thus personalizing the mode of communication. Voters can also be urged to go out and vote via text messages. Cell phones are also key tools in coordinating and mobilizing activism and protest movements. For example, the technicity of the software underlying text messaging and cell phone calls were used effectively by WTO protestors in Seattle in 1999 to coordinate protests at short notice so that police had little idea as to what protestors intended, and on the fly, reacting to events as they happened, enabling protestors to regroup quickly. The fact that the cell phone is also a potentially potent means of tracking people by the state, illustrates well the dialectical nature of such technology.

Conclusion

There is little doubt that the technicity of software can empower many people. It provides them with a powerful medium of work and expression that enables them to solve many of their everyday relational problems. If it were not so, millions of people would not entrust their time, energy, skills, and knowledge to using and developing software. Code is a medium and catalyst for invention, enabling unique kinds of new media and software applications that themselves afford creativity. As such, software offers a growing proportion of people with a set of tools to do work in the world, in ways that make their lives more convenient and productive; and they open up opportunities to do undertake tasks that were previously impossible due to issues of affordability, complexity, scale, or geographical separation; and also offer endless potential for recreation and new forms of play.

That said, as we noted in the previous chapter, software also regulates and disciplines. The freedom to participate and do certain kinds of work only exists if an application's underlying calculative algorithms and communicative protocols are encoded to support such actions. As the tactics of a number of national governments illustrate, however, such algorithms and protocols can be altered, for example, to try to restrict Internet access to designated content (Goldsmith and Wu 2006, RSF 2008). Empowerment then is facilitated by the Internet media, but its limits are defined by its fundamental operative protocols. Further, while Web 2.0 opens up new ways for people to add value to capta, to examine the world in new ways, and provides a new means of public expression and social organization, it also opens up capta on personal behaviors and social activities to greater state scrutiny and corporate monitoring. In particular, capta divulged and manipulated on social networking sites and blogs exposes individual intentions to wider audiences. A genuine ethical dilemma therefore exists between the benefits felt from revealing information and the desire to keep control over details deemed personal.

This dilemma is part of a wider dialectic between empowerment and control. At present, the majority of people seem content to negotiate this dialectic, trading the potential loss of privacy and control for participation and free services. This is likely to continue into the future as such arrangements become more mundane and routine, and people continue to use ever more software in their everyday lives. That is not to say that people will simply submit to any increases in levels of control, but rather that they will continue to trade the benefits of using software and online services against any perceived detriment. This trade-off will vary across people, place and context, so that what some people are happy to accept others will protest against (see chapter 11). What seems certain, however, is that people will continue to develop and use software because it empowers them to solve their relational problems.

III   The Transduction of Everyday Spatialities

7 Air Travel

The swift and affordable movement of people and goods is essential for society to function. Everyday people move around environments either through spaces that are increasingly monitored, augmented, and regulated by code or using modes of travel that are progressively more dependent on software to operate. Rather than discuss various different types of mobility, their infrastructure, and management, in this chapter we focus on how air travel has become dependent on software to take place (for a similar treatment of road transportation, see Dodge and Kitchin 2007a). Air travel consists of a passage through code/spaces that are governed by automated management. Tickets are bought online, whether individually or through an agent, check-in is automated and verified by unique passenger and ticket codes, security and surveillance rely on sophisticated captabases and sanctioned by pattern analysis programs, baggage transfer is sorted by bar code, planes are increasingly flown by computers and guided by air traffic control (ATC) systems, and immigration is verified by the scanning and processing of identification codes such as passport numbers and biometrics. The decision as to whether people and luggage can progress from one code/space to the next is more than ever before taken by systems that operate in an automated, autonomous, and automatic way (see figure 7.1).

These various coded infrastructures and processes entangle and fold together to form a vast coded assemblage that defines the practices and experiences of air travel. The relational problem to be solved is one of transferring people and goods from one location to another in a time-efficient, safe, and profitable fashion, and a key part of the solution is code. The whole apparatus of air travel, from initial transaction to exiting the airport at the final destination, is virtualized. As a result, the material transfer of people and goods has become *dependent* on the virtual. In this sense, air travel has become, in Castells's (1996) terms, a real virtuality *par excellence*, seamlessly blending the materiality and virtuality of travel.

That said, as we noted in chapter 4, how code/spaces are transduced in practice are contingent, relational, negotiated, and context dependent. Despite the desire of automated management to transduce an entirely observable, manageable, and predictable

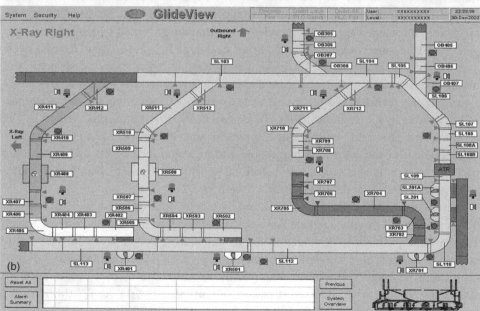

Figure 7.1
Visible surfaces of software in air travel. (*a*) Check-in kiosks with software interfaces. (*b*) Interface screen for a baggage handling system. (*c*) Cockpit view A320 airliner with multiple digital displays (*Source*: Guillaume Grandin, Air France). (*d*) View of the console of a U.S. immigration officer scanning a passenger's finger.

(c)

(d)

Figure 7.1
(continued)

assemblage, the code/spaces of air travel are not consistently produced, always manufactured and experienced in the same fashion. Rather, the connected sequence of airport spaces are beckoned into being in diverse ways, so that no one person's experience of moving through the sequence is identical to another, as it is shaped by the unfolding interactions between passengers, staff, material objects, and virtual systems. Consequently, air travel is never repeated exactly twice and never fully predictable or ordered. That is not to say that there is not a consistently repeating pattern and sense of order to the ongoing production of air travel, but it is to recognize that such patterns and orderly procession are mutable and open to rupture and resistance, and are reproduced through the citational performance of people, machines, and software systems designed to make air travel work in particular ways. As we illustrate below, even within the more software intensive transition zones, code/space is still negotiated—code is not simply law when people fly.

Transduction of Air Travel Code/Spaces

Air travel provides one of the key material supports to the global economic system connecting together people across a network that makes much of the planet accessible within twenty-four hours travel (for those who can afford it, and possess the right documentation and privileges). At any moment of the day, there are an estimated 1.5 million people in flight above the earth (Urry 2007). In many ways, the aviation industry has expanded in parallel to the growth in computing and information and communication technologies from the 1960s onward, drawing on these new technologies to improve efficiency, productivity, competitiveness, safety, and security. The result is that air travel is increasingly reliant on software engineering and networked computing, never more so than in the post-9/11 period, with its emphasis on creating a system that amasses voluminous amounts of capta about the people that pass through the assemblage in order to render it more safe and secure. Ironically, while code is used to make air travel more transparent to the authorities, how it is deployed is increasingly routinized and backgrounded, and many aspects remain invisible or unexplained to passengers and most employees. The progression of traveler from arrival at the airport to takeoff of the flight involves a whole host of processes and interactions between passenger (and baggage), the airline, and the state-sanctioned security apparatus (see figure 7.2). The result is that air travel consists of a passage through sequences of code/spaces.

In many ways, a passenger ticket is the material embodiment of code/space on which are printed several data codes, which while meaningful to the software programs that facilitate travel, are mostly meaningless to the passenger. With the move to e-tickets, these codes are often hidden further, reduced to a single unique code number that identifies the passenger at check-in. These capta's prime purpose is to

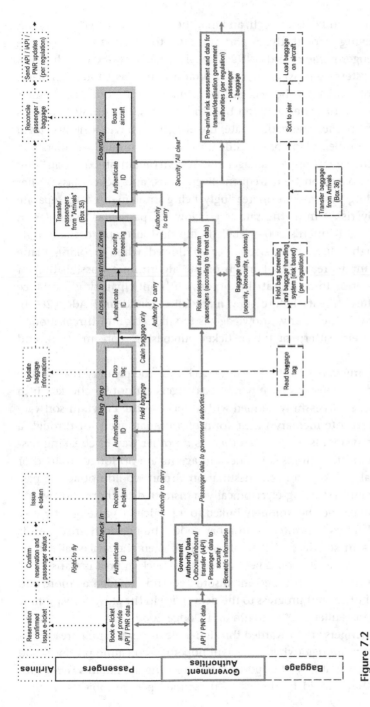

Figure 7.2

An inscription of orderly air travel created by an industry expert group called Simplifying Passenger Travel which shows the idealized flow in a typical passenger departure process. Many elements shown in this diagram are reliant on software. (Redrawn from SPT 2006, 5) verify that the ticket holder and ticket match, and that the person is cleared to progress to the next stage as moving through the airport and onto the destination. Ticketing details are held as passenger name records (PNRs) (see figure 5.2), stored on a handful of global distribution systems (GDSs) (under such brand names as Sabre, Amadeus, Worldspan, and Galileo) which can be accessed from many thousands of terminals across the world. PNR content varies between booking systems, but usually includes a minimum of passenger name, reservation date, travel agency, travel itinerary, form of payment, and flight number. Many of the code numbers are unique identifiers and references to comprehensive customer management systems maintained by airlines, which profile passengers based on their frequent flyer status, and ticket class. Other forms of security profiling systems are increasingly being implemented to separate the risky (or potentially risky) from the safe (see below for particular examples in the United States; also see Bennett's 2004 detailed empirical attempt to trace some of the locations through which his personal capta flowed when booking plane tickets). It also important to realize that much of the algorithmic classification of passenger risk happens prior to arrival at the airport, with anticipatory governance seeking to forestall future threats before they materialize (Budd and Adey 2009). Of course passengers have little, if any, knowledge as to what risk and threat models have been applied to their pattern of travel, ticket purchasing, consumption, and lifestyle characteristics.

The reliance on ticketing codes in the PNR for check-in is the primary reason that a departure area is now a code/space. Simply put, passengers cannot be checked into a flight unless they can be successfully verified with respect to the check-in software system, either through an intermediary in the form of a human agent or through a self-service kiosk. If this system is down, then there is no other way of checking passengers and baggage in or allocating seats. Check-in agents are no longer trained or authorized to do manual check-in, and the destination airport would not accept passengers without a full manifest being electronically transmitted to them, nor would they accept baggage that cannot be uniquely linked to a particular passenger by way of a software generated ID code printed onto a bar code. The check-in area then is dependent on the check-in software. If the software fails then the space fails to be transduced into a code/space as it should be. Instead, the check-in area is transduced as a large waiting room that will soon become disordered and crowded as more and more passengers arrive, but cannot progress to the next space in the store-forward flow architecture of the airport (Fuller 2009; Kitchin and Dodge 2009).

Beyond check-in, passengers are forwarded through a security screening area to the "store" of the predeparture lounge (where they will hopefully consume products and services that are vital to profitability of airports). The screening area marks the beginning of a sterile zone that should be devoid of proscribed people, objects (knives, scissors), and activities (filming and cell phoning). The security screening area is similarly a code/space, dependent on sensors to generate capta, and software to process and analyze it, along with human oversight to watch and interpret display screens, ask additional questions, frisk people deemed to be potential risks, and search bags. The boarding card bar code is often scanned for verification of identity; hand baggage is placed in a sophisticated x-ray machine that can visually slice through items; passengers are gazed upon by human eyes and also rendered "transparent" by channeling through metal detectors and new body scanners that use backscatter radar to look through clothing (Amoore and Hall 2009). Additional scans and tests can be done, such as using a GE EntryScan machine that blasts air onto a passenger's clothes and hair, capturing the particles driven off and automatically sniffing them for explosives and narcotics using an ion trap (GE Infrastructure Security 2007) or individually swabbing shoes and items within a bag for chemical residue indicative of explosives. Checked luggage takes a separate journey, usually through the bowels of the airport, and is also subject to software monitoring and automated scanning.

Once beyond the security area, the passenger is free to move around the store area of the predeparture lounge. This usually contains a mix of seating areas, shops, restrooms, and restaurants. In general, this area is produced as a coded space. Code makes a difference to the transduction of space, but is not essential to it (with the exception of certain retail processes which are dependent on software to handle payment transactions and manage their stock; see chapter 9). Here, passengers are subject to automated surveillance and airport management systems. They can also check the status of their flights via information screens, or use their cell phones or access Wi-Fi to communicate with the outside world. However, if these systems are down, the space still functions as a location to wait before a flight is called over the loudspeaker. Once the flight is announced, passengers walk to the relevant gate. Sometimes, they might pass through an exit passport control point to verify that they have permission to leave the country or enter the country they are about to fly to. At the gate, they walk onto the plane, again their ticket and identity are verified, and boarding cards are carefully scanned and tallied to confirm that the correct passenger numbers are on the aircraft.

Similarly, the plane itself is a code/space from the cockpit through to the in-flight entertainment system and digital maps displayed in the cabin. Over the past twenty-five years or so, avionics has dramatically changed flying for pilots. The increasing integration of sophisticated virtual geographic representations into the cockpit means that pilots now fly through real space virtually, using digital instruments (artificial horizons, inertial and GPS navigation), radio communications systems, real-time radar map displays, and so-called fly-by-wire controls, collision avoidance systems, and continuous feedback from onboard sensors and ground-based data streams. The Boeing

747-400, a leading long-haul jet aircraft, has some 400,000 lines of software code to power its numerous cockpit avionics systems, while the newer Boeing 777 aircraft has some seventy-nine different computer systems requiring in excess of four million lines of code (Pehrson 1996). The key control surfaces of the aircraft are not directly connected to the pilot's stick and peddles. Instead, commands are interpreted and approved by software before being physically enacted (see figure 7.3). Further, the pilot and plane's performance is continuously monitored and stored by black boxes, or flight data recorders. The flight itself takes place through the coded space of the atmosphere, which contains radio navigation beacons, GPS signals, and ATC systems that monitor all movements and direct planes on route to their destinations.

Once the plane has landed and the passengers have disembarked, they proceed to the immigration control hall. Here, their identity is verified again and a decision taken as to whether they can enter a country and under what conditions. We discuss the nature of how this verification occurs in more detail later in the chapter. Passengers then go on to baggage claim. In smaller airports, bags are taken from the plane to the carousel by hand. In larger airports, they are routed through mechanical systems that scan the bar codes on the bags and automatically direct them to the correct carousel. In the latter case, the baggage hall constitutes a code/space. If the code fails, the hall becomes a waiting area, not somewhere to collect bags and move on to the customs zone before exiting into the coded space of the arrivals hall.

Taken to their logical conclusion, we can think about the code/spaces of air travel extending to the Internet and the GDS systems through which tickets are purchased (travel web sites, booking databases, credit card encryption) and global financial markets (the networked spaces of banks, stock markets, financial districts, insurance centers) that, as the volatility across the aviation industry post-9/11 have demonstrated, play a large role in defining airline, airport, and aircraft manufacturers' viability and in restructuring routes, service levels, and plane production. The code/spaces described above are often simultaneously local and global, grounded through the passage of people and goods, but accessible from anywhere across the network. They are linked together across the whole architecture of networked infrastructure of air travel into chains that stretch across space and time to connect start and end nodes into complex webs of interactions and transactions that can be accessed from many thousands of terminals across the world. The massive assemblage of air travel is then widely distributed and diversely scaled.

Figure 7.3 (opposite page)
An illustration from a training manual for an Airbus airliner showing that lines of control from the pilot to the physical flight surface pass through the ELAC (elevator aileron computer) and SEC (spoilers elevator computer) where they are subject to algorithmic laws before being enacted. *Source*: www.smartcockpit.com/data/pdfs/plane/airbus/A320/systems/A320-Flight_Controls.pdf

PITCH CONTROL – SCHEMATIC

FOR INFO

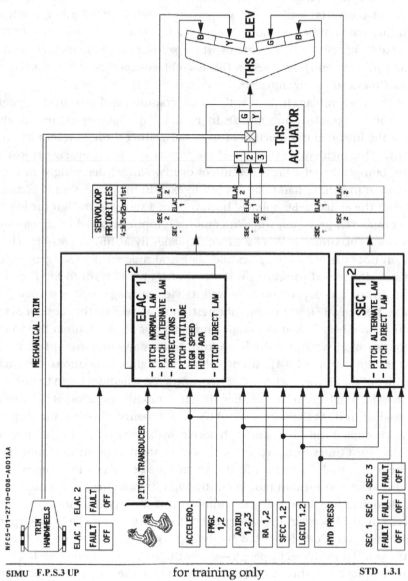

Why Code/Spaces Are Always Incomplete

It is important to note that code/spaces of air travel have accreted over time to no set master plan, with technological advances, a changed political and legislative and economic landscape, to create an interlocking assemblage. The components of this assemblage have a diverse range of owners, maintainers, and licensing, accompanied by a labyrinth of contracts, leasing, and service-level agreements. Further, a raft of national and international bodies and industry organizations are responsible for the setting and vetting of standards for systems where software is vital (such as aircraft navigation and ATC systems). As a result, the assemblage emerges as a constellation of many, sometimes competing, interests.

Such an accreted assemblage is riven with nooks, crannies, and gaps in the system which make them necessarily incomplete in nature. This incompleteness is also revealed when the intended transduction of space fails, either through minor glitches or rarer, catastrophic incidents. Examples of the former are when luggage is lost or passengers are bumped off of a flight because of overbooking. Interestingly, in these cases it is common for airline staff to be at a loss to explain the cause, simply blaming the computer for the problem. Bumping is, however, not a system error, but the logical outcome of commercial pressures, wherein complex (proprietary) yield management algorithms work to maximize profits by ensuring planes fly as full as possible. These systems rely on notional behavioral rules and statistical models of passengers which assume that not all reserved passengers will actual turn up and want to fly. The very survival of an airline can depend on how well its yield management is working, as every empty seat is revenue lost. In terms of catastrophic accidents, the cause of many incidents which have been traced to so-called human error are more often due to the complexity of technical systems and a breakdown in human–computer interactions, particularly for pilots (Baberg 2001). Airline delays and flight cancellations also highlight the fragility of the air travel assemblage. Once ordered schedules begin to unravel, perhaps due to ATC problems or bad weather, then the smooth operation of the airport can quickly be disturbed. As the store-forward flows of passengers become interrupted, the airport environment quickly changes character, with crowds of annoyed passengers and, at the worst times, stranded people forced to sleep in departure lounges.

Despite these potential disruptions to the air travel assemblage, the danger is to think about the store and forward movement through its code/spaces in a deterministic (that code determines how the space unfolds) and universal manner (the same processes occur in all airports in the same way). This is clearly not the case. Airports emerge in diverse ways. Code is not law by itself (Lessig 1999). Software's ability to do work in the world is mediated by people—either through a direct interface between passenger and employee, or through gatekeepers who take the outputs of a program, interpret the results, and are able to negotiate with passengers or co-workers to varying degrees. What this means, is that how travelers engage with software and its gatekeepers (the travel agent, check-in supervisor, security guard, and immigration staff), and react through embodied practice, varies between people and is contingent on their abilities, experiences, prejudices, and the context in which interactions occur. It is necessarily a social and cultural practice, not a simple, deterministic exchange or an act of raw governmentality, and it proceeds in multifarious, subtly mutating ways.

In this sense, the code/spaces of aviation are of-the-moment and performative. The ordering of flows in the store-forward nature of the airport assemblage in particular take continual tuning, and as Knox et al. (2005, 11) note from their study of a British airport, "the organization of 'flow' is always in danger of 'overflow,' of disintegration into confusion and flux, where people and objects become unstuck from the smooth operation of representations and get lost in the intransigent opacity of the 'mass'." Negating the occurrence of overflows, means the airport is remade continuously— cleaners clean; security guards patrol; food is prepared, served, cleared away; planes land, taxi, disgorge passengers and luggage, are checked, refueled, serviced, and reboarded, and they depart; travelers and their bags move through the various architectural spaces and inspection points, and are channeled in various ways (by signs and flight information display screens, by printed boarding cards, by audible announcements, by customer service agents, by automated barriers and doors). Airports require continuous routine maintenance, ad hoc repairs and planned renewal that is easily overlooked by passengers unless they are directly impacted (Graham and Thrift 2007). They exhibit metastability at different scales—"they are stable [only] in their constant instability" (Fuller and Harley 2004, 153).

Given this collective and incomplete nature, there is always scope for workarounds, as airport staff in different roles adapt their interactions with software systems to cope with the pressures of on-the-ground situations. Oftentimes these are unauthorized actions, undertaken with the tacit understanding of managers as necessary to circumvent systems in order to get the job done (for one example, staff may violate rules by sharing access accounts). There is also the ever present potential for errors, particularly in capta entry and translation within and between these software systems (see the numerous real-world stories reported on the RISKS List, http://catless.ncl.ac.uk/risks), while the output of software can easily be wrongly interpreted by workers and passengers (so-called human error). There are also opportunities for malicious damage to the vital software systems of air travel from insiders, and also external attacks. One example of this occurred in August 2006, when it was reported that a computer virus infected the US-VISIT immigration software system operated by the U.S. Customs and Border Protection Agency and caused considerable disruption to passenger flow (Poulsen 2006).

If one spends time in an airport observing what is happening, its diverse realities become all too clear (on the sociological interpretation of airports see Gottdiener 2001 and Pascoe 2001). Consider the example of checking in for a flight. The practices of checking in are not simply rote, but are part of a social exchange between the passenger, the check-in agent, and information systems. Passengers ask additional questions about their travel, for example, checking in to additional legs, or confirming the routing of baggage to the final destination. Check-in agents can ask for additional information, such as whether the bag was packed by the passenger. There can be frank exchanges between them when, for example, the system does not recognize the ticket or the passenger, or has seemingly lost details of pre-ordered seats. There is likely to be further exchange if the desk is closing as a late traveler arrives, or if the luggage is too heavy and the airline wants additional payment to carry it. Other examples of social exchange occur when the flight is overbooked and the airline is seeking to hold over or reroute passengers, or when the check-in agent will not check the passenger all the way through to a final destination, claiming a system glitch. These situations are resolved through a combination of dialog between people and accessing, updating, and modifying records of captabases.

Similarly, security checkpoints and immigration are *negotiated* zones of transition. Code is used to screen and identify passengers in the security area, but often with a human operator who is usually part of a team. The level of attention one receives is often gendered, aged, and raced (women, children, and Caucasians are generally perceived as less of a potential risk in the West), and agents have the authority to decide which items are confiscated and who receives extra screening (Parks 2007). These kinds of collaboration and negotiation are captured by the description below, drawn from observant participation research (Kitchin and Dodge 2009, 104–105).

The bag belonging to the passenger behind is moved into operator's frame. The operator performs a set of scans. He zooms in on one section, then zooms back out again, and performs the same scan routine. He then zooms back in once more and calls a colleague over. Pointing at the screen he indicates the suspected problem and they confer. The colleague then gestures to the bag's owner, a smartly dressed man in his fifties and they head off to one side. The bag is placed on a counter and the passenger is asked some security questions and for permission to search the bag. The man concurs and all the bag's items are emptied onto a counter. The offending item is a meter-long steel security cable. There is a brief negotiation, where the security official clearly sees the cable as a potential weapon and the passenger argues that it is simply for securing the laptop to a workstation. The official concedes that the man can keep the cable this time, but suggests that it not be carried in carry-on luggage in future. One is very much left with the impression that not every passenger would have been allowed to keep the cable (and there is a large perspex box nearby full of confiscated items, including cutlery, penknives, nail files, a metal ruler, a hammer, and other assorted, mostly metal, objects).

While the processes and practices are broadly similar for all passengers, they emerge in contingent and relational ways, and by no means is the code simply law. As a result, as Wood (2003, 337) notes, the security screening area can be viewed as a form of theater, consisting of the "spectacle of the frisk," within which, "we find ourselves tied within a web of individuation and de-individuation marked by perpetual surveillance." Likewise, when individuals pass through an immigration hall, they are subject to verification and examination. Here, machine-readable passports and, depending on location, biometric information are scanned, processed, and interpreted, with the results screened to gatekeepers (immigration officials), but not shown to the individuals themselves. The gatekeeper then decides whether a person gains entry to the country, often asking clarifying questions about the purpose of the visit, length of stay, and itinerary. Code is critical to the process, and is not easily overridden, but the decision is ultimately made by a person interfacing with software, sometimes in negotiation with the passenger. In the next section, we examine how new systems and procedures seek to minimize human interjection, and subject security and immigration to the law of code through the deepening role of automated management.

Automated Management of the Air Travel Assemblage

The use of software to manage passenger flow through the assemblage of air travel, along with a panoply of other routine but foundational management tasks, like aircraft scheduling, staffing levels, and accounts and payments, has a relatively long lineage. Such systems were originally used to make the business of air travel more efficient, competitive, and profitable. More recently, they have been used as a means to manage and regulate passengers and workers, especially in relation to security. Software enables airports, airlines, and states to identify, survey, and assess passengers and workers for potential risk, and to script air travel into more knowable and ordered environments. The aim is to render passengers and staff, in Foucault's (1978) terms, "docile bodies"; bodies that occupy the assemblage in an orderly, noncomplaining, compliant manner through visible systems of discipline (unique identification check-in and immigration, surveillance cameras, security checkpoints, warning signs, and architectural design), accompanied by a sliding scale of sanctions (delayed flight, termination of a journey, police questioning, arrest, criminal charges, threat of fines, and imprisonment). Both capture and automated surveillance systems are in evidence, often in conjunction with each other (see chapter 5).

Both passengers and employees are subject to capture systems. For example, as noted above, check-in can only be accomplished through the use of the check-in software system and the updating of PNR in a captabase. While check-in is a negotiated practice, the nature of the task is defined to a high degree by the software system that scripts the process. For the airline employee at a check-in desk, their activity is reshaped to that demanded by the sequence of prompts and commands generated by the system. Unless all of the required information fields are entered, the passenger cannot be successfully checked in to the flight. Moreover, the system captures much more than the passenger's details, but is also the means by which workers can be surveyed with regard to quality and quantity of their work. Similarly, the passenger using a self-service kiosk is directed through a sequence of screens and questions that must be answered appropriately. Their activity is entirely scripted and over-determined by the system, with appropriate capta collected (although see Kitchin and Dodge 2009 for examples of resistance). These capta are processed and evaluated using sophisticated algorithms that compare the records with various customer and security captabases, combine it with other known capta about a person, assess the passenger's status, and react appropriately (issue or deny a ticket, provide upgrades and access to airline lounges, or target for special security checks and questioning). These systems are automated, automatic, and autonomous in nature. For example, an iris scanner generates and evaluates capta, and has the authority to authorize passage without human oversight.

The development of such automated management systems, especially those related to security and immigration, has expanded dramatically post 9/11, alongside moral panics concerning illegal immigration and asylum seekers. Here, the aim is to upgrade the effectiveness of systems by introducing new grammars of action that deepen capta input and improve analysis, identify and deny potential security risks before a crime is committed, anticipate threats and predict future passenger behavior (Adey 2009; Graham and Wood 2003). In the United States, these systems include the U.S. Visitor and Immigrant Status Indicator Technology (US-VISIT), APIS (Advanced Passenger Information System), and Secure Flight programs. Elsewhere, equivalent systems are being developed; for example, in the UK there is the "e-Borders program" and in Canada, "Smart Borders." These systems use software with the aim to strengthen border controls by more reliably identifying and classifying people prior to and as they travel, verifying their departure, and building up a profile of individual movements over time. Here we outline in brief the three U.S. systems (as they operated or were planned in 2005; note these systems are subject to rapid change).

The US-VISIT system is operated by the U.S. Department of Homeland Security (DHS) and aims to automate the regulation of the flow of non-U.S. citizens in and out of the United States. For those needing a visa to travel to the United States, biometric data (digital fingerprint scans and photographs) is a key form of capta, collected at the point of application (usually a U.S. Consulate office in the country of origin) and checked against a system of interlinked captabases for known criminals and suspected terrorists. When the traveler arrives in the United States, the same biometrics are used to verify that the person is the same one that received the visa. For countries who have a visa waiver program (most OECD nations), travelers must travel with a biometric passport or be photographed and fingerprinted on entry. At its core, the system consists of the integration of three existing DHS systems: the Arrival and Departure Information System (ADIS), the Passenger Processing Component of the Treasury

Enforcement Communications System (TECS), and the Automated Biometric Identification System (IDENT) (DHS 2004). US-VISIT has a one-hundred-year capta retention
period and the capta are shared with "other law enforcement agencies at the federal,
state, local, foreign, or tribal level" who "need access to the information in order to
carry out their law enforcement duties" (DHS 2003, cited in Privacy International
2004). Indeed, the capta US-VISIT generates is used for:

Identifying, investigating, apprehending, and/or removing aliens unlawfully entering or present
in the United States; preventing the entry of inadmissible aliens into the United States; facilitating the legal entry of individuals into the United States; recording the departure of individuals
leaving the United States; maintaining immigration control; preventing aliens from obtaining
benefits to which they are not entitled; analyzing information gathered for the purpose of this
and other DHS programs; or identifying, investigating, apprehending and prosecuting, or imposing sanctions, fines or civil penalties against individuals or entities who are in violation of the
Immigration and Nationality Act, or other governing orders, treaties or regulations and assisting
other Federal agencies to protect national security and carry out other Federal missions. (Federal
Register 2003, cited in Privacy International 2004)

The final statement, "and carry out other Federal missions," effectively means the
capta can be used for whatever the U.S. government thinks is appropriate now and in
the future; this clearly opens the door to wider surveillance of mobility. Further, this
sharing of capta across agencies makes it available for use by several hundred mining
programs identified by the General Accounting Office in U.S. government departments
for purposes beyond security and immigration, and clearly raises issues concerning
function creep, privacy, and civil liberties (Privacy International 2004).

In addition to US-VISIT, passengers on international flights to the United States are
prescreened by U.S. Customs and Border Protection using APIS. APIS uses information
from the machine-readable part of a passport, along with PNR information supplied
by air carriers (this links to other layers, such as, international standards in the capta
ontology of passports determined by the International Civil Aviation Organization.)
APIS requires passengers to provide in advance to U.S. Customs details such as name,
date of birth, sex, travel document number, and destination. APIS targets suspected
or high-risk passengers by checking for matches against a multiagency database, the
Interagency Border Inspection System (IBIS), and the FBI's National Crime Information
Center wanted persons files. IBIS includes the combined databases of U.S. Customs,
U.S. Immigration and Naturalization Service, the State Department, and, most likely,
multiple other federal agencies.

The Secure Flight program monitors internal flights, and accordingly U.S. citizens.
Secure Flight is the replacement for the CAPPS (Computer Assisted Passenger Prescreen-
ing System) program, with the main differences being that the system only looks for
known or suspected terrorists, not other law enforcement violators, that it includes a
redress mechanism if passengers believe they have been unfairly or incorrectly selected

for additional screening (Sternstein 2004), and it does not have new capta requirements for airline reservations systems. Using PNR capta, Secure Flight verifies the identity of the passenger and conducts a risk assessment using commercial and government data, and updates the Transport Security Agency's (TSA), Passenger and Aviation Security Screening Records (PASSR) captabase (Hasbrouck n.d.). The risk assessment affects the passenger's assigned screening level—no risk, unknown or elevated risk, or high risk. Based on the risk level, the traveler could be subjected to additional searches, questioned by screening staff, or detained and interrogated by police. Importantly, the rules of grammar that lie at the root of these determinations are purposefully secret, being classified as "Sensitive Security Information" and, as such, are not open to scrutiny (in terms of independent verification of their effectiveness) or informed challenge (in terms of equity issues, such as potential racial profiling).

It is fair to say that these automated management systems have been subject to some expressions of concern and criticism. For example, CAPPS was criticized on normative grounds and replaced due to the ease with which the "system could be beat with fake identification, the system's reliance on commercial databases widely acknowledged to be riddled with errors, and the fact that the system compromised the privacy of airline travelers without making nation's airliners safer" (DHS 2004). In 2004, the American Civil Liberties Union published a list of seven reasons to question the design and deployment of such automated passenger screening and profiling systems (ACLU 2004). These reasons focused on errors, due process, cost, and impact.

First, passengers are judged in secret and without knowing the terms by which they are judged. Second, as the TSA itself acknowledges, these systems are not as infallible as their developers suggest, being open to both biographical and biometric errors. For example, biographical errors include recording mistakes, such as misspelled names and incorrectly keyed dates of birth, nonupdates (change of address), missing or misleading fields, and mismatching errors and false positives, especially based on names. These errors are particularly prevalent in commercial databases sometimes used as a component in profiling systems. Biometric errors include the "failure to enroll rate," wherein the biometric is either unrecognizable or not of a sufficiently high standard (worn fingerprints), a "false nonmatch rate," wherein a subsequent reading does not properly match the enrolled biometric (facial aging), and false positives, wherein a system is so large that there are many near matches leading to people being falsely identified. In 2005, the TSA was predicting an error rate of at least 4 percent, seriously undermining the effectiveness and integrity of the system (for every hundred million who fly, four million people will have errors in their capta that could adversely affect their ability to travel) (Kitchin and Dodge 2006).

Third, with respect to due process, the ACLU (2004) points out that findings are largely nondisclosed and there is a limited process of notification, correction, and appeal. Fourth, these new systems place an unnecessary burden on commercial airlines, travel agents, and the public by passing the costs of a flawed and ineffective security system onto them. Fifth, the systems infringe on privacy through the creation of lifetime travel dossiers that remain beyond the control of the individuals that they relate to. Sixth, they have the potential to foster the systematic unequal treatment of passengers on the basis of some arbitrary criteria (the so-called flying while Arab effect, where those of Arab or South Asian descent are subject to extra screening and profile based simply on race and ethnicity indicators in their capta shadows). Seventh, there is great potential for control creep, that is, capta being used for purposes beyond its original collection, and the system being rolled out to govern access to other kinds of environments such rail networks, national monuments, and key public buildings (Graham and Wood 2003; Lyon 2003).

Taken together, US-VISIT, APIS, and Secure Flight aim to create a capta shadow of travel for individuals that lasts a lifetime. In short, all air (indeed international) travel will be collected and linked to biographic and biometric information and used to screen individual travel behavior. These systems are representative of the capture model, wherein the grammars of action are the formalized rules of assessment at the heart of the classification and risk assignment process, and biographic and biometric capta are the basic ontology. Clearly, these systems actively shape, both implicitly and explicitly, the nature and procedures of travel (rather than simply externally surveying moving bodies). In explicit terms, travelers have to acquire machine-readable passports, repeatedly submit to biometric capta generation, and potentially experience extra security and immigration checks. In implicit terms (to travelers at least; explicit to workers), how the travel industry is organized, its procedures, operations, and work practices, are altered in ways not necessarily democratic or equitable to those directed affected.

As noted above, while these systems of automated management seek to create an exhaustive and infallible means of regulating air travel, they are open to negotiation and resistance. The drive is to limit such negotiation through improvements in system design and capta quality, that provides both passengers and workers fewer opportunities for finessing or overriding the work that code does, and which further empowers code to determine outcomes. Resistance is being tackled in a different way, through the creation of a powerful discursive regime that brings both passengers and workers in line with its logic.

The Discursive Regime of Travel Code/Spaces

The code/spaces of air travel, and the regulatory capacity of automated management, are supported by at least seven interlocking discourses. These are security, safety, anti-fraud, citizenship, economic rationality, convenience, and free skies. These discourses work ideologically to construct and position code/space as a commonsense method:

it benefits passengers and workers, society and the aviation industry alike, with few negative externalities (and these are more than outweighed by benefits).

Major airports and passenger aircraft have been, and continue to be, perceived as prime targets of terrorism. They are a means of international travel and smuggling for terrorists and criminals. Further, planes are involved in accidents, hijackings and attacks. Code/space, it is argued, is desirable because it creates a more secure and safe environment. Automated management allows the surveillance of passengers and workers to become more panoptic in scope, both widening and deepening the extent to which the complex and dynamic flows of air travel can be policed, thus making air travel a more secure and safe undertaking. Part of the power of code/space is what Foucault (1988) calls a "technology of the self": a sociospatial configuration where the presence of a technology persuades people to self-discipline their behavior; to act in ways prescribed by those controlling the space and technology. In the case of airports, this is reinforced through regular auditory security warnings about unattended baggage, check-in security questions, warnings not to tamper with the restroom smoke detectors, barriers, and access controlled doors, and blanket CCTV coverage.

Safety is not tied to security alone. There are other ways that automated management ensures safe passage. For example, the use of software is now integral to effective air traffic control—code reduces the physical and cognitive demands on pilots, and provides a means of remote detection and automatic response to system failures. Further, airlines stress their maintenance record, and the aircraft manufacturer's competence, based in part on the allure of digital systems.

Safety and security have often been accompanied by discourses of anti-fraud and citizenship, and indeed in some cases they have been explicitly linked. Here, the systems are seen as a means to enhance the effectiveness of policing state borders and to ensnare and return illegal immigrants and asylum seekers. For example, a press release for the Project Semaphore (the precursor to the e-borders program), UK Immigration Minister Des Browne stated:

e-Borders, along with biometric ID cards, shows how we are using new technology to develop embarkation controls for the 21st century. Access to information about passengers before they travel will help in the fight against illegal immigration, particularly document and identity abuse. It will also aid law enforcement and counter terrorism. At the same time, technology will allow us to speed through low risk passengers, helping British business and visitors to the UK. (UK Home Office 2004)

These interlocking discourses of anti-fraud, citizenship, and security are powerful because they are designed to enhance trust and confidence in the air travel industry as a whole, and address the concerns of legitimate, law-abiding citizens about illegal immigrants and bogus asylum seekers. Here, automated management is positioned as the foundation for confidence by providing infallible systems. Here, virtual code offers a solid solution to problem of porous, real borders. These discourses are further reinforced by government regulations, legislation, and a raft of international treaties (Butler 2001; Graham 1995; Van Zandt 1944).

Another set of discourses justifies the intense deployment of software by contending that it produces a more convenient or cost-effective journey. The transduction of code/space reduces the hassles of flying, and passengers supposedly gain through lower fares and faster progress through the airport. People can book online by themselves, meaning they do not have to interact with an agent, they can pass more smoothly and time-efficiently through the airport, and the systems can automatically acknowledge status such as frequent flyer, offer seating selection, and provide upgrades. The rhetoric produced contends that by automating aspects of the industry, airports and airlines can reduce their fares and fees, passing on savings to customers, while at the same time improving their profitability (a win-win situation). Further, code/space is economically rational because it facilitates global trade and tourism, creating and maintaining wealth creation for many. Here, code/space seduces people to its logic. In Althusser's (1971) term, code/space thus interpellates people to its ideas by enticing them to subscribe to and desire its logic and to willingly and voluntarily participate in its ideology and practice (rather than simply disciplining them into docile bodies).

This interpellation is key to another discourse, that of free skies, which paradoxically undermines the discourse of security. The ethos of air travel, from its very beginnings, has been one of freedom of the air and open skies. Implicit in the rhetorical messages of aviation is the deeply utopian logic that making the world a smaller place, will make the world a better place. Air travel is presented as a benevolent force that is inherently good for commerce and can bring greater understanding between people. The aviation industry strives to portray an image that it transcends geopolitics of the terrestrial world and offers travelers who can afford it an uncomplicated world without frontiers. The commercial aircraft manufacturers and major airlines spend heavily on marketing and advertising to promulgate this powerful, idealistic rhetoric, often utilizing universalist, visual tropes of the globe and world route maps (Cosgrove 1994). Code/space is now promoted as an integral part of making such utopian rhetoric a (profitable) reality.

While undoubtedly the aviation industry and its attendant code/spaces have detractors, it is fair to say that, at present, intensive software solutions are the hegemonic production of space associated with air travel. Indeed, given the potential for capture errors, flaws in procedures and structures, and potential impacts and misuses of the system, there has, to date, been remarkably little mass, organized resistance by individuals, unions, or activists to embedding of code into air travel. The resistance that has occurred is either expressed in disquiet, individual resistance, such as boycotts of travel to particular destinations, or legal challenges to state policy by groups such as the American Civil Liberties Union. This resistance, however, is a long way short of a tipping point, wherein opposition becomes so great that it starts to challenge the present hegemony and places pressure on governments, airport operators, and airline managements to modify or abandon software systems. We posit that this lack of overt, organized resistance is due to five reasons detailed in chapter 5 (people have been persuaded to the new emerging logic; the changes occurring are viewed as simply an extension of an existing systems; new grammars of action and surveillance are seen as an inherent part of the system; the point of contact for most travelers is relatively painless; they are worried about the consequences of protest).

Conclusion

Aviation consists of chains of code/spaces. Software purposefully mediates many of the processes and actions of passenger movement. However, code is not simply law—deterministic, fixed, and universal. Rather, air travel emerges through the interplay between people and software in diverse, complex, relational, embodied, and context-specific ways. Even when flying becomes routine for commuters, it is an event that unfolds in multifarious, ever-changing ways. Because airports are diversely (re)produced, through the collaborative manufacture of people and code, they are certainly not the nonplaces as described by Augé (1995). While airports share similar architecture and processes, they are places in the same sense that small towns are, albeit with a daily flux of a large transient population. They have diverse social relations and formations, engender meaning and attachment, and represent different values and images of the locale and nation (Crang 2002). This is especially the case for the hundreds or thousands of workers, and for travelers who live locally and pass through the airport regularly; for example, Santa Barbara, California's airport with its small number of regional flights per day is very different from Chicago O'Hare with its thousands.

The widespread use of software to organize, manage, and produce air travel is set to grow further, supported by a persuasive set of discourses that work to create a powerful logic. These discourses include security, safety, economic rationality, and increased productivity, and convenience and flexibility. Software enables securer and safer air travel by widening, extending, and automating the degree to which passengers, workers, equipment, planes, and spaces are monitored and regulated through "infallible" systems of detection and response; software enables the streamlining and automation of myriad routine tasks, speeding up processes, increasing throughput, improving efficiencies, and reducing staffing and resource overhead that can be passed on to the traveler (or to shareholders); and software can provide passengers with greater convenience and flexibility in terms of booking, itineraries of travel, progress through the airport, requesting certain seating, and racking up rewards. Collectively, these discourses work to justify further investment, to make code/spaces appear as commonsense responses to particular issues, and convince travelers (and workers) of the logic of their deployment. In other words, they work to ensure that air travel will consist of ever more densely interconnected code/spaces.

Despite these efforts to further deepen deterministic forms of automated management, the code/spaces of air travel will continue to be contingent and relational in nature, the products of complex and diverse interactions between people and code. As such, we believe these interactions warrant further attention and study, requiring detailed ethnographies of aviation across peoples (passengers by class, race, gender, age, disablement, and different kinds of workers), types of airports (local, national, and international hubs) and in a range of nations (with differing political economies, state policies, legislation, and business practices).

8 Home

Work across the social sciences documents how a home is a complex set of social and material relations (Blunt and Dowling 2006; Hitchings 2004; Mallett 2004; Miller 2001), and a site of continual technological adoption and innovating domestic practices. Home is a dwelling space in which important lived experiences take place, providing a locus for the fundamental aspects of daily social reproduction (eating, personal care, relaxation, and sleep). Home is also central to human psychological well-being; a place of familial relations, intimacy, and emotional ties; a place for personal life and privacy from others; a place with layers of memories and meanings from the past; a sanctuary that offers security and safety from the wider world. Home is important then, not least because people spend most of their time at home.

A great deal of emotional, physical, and financial effort is expended in the maintenance of the physical dwelling, along with the nurturing of home life. A significant part of this work in creating a proper home involves the continual ordering of time, spaces, and resources into configurations to solve ongoing problems of living. As part of ordering the routines of homemaking, a plethora of technologies are used. Indeed, typical Western homes function through the use of products, tools, machines, gadgets, and equipment, from toothbrushes to teaspoons. Cupboards, closets, shelves, and drawers are full of the things we live with, and the built fabric of the dwelling is itself a composite of hundreds more components and materials. Homes then are meta-machines of literally thousands of different technological components.

As detailed in chapter 3, the nature of a significant number of these objects are changing as they increasingly become infused with software. Domestic objects are gaining capacities that extend their technicity and enable them to do additional work in the world. Indeed, it seems likely that the majority of objects that currently use electrical power will become colonized by computer code in the (near) future, just as a wide range of manual and mechanical household tools became newly animated by development and integration of electrical controls and motors in the first half of the twentieth century (Cowan 1983). These capacities are helping to reshape home life and its complex spatialities by on the one hand, augmenting and supplementing domestic tasks, and on the other hand plugging the home into new, extended, distributed networks. In other words, coded objects are reconfiguring the social and material relations of home, often in banal and subtle ways. They do so, in part, because they transduce space; that is, coded objects bring new spaces and spatialities into being through their enrollment in practices. In this chapter, we explore the embedding and work of coded objects in the home, and consider how the home is represented and worked upon by a wide range of coded processes external to material dwelling spaces.

The Prevalence of Coded Objects

In this section, we illustrate the contemporary enrollment of coded objects to solve domestic tasks. We do this by providing audits of three typical (Western) homes. These audits are hypothetical, but are based on our broad observation of different homes, particularly in an Anglo-American context. They also highlight that the transition to the smart home varies depending on the person, place, and circumstance, with homes still possessing objects working in analog form (Rode 2006). In the audit, PCO refers to a peripherally coded object, HC to a hard codeject, CC to a closed codeject, SC to a sensory codeject; PL to a permeable logject, and NL to a networked logject (see discussion in chapter 3).

Audit I

Peter (age 43), Wendy (age 40), and their three children (Joshua, 12; Toby, 6; Milly, 3) along with their pet dog constitute a typical hard working family. They live in a twenty-year-old, mortgaged, semi-detached house, with three bedrooms and a converted attic bedroom, a single garage, backyard, and shed. Both parents work full time (in manual and lower managerial occupations), and they have a hectic home life raising their children. A range of technologies and an increasing number of coded objects are enrolled in the daily production of their home, beckoning into being a series of overlapping coded spaces and code/spaces.

Living room   The main family room is the focus of entertainment and information gathering, and an intense point of digital media use at different times of the day. Pride of place in the room is given over to a large, flat-screen, digital television (CC), partnered with a coterie of coded objects to provide it with various media sources. The family have recently upgraded from a separate analog video recorder and DVD player to an integrated digital video recorder (PL). A satellite decoder box (NL) is connected to the telephone line, necessary to access some of the more sophisticated interactive services, particularly pay-per-view sports. The move to a digital television system has increased the range of viewing options and enhanced flexibility of schedules with on-demand media consumption becoming the norm.

One corner of the living room has been semipermanently reconfigured to serve as a computing zone for the main family desktop PC (along with printer, scanner, and various accessories and cables for cameras and portable music players). It is permanently connected to the Internet via broadband and is the most obvious networked logject in the home. It is a source of information and entertainment services, and a store for growing amount of personal capta related to the household (documents, e-mail, photographs). It is used intensively and sometimes becomes a focus of family-activities, in competition with the television. At the moment, the digital camcorder, an expensive and relatively little used permeable logject, is on the table next to the PC. The living room also plays host to an Xbox360 video game console (PL) that can be connected to the Internet, and contains a multifunction cordless phone and answering machine that serves as the main contact number for the home, but is being usurped increasingly by the flexibility offered by the parents' individual cell phones (NLs).

Kitchen/dining room   Along with the living room, the kitchen is typically the busiest room in the house, serving various home functions such as preparing food, cooking, cleaning, and socializing. These functions are often aided by domestic appliances, many new models of which are now augmented by code. In Peter and Wendy's case, most of their appliances are more than five years old and are analog or peripherally coded in nature: oven/range (PCO), dishwasher, refrigerator/freezer, and clothes dryer. As such, they are largely uncoded objects, with electromechanical or electronic controls, but some will certainly become coded objects when next replaced. This has occurred with respect to the washing machine (SC), which is a new model that offers a raft of software-driven programs and options from its LED control panel. While the software has the potential to make a difference to the wash, in this case, the family typically only uses a couple of preset programs so that the code makes little, if any, difference to the household's laundry practices. The manufacturer may well assert, however, that the technicity of the code improves the energy/water efficiency of the machine, and facilitates maintenance by providing detailed diagnostics for the repair technician. In one corner of the kitchen is the thermostat for the central heating (SC), which was recently updated following the replacement of the furnace. The control is code driven, notionally providing much greater control over heating (variable timings and temperature levels), with settings held in memory for future use. The kitchen is also home base for the dog with her basket and bowls in one corner. She is rendered machine readable through an RFID tag implanted under her skin that uniquely links her body to a record in captabase run by PETTRAC (www.pettrac.co.uk) that provides details of her ownership and proper location should she ever get lost.

Bedrooms   These rooms are typically more private spaces and less coded than the living room and kitchen. The master bedroom contains several pieces of home gym equipment that includes digital performance monitors (PL), used on a semi-regular basis by Peter. Joshua's attic bedroom contains a growing number of coded objects, including a new laptop, a DVD player, portable media player, docking station, and speakers, digital camera, and what he perceives as an aging video game console that cannot play the latest releases (all PL unless actively networked). The room also has other media technologies including an analog television and radio. Toby's bedroom has a large range of toys, some of which use electronics and software to provide interactive features (HCs and CCs). The last bedroom is serving as a nursery for baby Milly and contains the base station for a Philips baby monitor (see figure 8.1) and electronic learning toys, some of which are enlivened by software (HCs and SCs).

Bathroom   The family bathroom is the most private space in the home and also the least mediated by electrical and electronic powered technologies. Yet, it is a highly technological space, one that is dominated by machinery and materials to effectively channel clean water and remove waste into the sewer system. As a pivotal space for personal care of the body it contains several portable coded objects, including Peter's digital "body monitoring" scale (PL) and Wendy's pedometer (PL), among other electrical gadgets like shavers and toothbrushes that can be purchased in coded models.

Garage and shed   These spaces, while peripheral to the main dwelling, are important components of the family's domesticity, containing a range of specialized objects and tools, some of which should not properly be located elsewhere in the home (with respect to their cleanliness, hygiene, and size; Bell and Dourish 2007). There are gardening implements, outdoor toys and bikes, camping equipment, shop tools, and miscellaneous items from past projects and hobbies. The majority of these objects are manually operated, lacking electrical power or embedded code. Many outdoor manual tasks cannot realistically be enhanced with software at this stage, and other objects are deemed to be so cheap, disposable, or insignificant as not worthy of coding.

Cars   The household has two cars. The vehicles are essential elements in household activities with many daily tasks configured around car-based solutions. Moreover, their interiors are so familiar and personalized through habitual use that they often feel like, and are treated as, an extension of home spaces. One car is a two-year-old Honda, and the second is a smaller run-about car that is over ten years old. The Honda has a significant array of integrated software systems that tune the car's performance and also augment the information provided to the driver through the digital dashboard,

Figure 8.1 (opposite page)
Promotional material for a sophisticated baby monitor that proffers several enhancements to parents in the care of their children, promising greater knowledge at a distance of the space in which the baby is sleeping. The monitor works as a sensory codeject. *Source*: Philips Electronics, www.p4c.philips.com/files/s/scd530_00/scd530_00_pss_eng.pdf

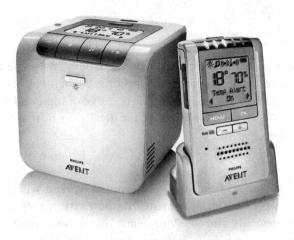

Healthy climate, total comfort

Zero interference guaranteed with DECT technology

Enjoy complete peace of mind. With the new Philips AVENT range of DECT Baby Monitors you can relax, safe in the knowledge your baby's happy even when you are out of the room.

Complete peace of mind
- Guarantees zero interference from any other device
- Humidity sensor to help maintain a comfortable climate
- Temperature sensor to monitor and keep baby's room healthy
- Indicates a continuous connection between the two units
- Uses lights to indicate if the baby makes a noise
- Adjustable sound sensitivity

Soothing sights, sounds and words
- Lullabies and night light
- Allows you to talk to the baby

Convenience for you and your child
- Adjust the volume of the parent unit to suit any situation

Mobility in and around the house
- The belt clip provides hands-free convenience and mobility
- Rechargeable parent unit for minimum 24 hours of monitoring

including a GPS unit that can reduce the risk of getting lost (see figure 8.2). The second car is largely devoid of software, being manufactured at a time when onboard computer monitoring and driver assistance systems were the preserve of high-end vehicles only (see Dodge and Kitchin 2007a and Thrift 2004c for details on how software is changing cars and wider driving spaces).

Audit II

Simon (age 43) and Iris (age 37) are both full-time professional workers with no children or pets. They live in a two-bedroom apartment in a new city center complex, with attendant security gates, keypads, and CCTV cameras. They have a small balcony but no garden; and they have a dedicated parking space for their single car in a secure underground garage. They have high disposable income, are technologically savvy, time pressured, and security conscious. They regularly work at home as part of their

Figure 8.2
The digital dashboard of a Honda Civic that includes code to calculate average speed, current fuel consumption, and estimates of the distance to next refueling, along with the display of the outside temperature. Software is able to provide drivers a greater range of real-time information than analog dials. This mid-range priced car also has much software in its mechanical guts that continuously monitors engine performance. *Source*: www.honda.co.uk/cars/_assets/downloads/civic5door/Civic.pdf

lifestyle. Their apartment is actively monitored by a buildingwide fire and smoke alarm system, and monitored externally by coded services in terms of metered gas, electricity, water, cable, broadband Internet, and television.

Living room   The living room contains a variety of very expensive, branded home entertainment technologies (all are coded objects). A large, high-definition plasma screen television (HC) is mounted on one wall, linked to a home theater amplifier and surround sound speakers. It is also connected to a cable television set-top box (NL), a DVR (PL), and to a Slingbox (PL), a wireless networking device that distributes the digital television signal into other rooms in the apartment. Simon and Iris are music aficionados, and the room has a state-of-the-art hi-fi system that is heavily coded, although it is not logging usage or directly networked. On the table is a year-old Apple MacBook laptop (NL) that Iris and Simon use as an everyday home PC for surfing the Web; including online grocery shopping; it is always networked via Wi-Fi to the household cable broadband. On the mantelpiece are two Kodak EasyShare digital picture frames (CC) showing a sequence of photographs from their summer vacation in New Zealand. They have no fixed line telephone, using the cable broadband for Wi-Fi and VoIP calls (using Skype) and have multiple cell phones (work and personal).

Kitchen   The space is purposefully designed as a luxury fitted kitchen with top of the line appliances and built-in media center (LCD television and DVD player), all of which are unitary coded objects and are programmable to some degree. The kitchen also has a DAB radio (CC), although the addition of software makes little difference to Simon's radio listening while cooking. He is always enticed by new digital gadgets, including a sophisticated kitchen scale that tallies the weights of multiple ingredients (see figure 8.3). On one wall is an LCD panel that provides a software interface to control the environmental system (NL) for the apartment, which offers individual room heating and air conditioning profiles, along with wireless connection and remote online access. In a closet, next to the vacuum cleaner, is a redundant coded gadget that Simon bought for Iris as a humorous present (see figure 8.4). This robotic convenience (SC) has only been a used a couple of times as they pay a housekeeper to clean the apartment two mornings a week.

Bedrooms   Their main bedroom has little coded technology except for a clock radio (CC), an LCD digital television, and a Slingbox receiver for cable television signal (PL). The room is often a transitory site for various mobile codejects (such as phones, Kindle e-book readers, PDAs, laptops, MP3 players). The second bedroom of the apartment is permanently configured as a home office and contains a range of computers and associated paraphernalia to support Simon and Iris when they want to work from home. There is a new desktop PC and an aging iMac (both NL), along with a laptop docking station and monitor (HC), plus a cradle for a PDA and an iPod (HC). On top

Figure 8.3
Advertisement promoting the benefits of a digital kitchen scale offering ease of use and greater precision than the analog equivalent. *Source*: Salter

**Programmed
to make a mess**

**Programmed
to clean up**

iRobot Roomba: cleans routinely...so you don't have to

The new floor vacuuming robot that really works

Keeping on top of the cleaning and floor cleaning in particular is a constant battle in any home. Thankfully, the new iRobot Roomba is designed to relieve you of this tedious chore and help you on a daily basis. It cleans floors superbly at the press of a button, using less energy than a standard vacuum.

How does iRobot Roomba work? Advanced sensors and AWARE® robot technology ensure this intelligent and energy efficient home robot covers your whole floor area. Whether it's carpets, rugs or hard floor surfaces, its highly effective brush system and smart vacuum picks up large debris as well as fine dust and dirt. It even gets right under most furniture to clean those difficult to reach areas.

Just turn it on, walk away and come back to clean, mess free floors.

For more information on iRobot Roomba call 0800 132 509

Navigates to clean right
under low furniture

Adjusts to clean any type
of floor surface

Cleans along edges and
in tight corners

Automatically returns to
homebase to recharge

www.irobot.com

Distributed by

omotec
home appliances

2007 iRobot Corporation. All rights reserved. iRobot and Roomba are registered trademarks of iRobot Corporation.

Figure 8.4

Magazine advertisement for domestic coded object that promises greater convenience and leisure through automation. It is also an overtly gendered representation of technology and domestic practice with the messy boy playing while a passive mother figure sitting in the background sees to the childcare role. *Source*: iRobot of one of the monitors is a Webcam (NL) that Simon occasionally uses. Under the desk is a wireless router (NL) for the cable broadband that provides secure Wi-Fi net-working throughout the apartment; also hidden away there is a redundant fax machine (HC), now inoperable as the apartment does not have a conventional landline tele-phone connection, and replaced by the PC. The bottom of a filing cabinet also contains several generations of digitals cameras (SC), a camcorder (PL), a couple of redundant cell phones (NL) and media players (PL), and an external hard disk (PL) for infrequently-made backups of their growing range of personal capta. On top of the filing cabinet is a wireless color laser printer (NL). Lastly, the office is the storing place for Simon's large digital keyboard synthesizer (PL) and the rugged new GPS (PL) that Iris uses for geocaching on weekends.

Entrance hallway   Next to the front door of the apartment is a video entry phone (CC) that allows them to control visitor access into the building. Nearby is the control panel for the apartment's burglar alarm (NL) that is connected to a central monitoring station. (There are four movement sensors in different points in the apartment, along with the sensors on several windows that are potentially vulnerable.) The storage closet in the hallway also contains two smart meters (NL), recording the household's utility usage.

Car   Their car is a top of the line Audi S5 coupe, which is saturated with software and is the epitome of a computer-on-wheels, with nearly every aspect of the vehicle being monitored and augmented by code. It also includes a raft of driver assistance systems that shadow their actions and help reduce the cognitive and kinesthetic load of driving. For example, the car has adaptive cruise control with radar distance warning and lane assist; a parking assistance system provides audio and visual cues to aid the driver; and headlights and windshield wipers activate automatically in response to external conditions. The setup of seats, mirror, and steering wheel positions for indi-vidual drivers can be memorized. The car is also a hub for entertainment and com-munication with Bluetooth connectivity to cell phones and other devices.

Audit III

Dorothy (age 85) has lived in the same two-bedroom duplex for over forty years and has been a widow for eight years. She has a limited fixed retirement income. She is still relatively active and enjoys visits from her great-grandchildren, but she has a growing number of medical problems that have reduced her mobility. She has come to rely on homecare and assistive quality of life technologies and tele-monitoring to keep her living independently, but much of her house is uncoded. She wears digital hearing aids that make a positive difference to her ability to interact socially. Such an everyday embodied mixture of code can be seen as a forerunner of wearable comput-ing for routine health monitoring and well-being assistance, and the future potential fusing of software and biological functioning to create cyborgian recombinations.

Living room   In the living room there is a limited set of home entertainment technologies including a television (analog), VCR (CC) along with a radio-CD player (HC). From television advertisements, Dorothy is aware of a "digital switchover" (the phased termination of analog television broadcasts), which means she will need to update her television set, but she is worried about costs and uncertain about the details of what she will need to do. There is a cordless digital telephone base station (HC) on the coffee table, and Dorothy usually takes the handset with her as she moves about the house during the day, otherwise she risks missing phone calls. She has no cell phone. The living room also contains the Lifeline control box for the telecare home monitoring system (NL) that unobtrusively watches Dorothy's daily activities and provides a safety net for summoning help if she has an incident in the house (see figure 8.5). It is wired to passive infrared (PIR) movement sensors in all rooms and several fixed panic alarms (including a pull cord in the bathroom) and the pendant alarm (HC) that she wears.

Kitchen   The kitchen contains a range of older electrical appliances, none of which are coded but remain perfectly functional and able to solve Dorothy's daily domestic tasks. The central heating control is an old clockwork timer with a manual thermostat. The exception is a new DAB radio (CC) on the kitchen counter, received as a Christmas present. It is permanently tuned into Dorothy's favorite local station and its additional functionality is ignored. A basic calculator (CC) is on the table, on top of a couple of utility bills, and the day's mail lies on a counter including a bulky padded envelope containing her repeat prescription of tablets ordered automatically for her by a health management database at the local pharmacy. In one corner are the food bowls for her aging cat, Norris. He has an identification tag and a bell on his collar but is not micro-chipped.

Bedroom and bathroom   These rooms have no coded objects beyond the PIR movement sensors on the wall, a panic alarm button/cord and a bed occupancy sensor—a pressure pad under the mattress (HC).

Car   Dorothy does not own a car and cannot drive. She is reliant on rides from friends, the dial-a-ride minibus, and the local bus. The degree to which public transportation is reliant on software varies and is not at all apparent to Dorothy as a passenger.

The Networking of Homes

In addition to the embedding of software into domestic settings, the home is becoming ever more porous to information flow and open to monitoring and regulatory networks. Every home is a node in multiple consumer and government networks relating to utilities, entertainment, communications, finance, taxation, health, and security, some of which work in real time, others asynchronously, all using electronic captabases structured and worked upon by software algorithms. Particular domestic

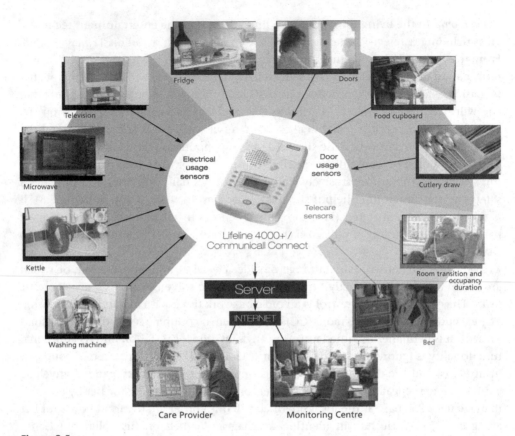

Figure 8.5
A promotional diagram of the range of everyday tasks that can be silently and continuously monitored by sensors and capta fed into software for analysis. This could alert a security company or caregiver if capta on certain activities falls outside of normal patterns or exceeds set thresholds (for example, the front door opening late at night) and can also model changing activity patterns that might predict declining health (for example, the refrigerator, or fridge, and hot water heater, or kettle, not being used frequently could be indicative of not eating properly). *Source*: ADLife Solution Sheet, www.tunstallgroup.com

objects connected to the dwelling are subject to intense scrutiny, the most obvious being cars which must be separately registered and taxed. Significant amounts of capta are also generated, processed, and analyzed with respect to the manifold infrastructures that make up a home. The use of these infrastructures binds them into overlapping grids of calculation through instruments of measurement, surveillance, and classification.

All three homes discussed above are serviced by various utilities, water/sewage, gas, and electricity. The provision and consumption of these resources are recorded and processed by their suppliers for billing purposes. Conventionally, billing has either been a flat rate charge based on dwelling size or per volume usage monitoring. There is now a move to install so-called smart meters that record more detailed capta on how a resource is consumed, revealing activity patterns in the household (when people get up and go to bed) and also the type of appliances being used. Some smart meters can also be read remotely. Another key infrastructural service for all three homes is waste collection. They all dispose of significant quantities of waste products, particularly packaging and excess food and domestic products. As a means of reducing landfill, encouraging recycling, and reducing the overhead associated with curbside collection, some municipal authorities are moving to pay-as-you-throw charging. These schemes use "spy" chips hidden in individual bins to link the weight of refuse to specific households (see figure 8.6) and constitute an initial move toward sustainability surveillance. Such surveillance is likely to become more common in order to force greater energy and resource efficiency and to reduce household carbon footprints.

Television viewing has been an iconic consumerist activity over the last fifty years, widely promoted and omnipresent in Western homes. The provision of television entertainment services in the UK and Ireland is subject to compulsory taxation (TV licensing in the UK funds the BBC). A captabase is used to monitor all addresses for enforcement of the tax. As such, all three homes, including Dorothy's, is known, reviewed, and billed. Television sets typically enjoy a prime location in the core space of most homes. The nature of these sets is changing significantly, however, through a reconfiguring of their relations to the wider world as they shift from analog broadcast and electronic controls to fully digital objects engaged in two-way networks.

Both Peter and Wendy, and Simon and Iris, have satellite or cable television with a contract to a commercial provider. While the service provider supplies a large range of programming, including pay-per-view options, it does so through a set-top box that "watches" the family and communicates back the log of their viewing patterns. As such, the service provider can build up a profile of a household's viewing habits and preferences, including such trivial information as when they rewind, fast-forward, pause, and turn off programming (Andrejevic 2007). As Carlson (2006, 111) notes,

BUG UNDER LIP

Figure 8.6
Example of RFID chips used to individually identify refuse bins to link them to households.
Source: www.dailymail.co.uk/news/article-402439/Germans-plant-bugs-wheelie-bins.html

"while viewers enjoy the freedom to create personalized experiences based on preferences, their individual behaviors are monitored and assessed for their commercial
value." Code renders the television a two-way mirror that watches the viewers as the
viewers watch it. Along with other new forms of feedback, such as voting in relation
to reality TV shows, stations and content providers no longer need to rely on probabil-
ity sampling to judge audience reaction. They now have detailed information concerning each household. Linked to geodemographic capta (see chapter 9), one can anticipate
that in the future each household will receive individually tailored advertisements
based on their viewing and status profiles (Andrejevic 2007). Yet, at the same time,
the ability to know the viewer is counterbalanced by the increasing fragmentation of
media consumption, with some people promiscuously utilizing multiple platforms
and sources (often unofficial, free, and copyright-infringing peer-to-peer sharing).

Similarly, communication and capta transfer using the Internet and cell phones
empowers individual households at the same time as it monitors and regulates their
actions. Internet service providers can monitor user browser and download habits.
Web site content providers try to identify and track users through cookies and forms

of spyware hidden in web pages. Cell phone companies can track phone calling patterns and deduce social networks as well as the geographic movements of a device. Consumers have traded their privacy for a service, and they are bearing the cost and labor of detailed capta generation in the name of their own empowerment (Andrejevic 2007—see chapter 9). In normative terms, such a trade-off works well so long as consumers do feel empowered, there is transparency over what capta is recorded and stored, there are alternative sources of service, and use is not compulsory. For Andrejevic (2007), the danger is that people are actively participating in their own passive submission to pervasive forms of surveillance that can be used against them, for example, by profiling them in order to apply discriminatory service plans or pricing.

Both Peter and Wendy, and Simon and Iris, have homes purchased through a mortgage. The building itself then is part of the bank's portfolio of investments, represented within its various captabases and assessed periodically for risk and profitability. Both couples have set up direct debit payments that automatically transfer money from their account to their lenders. Similarly, all three homes are insured, their level of risk calculated by complex algorithms that take into account a wide variety of predictive factors about the home owners, their lifestyle, the house size, and zip-code location in relation to the surrounding social and environmental milieu. These indicators of active consumption and proclivity to borrow mean that households are flagged as targets for unsolicited marketing literature. For example, the mail on Dorothy's table also contains a couple of pieces of junk mail sent to her because a direct mail marketing company has calculated the product on offer will appeal to the geodemographic profile for this zip code. As a result, Dorothy's home and domestic activities, relatively uncoded at the immediate scale of the dwelling, are nonetheless still represented and automatically worked upon by software at various distant sites.

Finally, Dorothy's home is linked to a health network that monitors for any signs of distress. The Lifeline control box is permanently networked via a landline phone connection to a remote control center, with software triggering alerts to human operators when an event occurs or a set threshold is exceeded. Simon and Iris's apartment is monitored by a burglary system that is connected to a central monitoring service. If the sensors detect movement, they alert the monitors, which then call the home to see if it is a false alarm, and then send a patrol or alert the police if needed.

Software Practices and the Spatialities of Home

These audits highlight that while the range and type of coded objects varies, software is already prevalent throughout Western homes. Furthermore, homes are being physically networked with new services and enveloped in a growing cloud of coded processes that distanciate domestic practices, and opens them up to routine monitoring and endogenous profiling. Coded objects alter the material, social, and spatial relations of the home in new ways; they offer members of households new affordances to undertake domestic living differently—to record television programs when they are away from the home; to have more choice of programming and to watch them at different locations about the house, to share them, keep them and potentially reuse them in a mashup (see chapter 6); to source information or purchase goods 24/7 without leaving the home; to cook food for a set time without being present in the kitchen; to play new kinds of games and with people located at a distance or interactively against a computer; to enjoy photographs and music in new ways; to be monitored for health unobtrusively; and to work at home while being in steady contact with the office and to move from room to room while doing so. Digital technologies are different from their analog equivalents, which might have performed similar roles, in several important ways: they offer more functionality, they are more interactive, they are often programmable, they work independent of human oversight, many can log their use, and some can communicate with other devices and with information systems across networks. In their physical form, coded objects are also often smaller and more mobile that electromechanical equivalents.

People take advantage of interactive software interfaces to time-shift and multitask. Some people prefer the impersonal process and sense of anonymity of software interfaces, and they can be convenient for those who cannot visit stores during normal business hours. Self-service by automated telephone systems and online transactions has also driven a new round of economic efficiencies and cost savings, meaning reduced prices for consumers (for example, in obtaining insurance) and profit gains for businesses. However, for some kinds of transactions, layers of software automation have the effect of disempowering consumers, working as barriers between the customer and the business, and leading to frustration as simple tasks become overly complicated by code or simply impossible to solve without human intervention.

Software thus makes a difference to the nature of domestic living by enabling a variety of coded objects to augment, supplement, and replace analog technologies, as well as providing new kinds of technology that undertake novel tasks. (We would also acknowledge that sometimes these technologies are by and large pointless upgrades, designed to encourage consumption of new products with little if any genuine benefit.) Coded objects make a difference to the transduction of home space; how the spatiality of the home is beckoned into being as coded space or code/space. Their supplementary capacities provide additional, partial solutions to the relational problems of domestic living (cleaning, cooking, entertaining, socializing, personal care) and enable other problems to be addressed from the home (managing household finances, work-related tasks, schooling, health monitoring).

For example, the computers and broadband connection in Simon and Iris's apartment transduces the space into a site of paid work; both Simon and Iris are able to undertake employee-related tasks at a distance while being coupled in real time to their colleagues and workplace servers. The apartment is spatially reconfigured to facilitate such a transduction, with a bedroom converted into space where office practices can proceed efficiently. The PC reduces the time to undertake tasks such as preparing, redrafting, and sending professional reports, and transforms where these tasks can be undertaken. Similarly, the Xbox 360 game console in Peter and Wendy's home transduces the space of the living room into a node on a global network across which people can play games in real time with opponents distributed around the world. The digital television, set-top box, and DVR alters how the living room is transduced into a space of entertainment by enabling a flexibility of choice of television content that can be watched at their convenience, as opposed to the schedule of the broadcasters. Simon's digital keyboard transduces the space of his office into a music studio where he is able to compose, record, manipulate, and play back multilayered and instrumented songs. Software applications allow digital music to be professionally edited, assuming one has the skill to use it. Dorothy's Lifeline control terminal transduces her home into a site of continuous yet unobtrusive healthcare monitoring, which enables her to live at home, rather than having to move to an assisted living facility. The environmental control system in Simon and Iris's apartment transduces the space into one with a comfortable climate that responds immediately to changes in temperature and humidity. These spatial transductions are made possible through the application of software locally that ties the home into wider networks and myriad layers of coded processes.

The home is also spatially reconfigured by domestic tasks being captured within and worked upon by external consumer and governmental processes, and by networked logjects deepening and widening of dwellings as nodes in a variety of physical and virtual informational networks. The result of this networking is twofold: rescaling and surveillance. Homes are increasingly being stretched out across space in networks of greater length and, as such, scaled in new ways. Information flow in an analog home was usually unidirectional or asymmetrical, and what was done with the information confined to the home (for example, television programs were beamed into the home, but what was watched was unknown except viewing figures extrapolated from Nielsen sampling). Through networked logjects, homes are being embedded in real-time, two way networks, so that the everyday nature of domestic practices (which television shows one watches and records; who one talks to on the telephone and for how long; what products one searches for or purchases on the Internet; the particular patterns of electricity and water usage) can be monitored by service providers at a distance, with the attendant capta being used to classify, profile, and potentially profile customers. Such expanding, and increasingly nonstop flows of capta, potentially render unseen domestic activities and personal behaviors visible to corporations, with little knowledge or control by those being observed.

Over time, it seems likely that this control by code will vary from subtle conditioning that is little noticed, such as the preselection of potentially interesting programs
to watch on television, or a body-monitoring bathroom scale chiding the user for
missing a target weight and urging greater effort (Schuurman 2004), to a more potent
form where coded objects refuse to perform because they determine that an action is
illegal (for example, copyright enforcement through digital rights management preventing the computer from playing movies not legally owned; see chapters 5 and 9).
The home, previously seen as a sanctuary from an overdetermined and regulated
world, becomes open to forms of automated management.

The "Home of the Future"

For many technologists, the embedding of coded objects into homes is evidence that
we are moving to the era of the smart home and widespread pervasive computing (see
chapter 10). Indeed, the home is the target of much investigation and speculation
within computing and digital design circles (Bell and Dourish 2007; Crabtree et al.
2003; Edwards and Grinter 2001; Taylor and Swan 2005). A central trope in such
research is the notion of a home that "anticipates and responds to the needs of the
occupants, working to promote their comfort, convenience, security and entertainment through the management of technology within the home and connections to
the world beyond" (Aldrich 2003, 17). This anticipation and response will be fully
automated, automatic, autonomous, and decided upon by sophisticated software
algorithms designed to be seamlessly reflexive to domestic users' desires and wishes.
This is the vision of the smart home—a home with computing power built into all
the objects contained within; a home that is aware of itself and its past activity, its
surroundings, its changing inhabitants and their activities, its contents, and its external service providers; and knows how to react appropriately to different scenarios. This
vision anticipates computing power to be integrated not just into objects within the
home, but also built into the fabric of the dwelling itself, with doors, windows, and
walls acting as sensors and also potentially ambient interfaces able to convey information to both humans and other digital objects.

While it is possible to argue that we are on the path to such an all-embracing
domestic digital assemblage, it must also be recognized that smart homes are a particular sociotechnical vision developed by technologists; the latest reincarnation of a
longstanding modernist fantasy of technology capable of producing orderly domestic
spaces and maximizing leisure time (see figure 8.7). Indeed, the premise of a smart
home has been common across several generations of home design (Spigel 2005),
promulgated by a nexus of product designers, house builders, and appliance manufacturers, and increasingly the software industry, focused on driving new rounds of
consumer fashions and home upgrades.

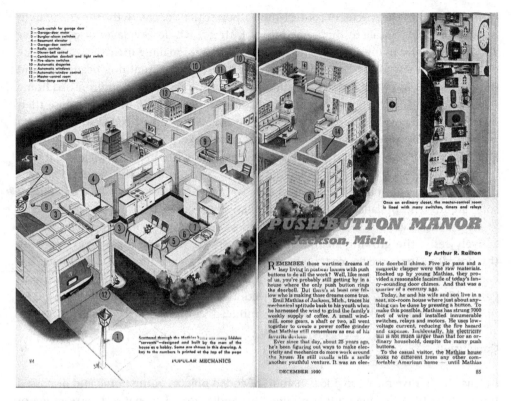

Figure 8.7
"Push-button manor," a 1950s exemplar of the recurrent fantasy of domestic automation facilitated by efficient technological service, in this case electromechanical motors and control circuits. *Source*: http://blog.modernmechanix.com

These visions of the smart home tend to focus on the supposed benefits, with little thought to its wider implications, the most obvious of which is the scope for greater control of the mundane and personal activities occurring in the home, and a concomitant impact on freedom and privacy. Yet control is not the whole story. Code opens up genuinely novel avenues for creative solutions to domestic tasks, particularly in terms of pleasure and play. How software can make things different is well illustrated by the present generation of toys and games, typically HCs and CCs but increasingly SCs. Indeed, creating fun is an important conduit through which software is seeping deeper into the sinews of home life. As Thrift (2003, 400) notes, toys are "rapidly becoming something else: something between a lumpen object onto which all manner of fantasies and all kinds of play could be projected and a kind of alternative life form, participating in the world on at least some terms of its own choosing."

In addition to the specter of control and empowerment of creativity, the enrollment of code on a wide scale in the home brings with it a whole new layer of complexity and risks to daily living, despite the rhetoric of software making life easier. A foretaste of this complexity is the real cognitive work required in maintaining home PCs and mobile devices in proper order. It is estimated that several million compromised home PCs are connected to the Internet (Leyden 2005; Markoff 2007), in part because their owners are technically unable or unwilling to invest the time needed to keep them patched and protected with updated software, and to keep passwords secure. As more and more everyday domestic tasks are undertaken with network logjects, it will become increasingly important to maintain them. The result will be the development of a whole new domain of "digital housekeeping" (Crabtree et al. 2007) to ensure software-driven appliances are stable and relatively secure.

Given these various issues, there will almost certainly be some populations who actively resist the growing encroachment of software into the home, concerned by the potential for surveillance by outside parties, along with those who will hack the code to subvert the deadweight of "technological paternalism" (Spiekermann and Pallas 2006) and those who will voice objections because of the frustration caused by function overload and excessive, software-induced, complexity (see chapter 10).

Conclusion

In this chapter we have provided an audit of coded objects in the home and discussed how these objects change domestic life. Our audits revealed that a diverse range of coded objects are already present within all the spaces of the typical Western home. In some cases, these objects have already become mundane and slipped into the background "technological unconscious" (Thrift 2004b), and yet they perform small but vital roles in holding together household routines. In other cases, coded objects are seen as novel and are feted as technological breakthroughs that provide new ways of being and acting. Indeed, many homes now contain multiple iterations of the same appliances (particularly those for entertainment), along with older and superseded versions (rendered obsolete by new functionality or mere changes in consumer fashion).

The audits also reveal that the transition into the fully software-enabled home is a slow, incremental process. Homes contain a mixture of electrical, electronic, and coded technologies which are enrolled together in multiple configurations daily to solve tasks of living and beckon home spaces in being. Homes then are made of an imperfect but functional bricolage of ordinary objects and coded components. Rather than making the domestic realm more orderly, the infusion of software into homes is perhaps leading to a new overcoding of routines and activities that often makes home life more complex and prone to unexpected and inexplicable failure and disruptions.

Yet, it seems clear to us that many parts of Western society are at a juncture in the production of home space, as domestic objects become more and more coded—either through software being embedded into their makeup or as machine-readable objects embedded in the Internet of things. While this is an incremental and not an epochal change, a useful parallel can be drawn between the contemporary coding of homes and the initial domestication of electricity at the end of the nineteenth century. At first, electrical power was a merely an expensive novelty (electric lighting over gas lighting) and there were initially very few electrical appliances. Over an extended period of time, existing technologies were converted to electricity (for example, cooking over an open hearth was overtaken by the electric oven, and washing clothes in a hand-crank washtub was improved by the invention of the electric washing machine), with small electrical motors being used to replace manual labor. At the same time, a raft of new domestic tools were produced (some of the most potent, but now mundane and ubiquitous, being the refrigerator and freezer that have significantly changed domestic practices relating to food consumption; Hand and Shove 2007; Watkins 2006). Just as electricity has pervaded every room and appliance, code seems destined to follow.

As a result, the spatiality of homes will increasingly be transduced in different ways. While the transduction of code/space is relatively rare in domestic settings, code certainly contributes to many domestic tasks, with the transduction of coded spaces common. In other words, the everyday use of coded objects reshapes the spatiality of the home by altering how domestic tasks are undertaken (and not always more conveniently for all), introducing new practices and sometimes greater complexity, and embedding the home into more diverse, extended systems of consumption and governmentality. How coded objects beckon space into being is not deterministic, rather it is contingent and relational. The spatiality of different homes, even if they were materially identical, would vary substantially because the technologies would be used in different ways, within varying contexts. These contexts are social and familial, but are also structured within the wider political economy (market-led pricing, fragmentation of consumer service contracts), legal arrangements and standards (health and safety), evolving cultural practices (when and where it is acceptable to use certain coded objects), and differential access to certain services.

9 Consumption

The latter part of the twentieth century witnessed the development in the West of a consumer society wherein the vast majority of people purchased goods and services not only out of necessity, but through choice. Individuals, regardless of class, started to accumulate items in excess of their basic needs and replaced these items not because they were broken or beyond repair but for other reasons such as desire, novelty, and status. In addition, there was the large-scale production of goods that were chiefly regarded as disposable—having short-term value before being discarded. In tandem, the practice of consumption, particularly shopping, became a major leisure activity for many, and retail and leisure spaces became the focus of development capital with large tracts of land and infrastructure devoted to them. In other words, there was a marked change in the nature of consumption.

In this chapter, we examine how software is reshaping the nature of consumption in a number of ways. Following the underlying approach of the book, we do so from a spatial perspective, arguing that one of the key reasons that software is making a difference to how consumption proceeds is because it reconfigures consumption's underlying spatial relations. For example, software has produced, to varying degrees, spatial fluidity and temporal flexibility with respect to retail activities—shopping has become an activity that need not be tied to any particular place. Instead, a growing range of goods and services can be bought from anywhere, and at any time, accessing networks using mobile devices; consumption practices unfold in code/spaces scattered across the space-time geography of everyday life (for example, sitting on the sofa at home buying music online, without regard to brick-and-mortar store opening times). Moreover, the spatial arrangement and logic of consumption supply chains and retail logistics has been radically reconfigured; a sophisticated profiling and marketing industry has developed focused on generated area-targeted sales; and consumers alter their spatial behavior to mesh with the evolving technologically mediated situations every day. While we do not want to overstate the necessity of a geographic perspective and sink into spatial fetishism, we feel it is important to acknowledge that the difference software makes is in part due to how it reconfigures spatial and temporal relations. We start by considering the way in which software has altered the nature of money and how people pay for the goods and services they consume.

Code and Money

At a fundamental level, software is having a significant influence on how monetary value is stored, mediated, and transacted, and on the nature of everyday consumption, by reshaping how people can purchase the goods and services they desire. As G. Davies (1994) notes, the way financial transactions are conducted has changed throughout history, for example taking the form of barter and exchange wherein goods and services would be directly swapped on the basis that they had equivalent and agreed value; primitive material forms of monies such as jade, gold, rice, salt, beads, and ivory, wherein these objects were conferred a certain known value that allowed them to be transacted in place of the goods and services themselves; and modern monies in the form of mass produced coins and paper notes that provide a more abstract unit of exchange, wherein these media are ascribed a monetary value but the coins and notes in and of themselves hold little intrinsic value (the symbolic power of the monarch or state guarantees their value).

The power of money in today's world is that it is simultaneously a unit of account, a medium of exchange, a measure of value, a means of payment, and a store of value (Pollard 2001). Software enables money to retain each of these qualities, but to also extend it in new ways by virtualizing it. Whereas barter, primitive money, and modern money all required the material exchange of some kind—the physical transfer of goods, valuable objects, coins/notes or credit notes—virtual money consists of nothing more than a digital record residing in captabases, and software mechanics that enable value to be transferred electronically between accounts. While some transactions might be entirely virtual and automated, such as direct debit payments for a regular bill, other exchanges are enacted explicitly through an embodied authorization process, such as chip-and-pin credit card payment, or people typing details into a web site to perform an online purchase. In both cases, through a sequence of software based transactions, the debit and credit account balances are accordingly adjusted; this usually occurs in a secure and accurate fashion, such that people come to trust virtual money as if it were real. Further, the transaction records within these captabases are subject to automated analyses in terms of monitoring for fee payments, system conformity, fraud detection, overdraft penalties, eligibility for a financial product, generating valuable additional meta-capta.

The scale of trades and transactions in virtual money is vast and hard to quantify with any precision. To give a sense of the scale of virtual personal consumption based on electronic payment in the UK, there were over 10.5 billion transactions made by debit/credit cards in 2008 representing spending of £603 ($962) billion. There were

148.9 million debit/credit cards in issue in the UK at the end of 2008, with the average person having more than three cards (UK Card Association 2009).

In a larger sense, the virtual abstraction of money has been critical to late modern capitalism as it has enabled a marked acceleration in economic life, radically reducing the turnover time of capital; it has made money more mobile and footloose with modes of electronic-fund transfers (EFTs) able to shift billions of a currency from country to country in seconds; able to rapidly invest and disinvest from sites of uneven development; and it has facilitated the creation of various forms of fictitious and speculative capital that leverage value from supposed present and potential future profits (Harvey 1982). Software has revolutionized and routinized the circulation of finance through global networks of banks, stock markets, currency exchanges, finance companies (mortgage lenders, insurers, credit risk assessors, brokers, investors, and pension advisors) by collapsing the space-time of money—in real time it can be monitored, transferred, tracked, repackaged, sold, revalued and de- and respatialized through financial software packages and their associated algorithms.

Such virtualization, especially in a poorly regulated context, has real consequences that can reverberate around the planet in a very short time period given the dense, global web of interconnections and interdependencies between financial markets and products. This was clearly illustrated by the 2008 global banking meltdown and subsequent recession, where risky lending (particularly in the U.S. housing market), accompanied by the dubious financial repackaging of mortgages and fraudulent overpricing of assets led to a significant property market downturn internationally, a steep decline in stock prices, the failure of some banking corporations, the propping-up of many financial institutions by national governments and taxpayers, and tens of thousands of businesses either going bankrupt or laying off staff, leading to rising unemployment.

The increasing role and popularity of virtual money, and the development of an efficient new mechanism in which it can be exchanged, has led to new ways of buying goods and services. The first "closed loop" debit cards (in which the issuer both authorizes and handles all aspects of the transaction and settles directly with both the consumer and the merchant) were issued in the 1940s (for example, Diners Club, with payments tracked through paper trails). Credit cards followed in the 1960s, with Visa and Mastercard operating as open loop systems requiring interbank cooperation and funds transfers (Sienkiewicz 2001). Both debit and credit cards were in mainstream use by the 1970s in North America, underpinned by computerization in the banking sector to process payments and debits and driven, in part, by aggressive target-marketing and the lure of status, convenience, and instant credit on demand. Importantly, the cards themselves are simply a convenient media to carry unique identification numbers for account verification. By the end of the 1970s, identification numbers were being encoded on magnetic strips added to the back of cards. This strip could be read by electronic dial-up terminals installed in retail locations to allow a customer's credit card to be swiped to access authorization. Although this took one to two minutes to process, it was still significantly more efficient than paper-based transactions (Marples 2009). By the late 1990s, credit cards had become ubiquitous in the West, especially with the rise of fully networked checkout counters in stores that quickly read magnetic strips. Next came the development of chips within the cards automating the exchange of funds and providing immediate authorization. After that came the growth in online shopping. The use of credit cards has also been extended to rudimentary identification and age verification, and some quite banal services cannot be easily purchased without them (booking a hotel room or renting a car).

The growing dominance of electronic payment, even for quite small values, might be more convenient for consumers and less risky for business, but it also has wider implications. The most significant is that electronic payments are by design logged and tracked by software. Paying on a card, rather than by cash, leaves an exact record of the time and location of the transaction and erodes the anonymity of cash, important for trust and for the maintenance of personal privacy. Each software-enabled purchase involves more than a trade of money for a product or service; it also involves an exchange of information. By using electronic payment, consumers passively submit, whether knowingly or unwittingly, to active forms of surveillance that are then used to regulate and socially sort them. Indeed, transaction capta provide states and companies with valuable information about the life a person lives, which can in turn be used to profile the person, and, as we discuss below, can be traded as a commodity in and of itself.

The Changing Nature of Consumption

In addition to changing the nature of money, software has altered the practices through which we purchase goods, enabling them to be bought routinely at a distance. There is a long history of mail-order shopping with postal payment using checks/ money orders or wiring money in advance, but the Internet has revolutionized such trade by lowering the entry costs of setting up shop, thus significantly widening the base of those selling goods and services, and enabling new kinds of products and transactions. The rise of mobile devices also enables virtual consumption on the move. Just about everything that can be bought and sold is available for purchase across the Web and then can either be shipped or downloaded across the network. Further, purchases are not restricted to the local area or nation states, so that the whole world becomes in effect a global market place, providing purchasers with a plethora of choice (although many practical and legal constraints remain). In addition, consumers are provided with a substantial amount of information on the items and services they are interested in, including detailed price and product comparisons across retailers and consumer reviews (although this is partly counteracted by the intensification of marketing and the degree to which online reviews are genuine). Barter and other forms of exchange have also exploited the online domain through auction sites such as eBay and secondhand listings like abebooks.com, as have services such as online dating, employment recruitment, utility bill payments, paying taxes, and government services.

The raft of connected software systems across the Internet has not just altered how goods and services are being purchased, but it is also changing the nature of the products and industries that supply them. A much documented case relates to the music industry (Leyshon et al. 2005; Leyshon 2009). The digitization of music in a compressed, universal, easily distributable MP3 format released in the early 1990s, coupled with faster broadband networks, rapidly led to file-sharing sites such as Napster that enabled people to freely (and mostly illegally) download tracks. In some respects, the practices of peer-to-peer sharing of music online has much in common with earlier rounds of tape-to-tape recording in the 1970s and 1980s. The key distinction, facilitated by code, is that reproduction is much easier and the sound quality much superior, and the scale of distribution is hugely increased in scope, so a single copied album could be downloaded by millions of people across the globe. The flexibility with which software can manipulate MP3 files, along with the huge savings in physical storage space, means people can carry a whole library of music in their pocket. Indeed, it is likely that the physical media (such as CDs) for distributing music (and much other media) will soon largely disappear from everyday consumption spaces.

Rather than embrace the new technology, the major record labels typically sought to control and regulate music online, with limited success. Eventually they were forced to modify their business model, embracing the MP3 format and facilitating the development of commercial and legal download sites such as Apple's iTunes Store, although large scale illegal file sharing still persists. In the meantime, some bands and new music entrepreneurs are using their own web sites and social networking services to launch their careers, and find novel ways to generate an income. For example, the band Gov't Mule sells recordings of every live show via its web site, www.muletracks.com, for around $13 per concert, grossing more than $600,000 between 2004 and 2008 (Goodman 2008). The growth of legal and illegal downloaded music has had knock-on consequences for other elements of the recording industry, including brick-and-mortar stores as well as artists, sound engineers, and studios (Leyshon 2009). Some of the former have either gone out of business or have had to adapt their retail model to diversify into other music-related merchandise (t-shirts, posters) and entertainment more broadly. For musicians and bands, royalties earned from packaged albums sales are becoming less important to their overall income, which is being supplemented by revenues from live performances, associated merchandise, licensing and publishing fees, airplay royalties, appearance fees, and advertising tie-ins. The ways in which music is created is also being affected by software (see chapter 6). Furthermore, software-enabled technologies are being used to fundamentally change the nature of consumption to that of prosumption, which will be defined and discussed in the next section.

Consumers to Prosumers

People have long played a role in the production of the goods or services they are consuming, such as buffets in a restaurant, or at a gas pump, or as members of an audience, or as part of a crowd at a sporting event. Arguably, the most radical innovation of supermarket shopping was the shopping cart for shoppers to gather goods for themselves. Many goods are now sold with integral elements needing to be completed by the consumer—the rise of cheap flat-pack furniture is perhaps the best example of this. Such participation has been conceptualized by the notion of prosumption—that people *prosume* rather than merely consume a service or good (Andrejevic 2007; Ritzer n.d.)—they fulfill a vital role or add crucial value in the delivery of a service for which they are paying. In the main, prosumers do this additional work for little or no recompense, either getting enjoyment from the task, or a sense of empowerment, or they save money/time as the cost of the service is reduced and often becomes more flexible in nature (such as online banking or printing out a boarding pass from a home computer). As such, a complex set of factors shape prosumption, including "choice, coercion, enjoyment, false consciousness, manipulation" (Ritzer n.d., 27). In return, the service provider or retailer receives free labor, talent, expertise, and opinions, and gains efficiencies (particularly through reduced staffing) and potentially valuable information by getting closer to the customer (Ritzer n.d.).

Software has deepened and diversified participation by enabling people to interact with, customize, and accessorize a wider range of services, media, and products; to move from being a consumer to a prosumer in more realms of everyday activity. The nature and level of contribution to the production of goods, media, and services purchased by active participants varies significantly from simple feedback mechanisms that shape present and future outcomes, to the highly involved production of key resources such as the writing of code to open-source software projects. As such, we would argue prosumption needs to be unpacked to think through the ways in which software reshapes the relationship between retailers and purchasers and what they prosume. For us, code enables at least six types of prosumption: feedback, customization, content, architectural, market, and self-service.

Feedback consists of prosumers actively and freely contributing information to service providers that then helps shape the product being prosumed. For example, audience voting on reality TV shows actively shapes which contestants stay in the competition and which ones leave, and potentially who will win. The mass solicitation of feedback is made feasible and financially viable at a large scale by software. Code can automate the capture of detailed information on viewer likes and dislikes for producers, signaling which act(s) will succeed in the marketplace, especially since the voters have already invested capital, time, and emotional energy into shaping the kinds of entertainment products they enjoy. Feedback used to be largely limited to studio audiences, but automated phone services, texting, and online voting now allow feedback from any viewer. As a result, huge numbers of votes can be cast. For example, over sixty five million votes were cast in the final of American Idol, series 3 in 2004 (580 million over the series) (Andrejevic 2007).

Customization allows prosumers to actively shape and configure the products and services they are buying, selecting from a raft of specifications, components, colors, and materials. In other words, the product is not simply bought off the shelf, but is tailored to meet the needs of the prosumer. Such services have long been available, such as bespoke furniture or tailored clothes, but only to those with the wealth to be able to afford it. Now customization is available to cheap, mass produced goods, such as running shoes and computers and peripherals, and can be selected at a distance and previewed through online ordering. For example, PC manufacturers like Dell allow customers to design the specification of their PC from an array of options; the choices are automatically fed directly into the production line and the computer is built to order. Complex products, such as cars, have so many possible permutations (engine specs, paint colors, interior trim levels, and accessories) that the each vehicle can be almost unique. For example, the web site for the BMW 3 Series allows customers to "design" their car with well over one hundred models (body style/engine types), around fifteen paint colors, nine types of alloy wheels, ten upholstery colors, and multiple accessories (see figure 9.1). Again, code is crucial for the tooling-up of manufacturing processes to cope with a high degree of customization and still make a profit.

Content prosumption consists of users actively supplying the substantive material for the service they are prosuming. For example, prosumers of online social media, such as Usenet, Facebook, or blogs, actively contribute material about themselves and their lives, and/or write comments in relation to other people or provide remixed content (such as new mixes of songs). Content is not supplied by service provider itself; their contribution is the platform (software tools and captabase) that enables prosumption. Similarly, information sites such as Wikipedia are both passively consumed (an individual reading an entry) and actively prosumed (adding, editing, and updating entries). Commercial or proprietary sites also enable prosumption such as the adding of reviews to products on Amazon or submitting videos, photos, or stories to news and entertainment web sites. Such is the commercial utility of so-called user-generated content, that companies induce participation through competitions for advertisement and product ideas, taking advantage of free creativity and labor.

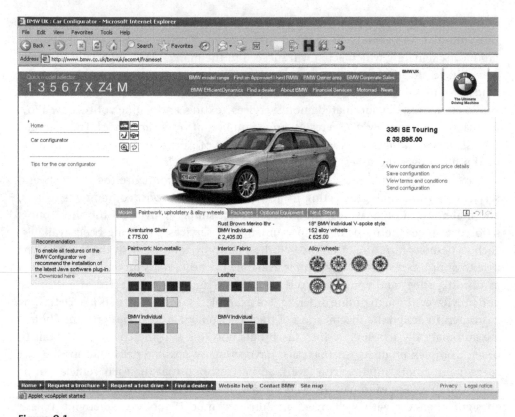

Figure 9.1
BMW's "car configurator" Web interface enables wealthy prosumers to purchase a bespoke vehicle that is manufactured to order on a highly automated production line. The standard options can produce in the region of 150,000 different types of BMW 3 Series vehicles.

Architectural prosumption concerns the active contribution of prosumers to the informational architecture that supports an activity or service. The most widely practiced example is that of open source programming, where scores of programmers work collectively to produce a software product that they themselves use. Linux, for example, is collectively produced by volunteer contributors, who then use the operating system they have added to. Other examples include mashups that enable different capta to be spliced together to create new applications (see chapter 6).

Market prosumption relates to the creation of online marketplaces to buy and sell goods. The goods on sale and their details are supplied by the users of the site. For example, eBay and craigslist enable people to sell a product, and others to bid on the sale; to take an active part in the marketplace. In other words, the process is interactive with respect to selling and buying.

Self-service prosumption refers to the increasing use of self-service kiosks and online processes that enable a person to access goods or services autonomously (see figure 9.2). Here, individuals do the labor that was formerly done by paid employees. Examples include using an ATM to withdraw money rather than interacting with a teller in a bank, or buying a train ticket using a self-service kiosk rather than from a ticket agent, or using a self-service supermarket checkout rather one that is staffed. This transfer clearly saves the provider significant staffing costs. For example, a grocery store generally aims for one cashier to oversee four self-service registers, thus reducing staffing needs by 75 percent while serving the same number of purchasers (Dean 2008). In some cases, such as checking oneself onto a flight either online or at a self-service kiosk, failure to act as a prosumer can lead to punitive penalties; for example, failure to self check in online with RyanAir, Europe's largest low-cost airline, resulted in a 40 euro additional fee in 2009.

These six forms of prosumption are significantly altering the relations between service provider and customer, leading to efficiencies and enhanced profitability for producers, and potentially empowering (or encumbering) consumers. Code makes this possible at a mass scale in a financially viable fashion. Over time, these types of prosumption—and one assumes new types will be added as new technologies and innovations are deployed—will become increasingly common. That is not to say, however, that such a rollout will be a simple process, since people do not predictably adopt software, and often adapt technologies to fit their needs. As Walker and Johnson (2006, cited in Dean 2008) note, there are several factors that influence the extent to which people are prepared to engage as prosumers, including: personal capacity (ability and self-belief that they can use the prosumption technologies and interfaces successfully); perceived risk (extent to which a prosumer believes the software system is reliable and their personal information is secure); relative advantage (the extent to which prosumption is believed to be more convenient, faster, more efficient, and more productive than the traditional mode of consumption); and preference for personal, embodied contact (the degree to which the customer prefers human interaction over interaction with software interfaces). As Dean (2008, 228) reports, these factors in turn are affected by a person's: optimism (the belief that software offers increased control, flexibility, and efficiency in daily life); innovativeness (the degree to which the consumer is a pioneer and thought leader); discomfort (perceiving a lack of control over computer code); and insecurity (a distrust of software and skepticism of its ability to work reliably and consistently).

What this means is that people will vary in the extent to which they embrace the practices of prosumption, and that any company adopting such a model of delivery will inevitably be circumscribing its market until unsure and skeptical consumers become convinced of its merits (or they are forced to do so by the company restricting or offering no alternatives), or gain access to suitable technology such as a home PC

Figure 9.2
A range of self-service kiosks and checkout terminals that are becoming increasingly prevalent on streets, in libraries, in post offices, and in supermarkets. All handle multistage processes with code and the software interface providing "conversations" with prosumers. (*a*) Library book self-checkout (*Source*: www.travelizmo.com/archives/000055.html). (*b*) Parking meter (*Source*: www. nelsoncitycouncil.co.nz). (*c*) Postage vendor (*Source*: www.wincor-nixdorf.com). (*d*) Grocery self-checkout (*Source*: www.authoritydirectory.com).

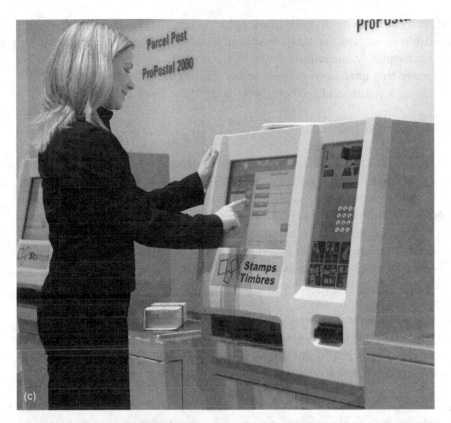

Figure 9.2
(continued)

with broadband connectivity. In both cases, age and class are important factors given their relationship to educational competence and likelihood of convenient and affordable access. Consequently, prosumption will be subject to similar inequalities of access and lags in usage that have been evident across the Internet's development and diffusion (see Crang, Crosbie, and Graham 2006; Rode 2006; Zook 2005).

Changing Consumption Spaces

Given that software has the capacity to significantly augment, supplement, and supersede aspects of how goods and services are supplied to purchasers, it is perhaps of little surprise that a plethora of code-enabled technologies pervade the material sites in which embodied consumption practices unfold (of course online spaces are entirely transduced by code); employed by companies to gain efficiencies, productivity, and competitiveness; enhance consumer experience; and reduce fraud and thus maximize profits. Like sites of mobility (such as airports) and domesticity (such as the home), consumption spaces—stores, recreation centers, gyms, sports venues, restaurants, cafés and bars, public plazas and streets, and visitor attractions such as theaters, theme parks, and museums—are increasingly brought into being through coded practices, transduced as code/spaces and coded spaces. Here, we want to concentrate on the consumption space itself, exploring the ways in which code has reshaped logistical networks and organizational structures of consumption in the next section.

Shopping

The experience of shopping in supermarkets in some ways has changed very little over the past sixty years, and the introduction of self-service, stacked, ready-to-eat products and checkout counters. The shopper collects a shopping cart on the way into the store, browsing the aisles to select items to purchase, and then heads to the checkout to pay. It is here that the work of code is most visible. It used to be the case that the checkout clerk at the electromechanical cash register had to hand enter the price of every item, and manually process payment, which was primarily by cash or check (even credit cards were manually swiped onto triplicate paper forms). With the industry-wide deployment of electronic point-of-sale (EPoS) technology from the late 1970s, the cashier now simply scans the product barcode and the price is retrieved automatically from a captabase and added to the running total, along with any reductions for items on sale. This is complemented with an integrated electronic funds transfer at point-of-sale (EFTPoS) unit that enables payment by credit or debit card. Cards are swiped through or placed in card readers and payment is authorized by the customer's bank in real time. This can be supplemented with the use of a so-called loyalty card, which identifies the customer and facilitates the tracking of that person's expenditure patterns, and provides related rewards such as discounts. A more recent development is the installation of self-checkout counters, in which the shopper becomes a prosumer, responsible for scanning the items and handling the whole payment process. These developments markedly speed up the process of payment; reduce charge errors and cash register fraud/theft; automate the monitoring of stock levels and inventory management and the reordering of goods from suppliers through electronic data interchange (EDI) software; and enable stores to collect valuable streams of capta about individual customers gleaned from credit card or loyalty card transactions, such as home address, the details of purchases, price sensitivity, and responses to special offers and promotions. As we discuss in more detail below, such information can be used to profile customers and socially sort them for the purpose of targeted marketing and enhancing revenue generation.

Large retailers must be able to manage a great variety of offerings that have differing expiration dates, are sourced from a range of suppliers stretched out across space; have varying sales volumes and customer traffic throughout the week; have a high number of relatively low cost transactions; and manage the complexities of running the store efficiently and profitably. A typical large supermarket in the UK carries thirty thousand or more product lines.

From the other perspective, customers expect retailers to offer more convenience, greater value, improved service, and increased quality (Al-Sudairy and Tang 2000). It is no surprise, then, that beyond the checkout counter, how the store is managed and run is also markedly different, affecting the shopping experience to some degree, but not necessarily in obvious or transparent ways. For example, software is used to manage and monitor inventory; automate warehousing operations and calculate delivery routes and timing; manage cash flow; track expenses and expenditures; monitor for shoplifting and general security; undertake store design and calculate optimal locations for product placement to maximize sales; manage staff and flexible scheduling to cope with longer opening hours and fluctuations in customer traffic; and help managers to make choices and decisions about product lines (Lockett and Holland 1991). Many items in supermarkets are chilled or frozen, and maintaining a continuous cool-chain system, monitored by software, is vital to providing edible and safe food. The efficiency of stocking and automated reordering in software-driven stores means customers have become accustomed to always having the product they want.

The application of software to stores means that most are produced now as code/spaces; software mediates the transduction of space into a code/space where consumption practices can proceed. This relationship is dyadic and is best illustrated with respect to the checkout process. If the software that controls the cash register crashes, product barcodes cannot be scanned and electronic payments are not possible, even cash sales. Given the huge range of products, and the automated linking of price to product through matching the barcode number to captabase record, cashiers are not expected to know the price of individual items, and even if they did, the cash register is designed to monitor its cash float, and to update the store's inventory system that feeds into the company's logistic chain through EDI. As a result, there is no way for consumers to purchase their goods. The store ceases to be a place in which goods can be purchased and instead is transduced as an inefficient and loss-making warehouse of goods. EPosS software is thus essential to the transduction of retail space into working stores where consumption practices can unfold.

In addition, retail space has been evolving in step with the introduction of online systems, wherein goods are ordered through a Web store interface and delivered to the purchasers. Murphy (2007) has classified these evolving processes into three types: bricks and clicks, pure-play, and infomediary. Bricks and clicks is where an existing store network is utilized to source the goods ordered online, with shop staff directed around the nearest store to collect items, which are then delivered to the customer (for example, Peapod home delivery service). Pure-play is an operator working entirely online with no brick-and-mortar stores, but rather a set of warehouses from which it dispatches goods to customers (for example, Amazon.com). Infomediary is where an existing retailer contracts out its Web ordering and customer management functions to an intermediary company whose core function is to manage and pass on orders to the retailer to fulfill (for example, Barnes and Noble online bookstore). In all three cases, retail space is being reconfigured by the application of code into a new spatial arrangement beneficial to both retailer and consumer to varying degrees.

It has been suggested that such online shopping will ultimately lead to the death of geography, but as we have argued elsewhere, this is hyperbole—retail space and its logistical underpinnings are being reshaped, not wholly substituted (Dodge and Kitchin 2000). The transfer to online enterprise has undoubtedly had some effect on brick-and-mortar retail and service businesses. Some small independent shops are finding it increasingly difficult to compete with big brand chains, in part because they cannot so easily exploit solutions offered by sophisticated software systems and automated management to more profitably serve customers. In many cases, they have either closed or had to become part of a large franchise chain, which can use the power of ERP (enterprise resource planning) and collective bargaining to compete effectively, in order to be able to survive. As a result, the retail landscape for many goods and services is becoming increasingly homogenous in appearance, with identical store formats and product ranges. Retail services such as banks, insurance, and travel agencies are withdrawing from physical sites, particularly in areas deemed to be sub-prime, to be replaced by call centers and online services. Indeed, retail banking is a sector that has gone through an enormous geographical reconfiguration over the past thirty years with the adoption of banking intranets—concentrating certain parts of the business in a small number of command-and-control centers, back-officing and off-shoring more routine administration to cheaper locations, and closing down bank branches in small towns and poorer parts of cities to be replaced with call centers or longer drive times to the nearest remaining bank (Leyshon, French, and Signoretta 2008).

Long-standing forms of self-service consumption such as vending machines are also being reconfigured by code. Vending machines, providing small dispensable products, such as drinks, snack foods, cigarettes, and tickets are most often sited at locations where demand is insufficient to cover the costs of an attended retail outlet, but still sufficient to make a profit. They offer convenience by providing goods quickly, anonymously, and during out of hours time periods. While they have been part of the consumption landscape for decades increasingly their electromechanical basis is being made smart with the addition of software for monitoring and control. They are also being linked into telemetry systems so the real-time status of the machine can be tracked by a central office and managed more profitably. Such smart vending machines are apposite examples of network logjects (see chapter 3).

Software enables vending machine operators to increase efficiency and potentially the profitability of their business. This can be achieved in a number of ways. For example, telemetric monitoring can diminish the risks of unnoticed machine failures. Such a failure may not be noticed for days, representing a significant loss of revenue to the business. It can optimize the labor intensive process of restocking in terms of scheduling and ensuring specific stock fill-lists. Much more detail on what is selling and when can be logged by the captabase, feeding into a sales trend analysis that seeks to optimize the effectiveness of site locations, product ranges, and pricing. Smart vending machines can also offer electronic payment options to customers and potentially dynamic pricing changes from the central office depending on circumstances such as a special event or temperature (for example, increasingly the price of drinks in a heat wave). The machine can also be surveyed with respect to vandalism and theft, and cash accounting can also be logged, helping to minimize the opportunities for employee theft of goods and fraud.

Leisure and Recreation Spaces

Similarly, leisure and tourist spaces such as restaurants, hotels, casinos, movie theaters, gyms, theme parks, and museums have become a mix of coded spaces and code/spaces. In these examples, code is being embedded into the architecture and infrastructure that constitute the spaces, and also to the systems that manage them (in terms of customer access, product supplies, staff scheduling, and building security), in order to augment and supplement the customer's experience to some degree, but also to provide consistency, efficiencies, productivity, and profitability to suppliers.

Hotel reservations are now entirely managed through software booking systems that track reservations and structure pricing to maximize yield. These are often complemented by customer relationship management (CRM) systems, that can analyze information about customers as a strategic necessity for attracting and increasing guests' patronage by building a personalized relationship with them through targeted marketing, loyalty rewards, special offers, appropriate upgrades, and providing prompts to staff so they can appear to know the customer when they check in. CRM systems are based on capturing patterns of previous bookings and purchases, and the preferences displayed during those visits, including detailed records of any services rendered, such as in-room entertainment, what meals were eaten, what additional tourist trips were booked, complaints made, and movement patterns based on electronic key records (Sigala 2005). Such CRM systems have become more significant to business operations because online search is providing prospective customers with a greater degree of price transparency across competitors. Online travel web sites also provide candid reviews by former patrons and not simply expert travel guides and advertisements. Individual hotels and franchises/chains are then faced with increased competition and greater customer turnover, along with rising customer expectations, so that to maintain and build brand loyalty and competitive advantage they have to work harder to create a value-added experience. Much of that work is being performed by software designed to manage the delivery of the service and generate valuable information that can be used to improve services, attract new customers, and anticipate future demands and pricing levels.

Within the leisure industry, large casino resorts are prime exploiters of software and automated management. Nothing is left to chance in the gambling business, and code is essential to how the sector works to make consistent profits for their owners. All but vintage gaming machines are controlled by sophisticated programs that offer the gambler the opportunity to play a variety of games with high quality graphics and music, with simple and complex play options, and a range of betting choices. The odds of betting on sporting events are calculated algorithmically, monitored, and updated using software that tracks previous performances and betting patterns, looking to anticipate future trends to maintain a profitable return to the casino. Given that casinos often consist of an agglomeration of hotel accommodation, themed entertainment, restaurants, bars, and retail units, they too use CRM systems to analyze customer preferences, spending and gambling patterns, and visit frequency, to personalize experiences, offer rewards, and target-market to encourage return visits and maximize profit (Kale 2003). Software is also a key actant in the monitoring of players and attempted fraud and security breaches. For example, some systems monitor the players of certain games, such as blackjack, and construct a player rating, providing information to the casino on how well a player compares to the basic strategy of play, average bet, and total amount bet. The software uses this information to calculate how much a player is likely to win or lose over a period of time, and thus an indication of how they should be treated by staff with respect to complimentary services. The software will also calculate how a player makes decisions with regard to strategy and betting, detecting attempted cheating by card counting, shuffle tracking, hole-card and top-card players, and will even measure a player's luck.

It is no longer enough for museums and art galleries to simply display their collections accompanied by printed caption and guidebooks. Museums are digitally cataloguing their collections and making versions of these available online, thus giving some access to the large number of items that cannot be displayed physically to the public due to space constraints (see figure 9.3). Museums also deploy automated audio guides and interactive devices carried by visitors as they wander through the galleries, and which give more information about particular exhibits and the museum itself. Museums are also using interactive digital displays that allow visitors to query and interact with objects and facilitate self-directed learning through quizzes and puzzles.

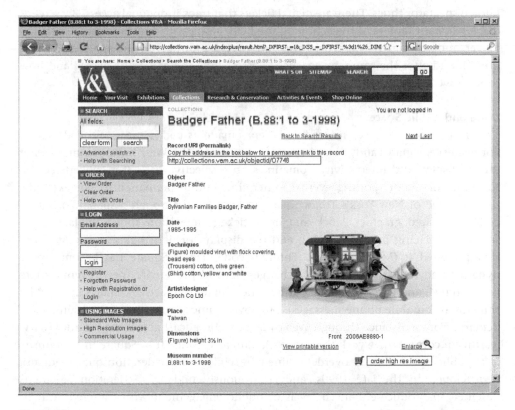

Figure 9.3
The Victoria and Albert Museum provides access to their collection online along with educational material, themed games, puzzles, and competitions, www.vam.ac.uk. Such services made possible by software that allows visitors to plan what they want to see before they arrive; the software also helps fulfill the museum's mission for outreach to people who may never visit in person.

Health and fitness has become a major area of lifestyle consumption in the West. The key space of practice, the gym, has become a coded space with equipment increasingly automated by basic software that enables certain settings to be chosen or for performance to be monitored. For example, treadmills, rowing machines, exercise bikes, and cross-trainers are now often equipped with heart and other physiological monitors; speed or effort feedback; preprogrammed settings, including simulations of real world conditions such as going up and down hills or against the wind; personal coaching based on an analysis of fitness; and a time-series analysis of performance.

Sports stadiums have also become increasingly dependent on software technology to deliver an audience experience in a safe and profitable fashion. English soccer stadiums, for example, rely on a range of software systems to monitor the game and also to control unruly fans. Automated digital surveillance cameras identify and track known spectator thugs. There are digital tickets that track individual access. Big screens display instant replays of the action on the field, along with real-time game statistics. Player and team performance is also intensively monitored and analyzed before, during, and after the game, by coaches to assess how the game was played and how to improve results.

Code and Public Space

Certain high-value public spaces have been remade as coded space and code/space. For example, squares and plazas in major cities across the West have become sites of digital display and interactivity, sometimes on a selective basis (for concerts or the screening of major sporting events), other times more permanently. For example, the spectacle of New York's Times Square is transduced through a spatial collage of code—animated graphics, stock and news tickers, television shows on large LCD screens—replacing print and paint, and the displays of light bulbs and neon tubes that preceded it (Mitchell 2004). Through code, Times Square has become more dynamic and reflexive—reacting to changes beyond the square (news events, share prices, travel, and weather updates) and in the square (interactive displays updated by cameras and mobile phone messages). Moreover, Times Square can be consumed-on-demand from a distance through Web cam access broadcast across the Internet (www.earthcam.com/usa/newyork/timessquare). Similarly, Federation Square in Melbourne is a public space that is overdetermined by code (www.federationsquare.com.au). Redeveloped in the late 1990s, and continuously updated, Federation Square is designed to produce enhanced levels of public engagement with the environment through the many different activities hosted there, including interactive displays, reactive digital and other forms of public art, open air projection of sporting and other live events, street theater and concerts, movie theaters, sidewalk cafés, exhibition spaces, free Wi-Fi, and a collection of public ventures including the National Gallery of Victoria, the Australian Racing Museum, the Melbourne Visitor Centre, the Australian Centre for the Moving Image, and an indoor amphitheater. Code is also being enrolled, in part, to achieve efficient securitization and privatization of public space for commercial gain. As such it clearly has political ramifications as well (Graham 2007).

The extent to which activities in public space will become coded practices is highlighted by the development of location-based services (LBS) and the possibility of context sensitive advertising delivered to mobile devices. Such information might relate to entertainment, such as what restaurants are nearby and what their menu is like, or what theaters are close by and what is being shown and at what times. It might be more general information concerning weather forecasts or traffic reports or a personalized map of the local area that updates as the person moves. In these cases, the user requests the information. Andrejevic (2007) details that in 2006, Google announced that it was exploring the possibilities of unsolicited information delivery through the provision of free wireless access in San Francisco. In return, users would be obliged to receive contextual advertising promoting partner businesses in proximity to where they are accessing the network. So, while browsing the Internet from a park at lunchtime, an advertisement for a nearby coffee shop might pop up on the screen.

Public spaces are also a major area in which illicit and illegal consumption practices often occur, as they offer some safety from surveillance and a degree of anonymity. A significant part of Western economies operate off the books, and seek to avoid taxation. Other types of consumption, such as prostitution and illegal drug use, often use cash and consciously try to avoid leaving behind evidence in capta shadows. Yet, even here, the conveniences of the Web and cell phones, which appear to offer degrees of anonymity in transactions, have become central to contemporary practices of prostitution and drug traffic. The centrality of digital communications to all aspects of criminal consumption means that phones and laptops are some of first items seized by detectives for their potential to provide revelatory forensic evidence for an investigation. As such, much illicit and illegal consumption is revealed by code.

Changing Logistics of Consumption

Traditional supply chains, such as in food production, are arranged as a complex sequence of producers, handlers, processors, manufacturers, wholesalers/distributors, and retailers (Buhr 2003). However, just as consumer practices in the supply chain is evolving, so too are the methods through which goods and services are being sourced by retailers, which in turn affects how companies organize their operations, including the location of shops, warehouses, administrative offices, customer support centers, their logistical supply in terms of the sourcing, tracking, and delivery of material goods and virtual flows of capta, and their relationship with suppliers. According to Sparks (1994, cited in Murphy 2007), rather than retailers being subject to the transport and storage whims of manufacturers and suppliers, as previously, over the past thirty years or so, they have exerted ever more control to shape the entire supply chain to their advantage, while at the same time massively increasing the range of products they sell. A key goal, made possible by inventory software, has been to significantly reduce stock levels throughout the chain, yet still ensure availability through just-in-time deliveries. Another strategy has been for the multitude of suppliers to deliver to a network of coordinating warehouses that are largely automated, that then create unique supply loads for each shop on an as needed basis that reduces on-site storage. As Murphy (2007, 947) explains, supplier "deliveries are now often already labeled with their destination stores and quantities, with the pallet contents bulk-broken and re-routed to the store loading bays without on-site storage, in a process known as 'cross-docking.' Full-truck loads are then sent to the store, with goods often already ordered and pre-stacked for easy shelf display in roll-in cages." The idea is that goods spend as little time in storage and transit as possible, reducing costs and shortening turnover time, and therefore increasing revenue flows and profit margins, particularly at the top of the logistics chain. In many ways then, the large numbers of vast warehouses, automated to a significant degree by software, characterize modern capitalism (see figure 9.4).

The result is that stores, particularly those in a chain or franchise, operate as nodes in a complex and dense assemblage of infrastructure and accompanying real-time processes. These distribution infrastructures and logistical processes are necessarily now increasingly coded, with all products and transactions fully enveloped by capta shadows and worked upon by software used to control, monitor, and regulate the flow of goods from production to consumption. Indeed, to a significant degree, code is the structural glue that binds distributed and distanciated activities together and ensures that products are (almost) always available for purchase and in a way profitable to the end business.

One of the key software technologies enabling such complex organization are so-called backstage technology infrastructures, such as ERP systems. ERP is an all-encompassing software system acting as a single portal that manages, integrates, and coordinates an organization's various subsystems (purchasing, warehousing, inventory, transport, marketing, accounting, personnel management and scheduling, project management, customer relations), and their multiple captabases into one whole, and ensures that processes are automatically and seamlessly available from one part of a business to another (Grant, Harley, and Wright 2006). It is promoted as a way to ensure greater coordination and control across and between organizations, reducing operating costs through gained efficiencies, and facilitating improved strategic planning by providing high quality capta on activities across time and space (Grant, Harley, and Wright 2006). While the product names of ERP systems are generally unknown to the general public, they have a major effect on the running of con-

Figure 9.4
The TurmFahrt (CarTower), a massive automated vertical warehouse for VW cars, in Wolfsburg, Germany. The locational status of all cars is tracked in captabase and the retrieval system is software controlled. *Source*: www.flickr.com/photos/swpj73/2775079437/

temporary society. The market leader R/3 is so successful that it has made its developer, SAP, into the third largest software company in the world, after Microsoft and Oracle, with revenues of $14 billion in 2007 (OECD 2008; see Leimbach 2008 for history of SAP). Campbell-Kelly (2003, 197), has argued that "if overnight R/3 were to cease to exist (say, if its licenses were made intolerably expensive), the industrial economy of the Western world would come to a halt, and it would take years for substitutes to close the breach in the networked economy. Were Microsoft's products to vaporize overnight, it would take only days or weeks to find substitutes, and the economic disruption would be modest."

ERP works by imposing a standardized set of procedures, especially in relation to capta input, handling, sharing, and applications, across an organization, and to integrate a myriad of processes and work flows (Dery, Hall, and Wailes 2006). Given the complexity of running a large business such as a supermarket chain, the lack of some kind of ERP system is likely to result in a plethora of department specific software applications and captabases that lack interoperability and hinder information sharing and an integrative view of the business. As a result, by 2003, over 30,000 companies worldwide had implemented an ERP system (Mabert et al. 2003, cited in Dery, Hall, and Wailes 2006). This is not to say that ERP is either easy to implement, or is without problems. Furthermore, given its pervasive reach across an organization, if it does not work appropriately, it can seriously hamper operations. Indeed, Dery, Hall, and Wailes (2006) report that implementation costs can be very high and that between 20 to 50 percent of ERP systems are scrapped as failures.

While a major part of the drive to more intensively manage supply chains in retail has been to control costs and increase profit, it has also been a response to customers' concerns and greater scrutiny over issues such as product safety, ethical standards, socially responsible production, and environmental sustainability. Retailers, especially the very large supermarkets, have been pressuring suppliers to implement systems of hazard analysis and full traceability for products, and to change their sourcing and manufacturing practices to enable greater visibility and verification (Buhr 2003; Friedberg 2007). This has meant the development of new captabases and software-based audit systems that extend back from retailers to food, clothes, and goods manufacturers, so that the means of production can be tracked and traced in order to reassure the consumer about a product's quality, safety, ethics, and environmental impacts. This is made more challenging as a single product or food item might be made from multiple components or ingredients, each with its own history. The depth of this monitoring can be pervasive. For example, Buhr (2003) details six different track-and-trace systems relating to meat supply demonstrating that in each case, individual animals, their products (such as eggs), and even specific cuts of meat are monitored through various means (such as wing tags on birds, barcode ear tags on livestock, cattle passports, or farm codes laser-etched on eggs), and included the recording of feed, farm, slaughter, packaging, processing, distribution, and retail (see figure 9.5). As Friedberg (2007) notes, the captabases that underpin these systems, and the software processes themselves, largely dictate to suppliers how they should run their farms or factories, how they should regulate labor practices, and how to prove that they were effectively self-policing them; in other words the systems constitute a disciplining regime working to ensure that profitable consumption can proceed and depending on code to work as intended (see chapter 5).

Software and the Profiling of Customers, Products, and Places

It is perhaps in relation to the processing of capta about the ongoing patterns of consumption, and using the information generated to produce new knowledge that help inform business decisions, that software is having its most noticeable influence on retail practices and the customer experience. With the ubiquity of EPoS and EFTPoS in stores generating transaction capta, along with the development of a myriad of

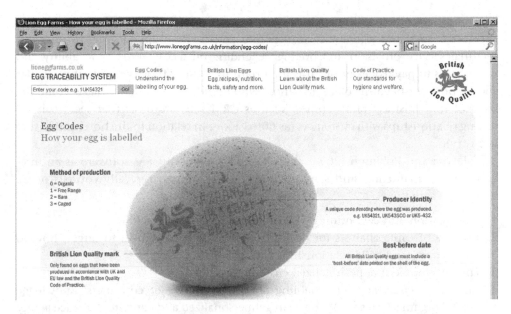

Figure 9.5
The public Web interface to the UK's egg traceability system that is made possible by software systems to generate the captabase of the production identification numbers.

other commercial and public captabases (from shopper surveys and lifestyle panels to marketing questionnaires), a huge amount of information is now harvestable for analysis and use by retailers anxious to understand their own business organization, the products they sell, and the shifting demands of customers in order to increase sales revenues and profitability. Indeed, capta harvesting and analysis has developed into a large and significant business, either conducted by an organization itself, or using specialist companies such as Experian, Equifax, Nielsen Claritas, and Global TGI. In general terms, the analysis seeks to model three components of the retail system— firstly, profiling customers; secondly, profiling individual products; and thirdly, profiling neighborhoods and individual stores—and the shifting interactions between them, with the resulting knowledge being used to more efficiently manage and plan the business, build relationships with new customers and suppliers, and geographically locate the various components of the business. We look at each of the three components of the retail system in turn.

The aim of customer profiling is to rationalize the market by identifying people who possess the characteristics that make them a potential purchaser of a product, to encourage them to buy it, and to reward them for the purchase in order to maintain brand loyalty (Gandy 1993; Andrejevic 2007; Lyon 2007). It is conceptually about understanding a mass of consumers, in order to persuade individuals to consume in ways more profitable to the business. Software tools for profiling are widely used to categorize, sort, and segment customers into particular groups in order to offer differential service provision and pricing depending on usage, status, and ability and willingness to pay. For example, it is important to identify those who merit particular special offers or payment plans and those who do not. This profiling has become the basis of new business philosophies, such as CRM software tools that seek to build lasting relationships with customers (as noted above in relation to the hotel and leisure industry).

Kalakota and Robinson (2000) characterize the work of CRM software as an integrated sales, marketing, and service strategy. CRM systems typically consists of six integrated activities.

1. The creation and data mining of a captabase of customer activity
2. The use of capta analysis for deciding about which customers to target, how to target, contact, and build relationships with them
3. The development of personalized customer experiences
4. Channel management for enabling an efficient share of customers' knowledge across the organization so that they can get personalized and consistent service at any time, any place, any where, and on any platform
5. Management of privacy issues
6. The development and gathering of metrics for measuring CRM success (Sigala 2005)

In short, CRM scrutinizes information about people, their characteristics, and their history of purchasing with a company in order to manage (and better exploit) the relationship between the business and the customer (Lyon 2007). Such software systems seek to identify who are the most profitable customers, who are loyal customers, and also those who pose the highest risks (for example, in terms of likelihood to default on payments), and how they should be differentially treated to the benefit of the company. For example, Lyon (2007) discusses how the Canadian company RBC Financial profiles and software-sorts its customers using an algorithmic metric of customer lifetime value (CLTV, a quantifiable measure of their worth to the business) and also KDD techniques (see chapter 5) in order to determine who should be nurtured with superior customer service, and who should just receive basic services or be actively discouraged or denied. CRM's "rationale is to enhance long-term profitability by moving from transaction-based marketing and its prominence in attracting new customers, to customer retention by means of effective management of customer relationships" (Sigala 2005, 392).

The ways in which customers are segmented by software by their monetary value raises important issues of accountability and social equity, because as Graham (2005, 566) notes, "most processes of software-sorting are actually invisible from the point of the users, these prioritizations are often not evident either to the favored groups or places or to the marginalized ones." Some consumers gain from profiling and software sorting, yet the differential pricing and service models that result can mean the poor pay more and the de facto redlining of areas, which has significant political implications in democratic societies relying on the market to deliver goods and services.

A different type of customer profiling used for marketing purposes is collaborative filtering, now commonly used by Web retailers and online markets. This technique takes multiple capta streams supplied by an individual, either by answering a series of questions in a online survey, or through personal interests expressed in terms of information posted on social networking sites, search terms, and ratings, or through transaction patterns of purchases. Collaborative filtering then uses these data to construct a personal profile. This profile is then entered into a pool of other profiles and compared to them to construct other aspects of an individual's profile, or to suggest other potential purchases based on the similarity of the profile to other people in the pool (Galloway 2004). Amazon's "personalized recommendations" works on this principle, tracking the browsing history, keyword searches, and purchases of individual customers to build a multi-dimensional profile of taste in reading or music or other consumer items, to then make recommendations for other purchases based on what other people with similar profiles have bought. In this sense, as Galloway (2004) notes, collaborative filtering seeks to both reflect and inflect an individual's identity.

The second type of profiling relates to understanding the nature of individual products. Brick-and-mortar retailers (and even pure-play online stores) have constraints in shelf display and storage space. There are hundreds of thousands of possible products that a given retailer could try to sell, and so they have to make choices about what to stock, how to price it, where to locate it in a store, how to position it on the shelf, and whether to promote it. Moreover, in order to satisfy as many customers as possible (or the most profitable segments), they have to balance product range against the profitability of different lines, pack sizes, and promotions. As a consequence, retailers monitor which kind of customer buys particular products, and in what kind of quantities, what products they buy in combination with each other, and how loyal a customer is to a particular brand. They also monitor how well a product sells in different locations in a store (for example, chewing gum sales are highly related to being stocked at the checkout counter), and how a product sells in stores at different geographic locations, and the effects of price promotions and display marketing. As a result, the range of products on sale in different stores of the same chain, and even the layout of the store and pricing, might be markedly different given the profile of the customers who shop there—their tastes and their willingness to pay certain prices for products. This kind of analysis is only feasible with the scalability and automation offered by coded, algorithmic processing.

Geodemographics spatializes profiling, marketing, and decision making by analyzing how patterns of consumption occurs across geographic space. Clearly, different kinds of people live in different kinds of areas, with a zip code working as an effective indicator of customer type. An expensive boutique shop will not fare well in a less affluent, working class neighborhood; targeting the residents of that neighborhood with marketing will similarly not be cost-effective. Geodemographics analyzes the characteristics of consumers and housing in an area to inform firms where best to locate their stores to maximize profit, and in which neighborhoods they should concentrate their marketing efforts. Geodemographic models of space are constructed from a variety of public and private capta using sophisticated statistical clustering algorithms, dividing up cities into profiled areas at fine spatial scales (see figure 9.6). For example, the UK-based CACI sells a geodemographic system, ACORN, which classifies every postcode in the UK into one of fifty-four "life-style" categories (see figure 9.7). The descriptions of each category include information concerning typical house size, area characteristics, likely earnings profile, car ownership, and so on. Other companies can then purchase this information, and through the use of relational captabases, combine it with their own customer profiles or other purchased capta.

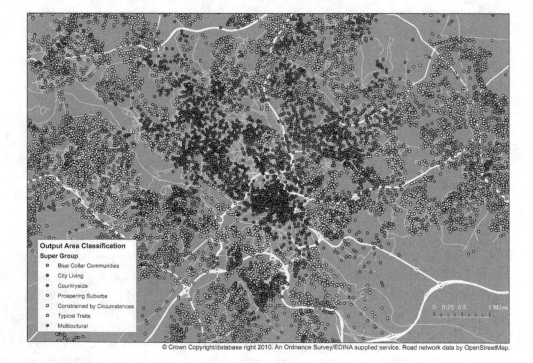

© Crown Copyright/database right 2010. An Ordnance Survey/EDINA supplied service. Road network data by OpenStreetMap.

Figure 9.6
Revealing the varying pattern of social geography captured by a software calculated classification. Postcodes in central Leeds are mapped according to their geodemographic classification. *Source*: Courtesy of Alex Singleton, University College London

	Group		Type	% of GB population
Group 1	Wealthy Achievers, Suburban Areas	Type 1	Wealthy Suburbs, Large Detached Houses	3.0%
		Type 2	Villages with Wealthy Commuters	2.7%
		Type 3	Mature Affluent Home Owning Areas	2.8%
		Type 4	Affluent Suburbs, Older Families	3.8%
		Type 5	Mature, Well-Off Suburbs	2.7%
Group 2	Affluent Greys, Rural Communities	Type 6	Agricultural Villages, Home Based Workers	1.5%
		Type 7	Holiday Retreats, Older People, Home Based Workers	0.6%
Group 3	Prosperous Pensioners, Retirement Areas	Type 8	Home Owning Areas, Well-Off Older Residents	1.4%
		Type 9	Private Flats, Elderly People	1.1%
Group 4	Affluent Executives, Family Areas	Type 10	Affluent Working Families with Mortgages	2.8%
		Type 11	Affluent Working Couples with Mortgages, New Homes	1.1%
		Type 12	Transient Workforces, Living at their Place of Work	0.4%
Group 5	Well-Off Workers, Family Areas	Type 13	Home Owning Family Areas	2.1%
		Type 14	Home Owning Family Areas, Older Children	3.2%
		Type 15	Families with Mortgages, Younger Children	2.0%
Group 6	Affluent Urbanites, Town and City Areas	Type 16	Well-Off Town & City Areas	1.2%
		Type 17	Flats & Mortgages, Singles & Young Working Couples	0.9%
		Type 18	Furnished Flats & Bedsits, Younger Single People	0.4%
Group 7	Prosperous Professionals, Metropolitan Areas	Type 19	Apartments, Young Professional Singles & Couples	1.0%
		Type 20	Gentrified Multi-Ethnic Areas	1.0%
Group 8	Better-Off Executives, Inner City Areas	Type 21	Prosperous Enclaves, Highly Qualified Executives	0.0%
		Type 22	Academic Centres, Students & Young Professionals	0.7%
		Type 23	Affluent City Centre Areas, Tenements & Flats	0.9%
		Type 24	Partially Gentrified Multi-Ethnic Areas	0.7%
		Type 25	Converted Flats & Bedsits, Single People	0.9%
Group 9	Comfortable Middle Agers, Mature Home Owning Areas	Type 26	Mature Established Home Owning Areas	3.0%
		Type 27	Rural Areas, Mixed Occupations	3.4%
		Type 28	Established Home Owning Areas	4.4%
		Type 29	Home Owning Areas, Council Tenants, Retired People	2.3%
Group 10	Skilled Workers, Home Owning Areas	Type 30	Established Home Owning Areas, Skilled Workers	4.1%
		Type 31	Home Owners in Older Properties, Younger Workers	4.0%
		Type 32	Home Owning Areas with Skilled Workers	4.7%
Group 11	New Home Owners, Mature Communities	Type 33	Council Areas, Some New Home Owners	2.8%
		Type 34	Mature Home Owning Areas, Skilled Workers	2.6%
		Type 35	Low Rise Estates, Older Workers, New Home Owners	2.7%
Group 12	White Collar Workers, Better-Off Multi-Ethnic Areas	Type 36	Home Owning Multi-Ethnic Areas, Young Families	0.9%
		Type 37	Multi-Occupied Town Centres, Mixed Occupations	1.8%
		Type 38	Multi-Ethnic Areas, White Collar Workers	1.3%
Group 13	Older People, Less Prosperous Areas	Type 39	Home Owners, Small Council Flats, Single Pensioners	1.9%
		Type 40	Council Areas, Older People, Health Problems	1.3%
Group 14	Council Estate Residents, Better-Off Homes	Type 41	Better-Off Council Areas, New Home Owners	2.6%
		Type 42	Council Areas, Young Families, Some New Home Owners	2.7%
		Type 43	Council Areas, Young Families, Many Lone Parents	1.7%
		Type 44	Multi-Occupied Terraces, Multi-Ethnic Areas	0.8%
		Type 45	Low Rise Council Housing, Less Well-Off Families	2.0%
		Type 46	Council Areas, Residents with Health Problems	1.5%
Group 15	Council Estate Residents, High Unemployment	Type 47	Estates with High Unemployment	0.9%
		Type 48	Council Flats, Elderly People, Health Problems	0.9%
		Type 49	Council Flats, Very High Unemployment, Singles	1.1%
Group 16	Council Estate Residents, Greatest Hardship	Type 50	Council Areas, High Unemployment, Lone Parents	1.8%
		Type 51	Council Flats, Greatest Hardship, Many Lone Parents	0.7%
Group 17	People in Multi-Ethnic, Low-Income Areas	Type 52	Multi-Ethnic, Large Families, Overcrowding	0.5%
		Type 53	Multi-Ethnic, Severe Unemployment, Lone Parents	1.1%
		Type 54	Multi-Ethnic, High Unemployment, Overcrowding	0.5%

Figure 9.7

Listing of the names of the groups and subtypes in a typical geodemographic classification of the British population. *Source*: CACI ACORN promotional brochure

The investment in capta harvesting and analysis can be significant. To take one case study by Whitelegge (2004), Marks and Spencer's, a major UK-based retailer with three hundred stores in twenty-nine countries, employed fifty-six people in its Customer Insight Group, an arm of its marketing division. This group included twenty-three statisticians and modelers, six GIS specialists, and four data planners. Their core task was to analyze the massive amount of capta generated by Marks and Spencer customers—at the time over ten million transactions per week, with details relating to products purchase, credit/loyalty card usage, basket value, along with customer traffic data—in relation to a wide range of external social, economic, and retail capta (such as the census, local market condition capta, and market capta) in order to understand the evolving relationship between its customers (demographics, segmentation, life stages, behavior/attitudes), stores (catchments, gravity modeling, store estimates, new formats), and products (basket analysis, customer affinities, product associations). The knowledge generated by such information was used to profile customers, offer promotions, change product ranges, and decide where to locate new stores or close underperforming stores.

A number of critiques have been leveled at the development of the geodemographics industry that questions the process of drawing ever more detailed social and spatial capta together to produce segmentations of space in terms of "purchasing power" and fetishized lifestyles. According to Goss (1995, 191), "the genius of geodemographics is that it systematically produces such lifestyles both from us and for us: it presents descriptions of our consuming selves that are actually normative models, or mean characteristics of our consumption (stereo) type to which we are exhorted to conform." While easily portrayed in a positive light, using the simple premise "that birds of a feather flock together," there are negative consequences to geodemographics (Curry 1997; Goss 1995). For example, the ability to determine the kinds of people who live in particular places, and their propensity to consume, implies an inherent ranking based on net worth, and has led to discriminatory practices, such as the redlining of communities deemed unprofitable or high risk by insurers and banks.

In classifying people as consumption prospects, geodemographic software reductively collapses the infinite complexity of human feelings, desires, motives, and emotions into a simple exploitable model. Importantly, this model is often then assumed to be how reality should be working, and thus becomes an tool for overt action to impose normative solutions onto people and places (Burrows and Gane 2006). But consumers are not rendered inert by these software models. They evolve more complex everyday behaviors and people slip through the gaps in the "cage of codes"; as Goss (1995, 192) notes, "the very necessity for continuously expanded surveillance and sophisticated modeling suggests consumer responses to marketing are always more complex and run ahead of predictions."

Regulation of Consumption

Code has had also been important in reshaping how consumption practices are regulated. Initially, consumption spaces were surveyed and controlled by the owner and any security they employed, with the police or legal system enacted where and when it was deemed necessary. More recently, this has been complemented by the widespread use of software surveillance and automated management systems, and new forms of contract designed to protect a company's rights and exploit prosumers rights (or the opposite, to reassure customers) (see chapter 5).

Digital CCTV systems are ubiquitous across the retail and leisure industry; so much so that Lyon (2007, 108) refers to them as "surveillant playspaces." The discourses underpinning its rollout focus on issues such as crime reduction (both among customers and employees), crowd control, and safety. Importantly, the effects of surveillance are differently enacted; "through CCTV, people and behaviors seen not to 'belong' in the increasingly commercialized and privately-managed consumption spaces of British town and city centers tended to experience especially close scrutiny" (Graham 2002, 240). The footage from networked CCTV cameras is being complemented by more and more sophisticated analysis, such as face and gait recognition, and with other kinds of security, such as biometric scanners and airport-style security to enter stores. For example, biometric scanners are in use in all four major theme parks in Orlando, Florida, for accessing areas and rides, and x-ray security checkpoints are used to scan bags and people entering many national monuments in the United States. While CCTV is being used to enforce modes of self-discipline, biometric scanners and security checkpoints enforce a particular grammar of action on both customers and employees.

Given the growth of delivery of services across the Internet, and the development of new kinds of online consumption and prosumption, there has been a rapid growth in new forms of software specific regulatory practices. This growth has been driven by companies seeking to protect their digital product from piracy and ensure that they can maximize the profit from it, while also finding new ways to exploit the widespread development of prosumption for commercial gain. With respect to companies protecting their digital rights, software is increasingly being produced in such a way as to protect the rights of manufacturers, content providers, patent holders, and copyright owners (Berry 2004). Tactics include restricting access to software and content, asking users to sign restrictive licensing agreements, limiting how many or what type of machines the software can be installed on, and preventing copying or conversion to other formats. Digital rights management (DRM) seeks to prevent the unauthorized, unforeseen, or undesired use or alteration of digital content and copyrighted works (music, film, literature, games) as well as specific devices. As Berry (2004, 68) notes, "software is delegated the legal restrictions of the copyrighted work and then pre-scribes these restrictions back on the user." DRM thus works to restrict the copying and moving of digital capta, such as music files, and also how often it is played. This level of control, enacted in software, is quite different from earlier analog media such as VHS cassettes. The same controls are applied to some packaged software, which requires a registration key to unlock it, and which confers differential access to func-tionality depending on the payment made, and ensures it can be copied and used on different machine.

While often giving the impression of empowering users to utilize a service in what-ever ways they want, whether online or on the go, phone service, media, and content providers do actively regulate users in relation to what content they post and their actions while using the service. They also ensure that when signing up to a service, the user ascribes certain rights and privileges as to how a company might exploit any content the user adds to a service. Such regulation is detailed in the terms of service and privacy statements that set out the legal framework underpinning how the site and users are regulated, and detailing the entitlements and protections afforded to service owners and users. They are often unread, as people simply click on the "I agree" button to complete the sign-up process as smoothly and quickly as possible, but they are important as they exert ownership and exploitation rights.

Conclusion

In this chapter, we have examined, in brief, some of the ways in which code is alter-ing the nature of consumption. Software has led to the virtual abstraction of money, enabling finance to circulate through dense, interconnected and interdependent net-works of companies, products, and property, and creating new, fictitious, and specula-tive capital which is highly mobile. As a consequence, capta and software algorithms are at the heart of the global financial system, underpinning how monies were, and continue to be, monitored, transferred, tracked, repackaged, sold, and leveraged; it was software that enabled fraudsters such as Bernard Madoff to run highly elaborate Ponzi schemes with a tiny insider staff, where investments were leveraged, shifted, posted, hidden, recirculated, and presented through a coded smokescreen that, when it finally unraveled, lost investors over $65 billion. And it is software that has enabled financial services to spatially reconfigure their operations so that some businesses become geographically centralized and others disappear from brick-and-mortar stores and exist only as call centers, back offices, and server rooms.

Code is changing the processes through which people purchase goods and services, opening up new forms of e-commerce and deepening and diversifying participation in their production by enabling motivated individuals to interact with, customize, and accessorize their products; to potentially take an active role in the prosumption of media and products. Prosumption, we feel, will become an important means through which people will take part in everyday life. No longer will most people passively consume predetermined products. Instead they will become ever more active agents in the nature of those products, service, and media. In so doing, they will become willing participants in processes designed to profile their tastes, behaviors, and desires. These processes will build relationships with customers in order that companies can more effectively market their products to them and to encourage them to remain loyal to the brand.

Code has also has reconfigured the spatial relations of how and where people purchase goods and services, and how companies restructure their organizations and supply chains to gain efficiencies and competitiveness, with consequent changes to the geographies of retail and service and some new forms of consumptive spaces—spaces reliant on code to perform as intended. These spaces, and the new processes of consumption and prosumption, have become the subject to new forms of surveillance and automated management that actively discipline and reshape consumer/prosumer and employee behavior, and seek to protect and extend companies' rights and profit making. The consequence of the pervasive embedding of code into retail, leisure, and public space is that they have become coded spaces and code/spaces.

IV Future Code/Space

10 Everyware

You walk into the [the conference room, living room, museum gallery, hospital ward], the contextual intention system recognizes you by your [beacon, tage, badge, face, gait], and the [lights, music, temperature, privacy settings, security permission] adjust smoothly to your preferences. Your new location is announced to the [room, building, global buddy list, Homeland Security Department], and your [video conference, favourite TV show, appointment calendar, breakfast order] is automatically started.
—Gene Becker

Now, nothing need be without processing power, and nothing need be left unlinked. . . . Networked intelligence is being embedded everywhere, in every kind of physical system. Code is mobile. Code is everywhere.
—William J. Mitchell

At stake is how the destabilization of time and space by data-intensive environments will be interpreted and employed: as time and space become more malleable, will this flexibility be used to enhance and amplify human life, or to drive humanity closer to thinghood?
—N. Katharine Hayles

The last three chapters have explored, in some detail, how software is increasingly being embedded in objects and space and enrolled in a range of practices with diverse implications. Given the trends outlined, it is easy to conclude that Western societies are advancing toward a situation in which code is routinely employed to undertake tasks and solve problems across all aspects of everyday life. This broad use of code is being actively explored by a wide range of computer scientists, new media designers, technology analysts, and IT corporations keen to explore such a scenario. The outcomes sought are to advance technical understandings and conceptual thought; produce prototype systems; and to exploit new commercial opportunities. These ideas are driven by the idea that rather than always taking work to the computer, computation should be available wherever it is needed; computation should be organized around people and their everyday lives, and not human lives around computation, as is presently the case (Dourish 2001). The new paradigm they are seeking to introduce has been termed "everyware" (Greenfield 2006).

Everyware is the notion that computational power will soon be distributed and available at any point on the planet—calculative capacity will be literally available everywhere, with multiple computers operating for every person. Many everyday objects will become computational devices and be promiscuously networked as micro-servers that are continuously accessible across an Internet of things, unobtrusively chatting to each other about small but significant matters. In other words, everyware is a state in which computation can be continuously on-hand, regardless of location, and thoroughly interwoven into the fabric of society. With everyware, life unfolds enveloped within software-enabled environments (Mitchell 2004). Software will become truly hospitable to social life, and the type of computers we have lived with for last two decades will disappear from view.

It is apparent that nascent forms of everyware already exist, at least for some people, and in some parts of the world. Much of the West is saturated with software-enabled, networked technologies supported by fixed line and wireless infrastructures (near field and proximate communication with Bluetooth, local Wi-Fi coverage, national GSM/3G networks, satellite connectivity); nations such as Finland are approaching 100 percent cell phone penetration (OECD 2008). Many daily practices are overdetermined by code. With access to the appropriate technology, it is possible to connect to ICT networks from anywhere on the planet. However, everyware in its contemporary deployment is highly partial in nature, uneven, and unequal in distribution, density, penetration, sophistication, and form. Access is dependent upon economic resources, knowledge to use technologies, location, and whether appropriate infrastructure is available, and devices and networks being interoperable. Computer and network usage is constrained by social conventions, cultural differences, language barriers, and legislative mandates; the freedom of access is also subject to surveillance, censorship, and control by the state and corporations (RSF 2008).

In this chapter, we detail how advances in different forms of computing, pervasive, ubiquitous, sentient, tangible, and wearable, are creating the technologies and infrastructures to make everyware a reality. We then examine three discursive regimes that are driving the development of everyware—empowerment (convenience, utility, productivity, play, military enhancement), securitization (surveillance, discipline, crime preclusion, risk reduction), and sousveillance (the personal monitoring and management of one's life, as opposed to endogenous surveillance that seeks to control; Mann, Nolan, and Wellman 2003). In the second half of the chapter, we examine why we believe everyware will always remain partial in nature, focusing on the desire of people to adopt core technologies, the persistence of gaps in the production and deployment of everyware, and how people already avoid and resist software-enabled technologies and will continue to do so for a number of reasons.

Defining Everyware

Following Greenfield (2006), we conceive of *everyware* as an umbrella term that encompasses a range of related forms of computing and social software that are often used synonymously, including: pervasive, ubiquitous, sentient, tangible, and wearable computing and ambient intelligence. These forms of software interaction are linked through the shared aim of opening up computation to everyday tasks, rather than tailoring a task to fit the constraints of current computer interfaces. Moreover, many tasks, it is envisioned, will be performed automatically such that people are not aware that software was active in the solution. There are, however, some subtle differences as to what these various forms of computing constitute, despite the fact that the terms are often used interchangeably and the forms of computing are used in conjunction with each other.

Pervasive computing seeks to augment aspects of everyday life and activities by adding value through the embedding of sensors and some degree of decision-making capacity in everyday objects and infrastructures rendering them interactive and smart, yet also mundane and routine. As we have detailed throughout this book, code is now being embedded into all manner of objects, very few of which present themselves as computers (see chapter 3). By 2005, less than a quarter of the microprocessors made by Intel were for desktop and laptop computers. The overall aim of pervasive computing is to ensure that an individual can interact naturally with and within an environment as opposed to operating a single digital device; tasks would be automatically coordinated, distributed, and shared across multiple devices where there is no one point of control (Dourish 2001). Over time it is hoped that systems will not only adapt themselves to their users, but that they will observe, learn, and, in some sense, be able anticipate the user's needs (Aarts, Harwig, and Schuurmans 2002). Successful pervasive computing, for Weiser (1991, 3), weaves itself "into the fabric of everyday life until they are indistinguishable from it." As such, processing power becomes so pervasive in environments that computers per se effectively disappear. This is the mission of projects such as MIT's Project Oxygen:

We will not need to carry our own devices around with us. Instead, configurable generic devices, either handheld or embedded in the environment, will bring computation to us, whenever we need it and wherever we might be. As we interact with these "anonymous" devices, they will adopt our information personalities. They will respect our desires for privacy and security. We won't have to type, click, or learn new computer jargon. (www.oxygen.lcs.mit.edu/Overview .html, January 15, 2009)

As this quote illustrates, interaction is facilitated by sentient and tangible computing. Sentient computing is where objects and systems sense and react in a contextual fashion to an individual's presence, without having to be asked or directly instructed

(Addlesee et al. 2001). The opening quote of the chapter provides several examples of sentient computing—wherein an individual is automatically recognized and depending on circumstance and context, the software reacts appropriately (for example, opening a door lock, increasing the thermostat temperature, showing datebook appointments). Other kinds of sentient computing include occasions when peripheral devices, such as networked printers and data projectors, make themselves known to codejects that come into their wireless network and react accordingly; or toys that know they have been picked up or interacted with in some way and react in a contextual fashion to the nature of play. It is thus argued that sentient computing allows people to personalize their network appliances so that environments know who they are and what they have done in the past, and can consequently react to them in ways that are appropriate or helpful.

Tangible computing, on the other hand, is an individual controlling computation, but in a manner that employs more natural modes of communication such as voice and gesture recognition and touch, rather than being statically positioned in front of a screen and typing at a keyboard or clicking a mouse—modes of interaction that have varied little since the invention of the digital computer (Dourish 2001). Indeed, in many ways, computers remain hard to use for many simple tasks. The aim of tangible interfaces is to make interaction with software into a normal, natural, tacit practice; something much less cognitively taxing and intimidating, thoroughly intuitively usable, and little different from conversing with a person. In this sense, everyware should be a "calming technology," as envisioned by Weiser and Seely Brown (1998). As Dourish (2001) notes, thinking about and developing these more intuitively humanistic modes of interaction with software requires moving from fixed hardware input devices and constrained metaphorical ideas, such as desktops, folders, and menus to ideas centered on the ways people "naturally" experience and engage with the world through voice, embodied gestures, and innate touch. All manner of objects and surfaces will receive digital inputs and give outputs; other digital objects will operate touch free. Recent innovations in touch screens and interface designs, as exemplified by Apple's iPods and iPhones, provide some hints toward the much more intimate interaction that tangible computing promises, but natural speech interfaces, long held as the apogee of human-computer interaction, are still presently in their infancy.

Whereas pervasive computing is software capacity embedded in environments that then interact with people moving around within them, ubiquitous computing is computation power that moves with the person regardless of environment. As such, ubiquitous computing refers to coded objects that people carry or wear that can solve tasks as they move about, or will react automatically and appropriately to changing environments and activities, depending on communications with local informational resources and infrastructural networks. Pervasive computing exhibits processes of divergence—software being embedded into more and more devices—whereas ubiquitous computing exhibits convergence, with single coded objects undertaking more and more tasks (see figure 10.1). While pervasive computing needs to be situationally aware to be successfully implemented, ubiquitous computing requires continuous context and location awareness. It is hypothesized that in time, how a coded object behaves will vary seamlessly with where one is, who one is with, and what one is doing (Greenfield 2006). A obvious example would be cell phones that would ring audibly only when it was appropriate to do so (this is simple for people to judge but actually hard to program algorithmically).

Wearable computing is where software migrates from specific coded objects to become embedded into the clothes, shoes, jewelry, and accessories that are commonly worn. The fibers and fabrics of clothes and accessories gain digital functionality, some awareness, and become programmable to a certain degree; they can identify and sense the person wearing them and something of the environment around them; they can potentially communicate with other wearable devices and coded infrastructures; and they can act as interfaces to other devices (Mitchell 2004). An early example would be a digital hearing aid, but envisaged examples include a shirtsleeve used to interface with an iPod (brushing down to decrease volume, up to increase volume, tapping to start and stop tracks); a jacket that could keep its wearer warmer in cold weather or change color on demand; shoes and socks might tighten and stiffen to alter gait and prevent injuries. In addition, the clothes and accessories might also automatically record where they go and who they encounter, monitor vital signs, and contain conductive fibers that can generate their own electrical power from body heat or movement (Andrejevic 2007). Mann (1998) suggests that genuine wearable computing can be characterized by the following qualities:

Unmonopolizing   It does not demand full attention.

Unrestrictive   Other tasks can be completed while using it.

Observable   The wearer is aware of its work.

Controllable   It is responsive and the wearer can take control of the process at any time.

Attentive   It has some awareness of the situation and/or environment around it.

Communicative   It can communicate with other devices and express the wearer's desires.

Constant   It is always on and ready to solve tasks.

Personal   It becomes prosthetic-like in its use (it becomes an unthinking extension of the body); it is private to the individual wearer.

If the mantra of pervasive computing is computation in every thing, then the mantra of ubiquitous computing is computation in every place. Ubiquitous computing requires, on the one hand, the development of much more effective mobile devices and, on the other, a rollout of universal networking coverage so that interactive com-

iPhone Applications

Press the Home ▢ button at any time to see the iPhone applications. Tap any application button to get started:

Phone	Make calls, with quick access to recent callers, favorites, and all your contacts. Visual voicemail presents a list of your voicemail messages. Just tap to listen to any message you want, in any order you want.
Mail	Send and receive email using your existing email accounts. iPhone works with the most popular email systems—including Yahoo! Mail, Gmail, AOL, and .Mac Mail—as well as most industry-standard POP3 and IMAP email systems.
Safari	Browse any website over the EDGE data network or over Wi-Fi. Rotate iPhone sideways for widescreen viewing. Double-tap to zoom in or out—Safari automatically fits sections to the iPhone screen for easy reading.
iPod	Listen to your songs, audiobooks, and podcasts. Watch TV shows, movies, and video podcasts in widescreen.
Text	Send and receive SMS text messages with anyone who has an SMS-capable phone. Conversations are saved in an iChat-like presentation, so you can see a history of messages you've sent to and received from each person.
Calendar	View your iCal, Microsoft Entourage, or Microsoft Outlook calendar synced from your computer. Enter events on iPhone and they get synced back to your computer. Set alerts to remind you of events, appointments, and deadlines.
Photos	View photos transferred from your computer or taken with iPhone. View them in portrait or landscape mode. Zoom in on any photo for a closer look. Watch a slideshow. Email photos, assign them to contacts, and use them as wallpaper.
Camera	Take clear, crisp photos at two megapixels and view them on iPhone, email them, or upload them to your computer. Take a friend's picture and set iPhone to display it when that person calls you.
YouTube	Play videos from YouTube's online collection. Search for any video, or browse featured, most viewed, most recently updated, and top-rated videos.
Stocks	Watch your favorite stocks, updated automatically from the Internet.
Maps	See a street map or a photographic satellite view of locations around the world. Zoom in for a closer look. Get detailed directions and see current traffic conditions. Find businesses in the area and call with a single tap.

Figure 10.1

Apple's iPhone, at the vanguard of cell phone technology, is a single coded object with software to solve tasks of telecommunication, Web browsing, personal organization, taking a picture, and serving as an MP3 player and a game device. Code can offer multiple functions in a single object. This computer is, in a profound sense, the universal machine.

munications can occur regardless of any particular location. Clearly, there have been significant strides made in both of these areas in the last two decades with the development of increasingly sophisticated handheld, mobile, multifunctional devices, such as hybrid phone/PDAs and the rollout of GSM/3G telephony and wireless Internet broadband in many countries (see figure 10.2). However, a key constraint with ubiquitous computing, based on mobile devices, is the availability of electrical power and the limited life of batteries (see figure 10.3).

Conceptually, it is possible to imagine the interlinking of all of these forms of computing because, as Greenfield (2006, 97) notes, "everything digital can by its very nature can be yoked together." After all, at a fundamental level, they all they share a universal language—zeros and ones. That is not to say that such convergence is practically possible or desirable—after all, at present and for the foreseeable future, coded objects, infrastructures, and processes use different capta formats, incompatible standards, inconsistent protocols, and a raft of legal barriers and political economy constraints.

Taken together, it is envisioned that these various forms of everyware will generate "ambient intelligence"—objects and spaces that are sensitive and responsive to the presence of people or other coded objects. Such ambient intelligence is defined by being context aware (a space recognizing the people occupying it and understanding sufficient aspects of the ongoing context), personalized (a space that can be effortlessly tailored to the desires of the occupier), adaptive (a space that changes automatically in response to the actions of the occupier and the unfolding situational context), and anticipatory (a space that predicts likely future desires based on prior interaction and unfolding context) (Greenfield 2006). In this sense, everyware is driven by adaptive software—code that is self-organizing and self-learning. It is not intelligent in the classical sense of producing devices and environments that have consciousness, and can socialize on some higher level with people, but smart in that it is aware and responsive. As Sterling (2002) notes, people want to be facilitated, but no one wants to be bossed around by algorithms.

All of the forms of novel computing we have outlined so far are in the process of being explored by university labs and corporate research centers, and some have made it to market in various guises. While prototypes are often rudimentary when compared to end visions of everyware, they nonetheless point to what is possible and the likely trajectories of development. Indeed, all ten of the essential characteristics of everyware detailed by McCullough (2004) presently exist to some extent, as we have illustrated in a range of contexts and practices in the previous three chapters.

• Space and objects are embedded with software functionality.
• Sensors detect some kind of action and generate capta that represents it.
• Communication links form an ad hoc ecology of coded objects.

Figure 10.2
The extensive 3G wireless coverage provided by Orange network in the UK at the end of 2008.
Despite the apparent gaps for some rural areas, the majority of consumers have access. *Source*:
Ofcom 2009, www.ofcom.org.uk/radiocomms/

Figure 10.3
A creative business solution to overcome battery constraints. A street charging-service provider in Kampala, Uganda. *Source*: Jan Chipchase 2006, www.janchipchase.com/sharedphoneuse

- Tags identify actors.
- Actuators close the loop (a system regulates itself by monitoring its own performance).
- Controls make it participatory (a system you interact with rather than react to).
- Display spreads out (interfaces becoming more ubiquitous).
- Fixed sensor grids can track mobile positions.
- Software models situations.
- Tuning and adaptability overcomes rigidity.

   The development and diffusion of everyware then appears to be inevitable in the long term, although the exact form is impossible to predict. Indeed, some spaces are already prototypical everyware environments such as airports and many other significant coded assemblages. However, it should be noted that everyware is developing differently between locations (McCullough 2004; Greenfield 2006). For example, in Japan the trend has been toward ubiquitous computing primarily using cell phones (Greenfield 2006). In North America, the trend is toward pervasive computing and the embedding of code into environments. One of the most ambitious rollouts of a proto-everyware environment at present is the conceptualization, design, and development of Songdo City, forty miles from Seoul, South Korea (see figure 10.4). This new city, built on a green field site, is conceived as a "ubiquitous city," thoroughly infused with software technology where "all major information systems (residential, medical, business, etc.) share data; computers are built into the houses, streets and office buildings; and the technology and facilities infrastructures are integrated and pervasive" (Songdo 2009a). The developers' aim is that the people who live and work in Songdo "will experience an unparalleled Quality of Life as technology, resources and innovation all come together to create the ideal environment" (Songdo 2009b).

The Drivers of Everyware

. . . will ubiquitous computing be co-opted as a stalking horse for predatory capitalism or can we seize the opportunity to use it for life-enhancing transformation?
—N. Katharine Hayles

As we detailed earlier in the book, the embedding of software into everyday life is supported by a powerful discursive regime consisting of sets of interlocking discourses relating to efficiency, productivity, safety, sustainability, and consumer choice. It seems to us that the drive to develop the conditions of everyware draws on these

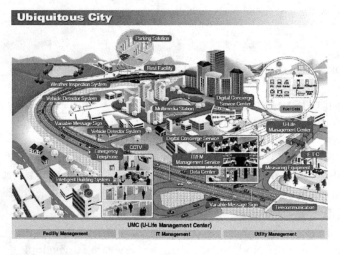

Figure 10.4
Songdo City, a self-styled ubiquitous city in the making. *Source*: www.korea.net/korea/view.asp?murl=/image/news/today/

discourses, but more particularly those relating to empowerment, securitization, and sousveillance. Everyware offers a future that enables and empowers individuals on the one hand, but can also greatly augment the capacity of states and corporations on the other.

Empowerment through Everyware

As we discussed in chapter 6, software affords its users a mechanism and media for creativity, and empowers them to do new kinds of work in the world. Software helps people solve relational problems in a more effective, cost-efficient, and innovative way. The central premise of much everyware is to take the affordances that software makes to people's lives to a qualitatively higher level. The calculative capacity of code will become instilled deeply into all aspects of everyday lives in order to enhance enjoyment and productivity and also empower people in diverse ways, as the opening quote below illustrates. In this section, we examine in brief some of the forms of everyware being envisioned and developed by technologists that potential to empower people.

An individual is walking down a street in a U.S. city in the near future. A Bluetooth-enabled jacket relays music wirelessly from a multipurpose device in a pocket to the person's earphones. The controls of the music player are embedded in the jacket's fabric. A pair of ordinary-looking eyeglasses is wirelessly connected to the same device, providing an augmented reality overlay on the environment being navigated, supplying contextual information about the buildings being passed or the route to be taken. The system software notes from historical capta that this is the fourth time this month that the person has walked down this street, while it also logs ambient noise levels and air temperature. By tapping on a sleeve, the device can be used to query specific information requests, such as looking at a restaurant's menu and making a reservation for later that day. Sitting on a bench, the glasses can be tuned to watch television, play a movie, or browse the Web. Also built into the glasses is a lens and CCD sensor that allows them to mediate reality, enhancing what the wearer is viewing by projecting a high resolution image onto the lens of the glasses, perhaps enlarging text or allowing the person to zoom in on a faraway scene. The glasses could also be connected to a captabase of people previously met, or a centralized store of capta, that is enabled by face-recognition software, so as to identify the people in vision and to provide subliminal or explicit cues on who the person is and how to act. Sensors and actuators in shoes react to foot form, terrain, and walking or running speed to absorb the most impact and support joints. A wristwatch not only tells the time but measures pulse, body heat, and blood pressure to monitor stress levels, all of which is logged and stored in a compressed form. Bluetooth enabled, it will also communicate with a cell phone to display text messages.

The individual arrives at home. The house's coordinating software system recognizes the person remotely from an identity tag (such as an RFID) and after a quick authenticating fingerprint scan on the door handle, it is automatically unlocked and opens. The time of the door being unlocked and who enters is logged. On entering the house, the lights come on as necessary and a small mirror display in the hallway subtly indicates the presence of other family members in the dwelling, their location, and their activity. As the person walks into the kitchen, a wall surface acts as a screen displaying any new messages. The person places a meal into the microwave, and the 2D bar code communicates to the machine the optimal cook settings. The person loads dirty laundry into the washing machine, and the RFID labels on the clothes inform the machine of the appropriate wash cycle. The person verbally tells the house's coordinating software systems that they will want to take a bath shortly at the usual temperature setting. Next, the person deals with messages. To add the contact of a potential client from that afternoon to the person's address book, the prospect's business card is placed next to the screen and the details are transferred electronically and stored for future use.

This kind of scenario aims to make people information rich and able to make more informed decisions. While such scenes were very much science fiction a couple of decades ago, they are now actively being developed and prototyped. For example, companies are already developing wearable computing. Burton and Motorola were selling Bluetooth enabled jackets in 2004–2005, and Adidas marketed a running shoe that would respond to the runner's biomechanics (Greenfield 2006). Several university research labs, such as the MIT Media Lab, ePi Lab Toronto, Wearable Computing Oregon, and IfE Zurich, are working on prototype smart clothing, watches, accessories, and video enabled glasses. Much work has focused on military applications designed to improve the performance of soldiers and their safety. For example, the development of voice-activated, heads-up displays attached to helmets that can map overlays, including the real-time location of comrades, images from a camera mounted to a gun (that enables the soldier to see and fire round a corner without visibly exposing the body), and the results of face recognition processing of people at checkpoints, built-in communication devices, digital cameras, and GPS, as part of modular wearable computers that enable soldiers hands-free access to data and video (Rensing et al. 2002; Page 2007; Crane 2008). To date, companies such as Xybernaut, CDI, and ViA Inc. have tried to develop more mainstream commercial applications, but so far they have largely failed. Indeed, one must be wary of the exaggerated claims of the weapons industry surrounding the potential of techno-warriors and the role of code to somehow sanitize the embodied practice of killing on the battlefield (Graham 2007).

As detailed in chapter 8, companies and research labs are also seeking to envision and build the homes of the future. The goal, as with much previous domestic technology, is to increase convenience by delegating more components of routine tasks to machines. In most cases, software is used to enhance the functionality of domestic appliances and to ensure they work appropriately without explicit instruction from a human. In effect, the home is envisioned with a set of smart networked peripherals.

Other researchers in university labs and commercial companies are seeking to bring location-based services (LBS) to the mass market, building on the success of personal satnav systems provided by companies such as Garmin, NavTeq, and TomTom. Morville (2005) characterizes GPS navigation as Wayfinding 2.0—navigation that extends beyond human memory or analog aids by tracking in real time the path taken while providing person-centered directions to a location. LBS adds significantly more capta to the system by enabling the mapped environment to act as a geographical interface to spatially relevant information about that environment. For example, by clicking on part of the map that represents a particular feature—such as a town or a building—contextual information regarding that place can be offered and locationally relevant responses and feedback given. Querying a train station would list the services leaving and arriving over the next couple of hours; querying a museum would provide details about the current exhibition, opening times, and admission charges; looking at a store could link to its online catalog. LBS envelops people within an "ambient findability," wherein the environment surrounding them is rendered transparent to enquiry and interaction—a world in which we can find anyone or anything from anywhere at anytime (Morville 2005). (Note, this of course resonates with deep-seated modernist fantasies of the individual being able to make the world into an ordered and knowable place working in service of their need.) In effect, software enables navigating the world to become a means of navigating information.

It is envisioned that consumers will be empowered by everyware technologies through the provision of richer information concerning the products that they buy. As detailed in chapters 4 and 9, it is projected that consumers will be able to easily query the ingredients or components of a consumer good, examine their history, the conditions under which the product was manufactured, or its capacity to be recycled (see chapter 11). In addition, it will be trivial to track and trace the use and location of things owned. For example, a mislaid pen could be easily located, queried as to when it was bought, how much it cost, the name of the pen design, and how much ink is left. Clearly this is useful to a certain degree, but also introduces unnecessary and largely redundant surveillance.

There are many other potentially socially productive applications of everyware for individuals and communities. For example, with respect to environmental monitoring, networks of sensors will be able to monitor different land-based ecosystems, the oceans, and the atmosphere, and relay information in real time about their status (Butler 2006). This kind of information might have a positive effect on communal consciousness about resources, and could aid democratic decision making (Dennis

2008). We can also envision a network of sensors in hospitals or homes that constantly scan the air, surfaces, water, and food for germs, viruses, and contagious diseases and various forms of pollution, with automated software analysis that can alert people when pathogens are detected or when thresholds are exceeded. For example, water faucets might scan and test the quality of the water supply as the water flows through them, alerting users if there is a problem; this clearly plays on the common discourses of hygiene and contamination that are entrenched in social psychology, along with more consumerist desire for health and well-being.

Securitization through Everyware

Clearly, one of the main implications of the development of everyware is that it opens up the possibility of widening and sharpening surveillance. Everyware encompasses the threat of universal panopticon (of being monitored at all times in all places), or at the very least, a series of strongly overlapping oligopticons covering many more aspects of everyday activities. Indeed, the preeminent discursive driver in the development of everyware technologies is the rhetoric concerning enhanced safety and security, especially with respect to reducing crime and tackling the threat of terrorism. Everyware promises new opportunities to monitor, link, and make sense of the interactions, transactions, and mobilities of people, goods, and information, at a spatial and temporal resolution previously impossible: to produce a dense, spatialized, rhizomic assemblage of oligopticons that will enable its users to know simultaneously and in the near real time the what, when, and where of everything in the world. Here, a key goal is anticipatory governance (Budd and Adey 2009), wherein three overlapping technologies—those that identify, those that read, and those that interpret—work in unison to create a fine-grained net of automated management (see chapter 5).

If we project this forward, we can imagine a world in which every action is monitored on an ongoing basis and actively shaped by different privileges and entitlements. In the home of this future world, all the activities and every conversation of the occupants would be visible, recordable, and analyzable by software. The household management system would note what time each person went to bed and woke the next morning, and movement patterns between rooms. The system would track the use of appliances; what each person ate, and the intake of any toxins, junk food, or excessive stimulants. The system would note the standard of personal hygiene of each person, the information browsed, television watched, and the e-mail read, written, and sent, as well as discussions on the phone and their content.

Passivity can also be observed in an everyware home; when everything electrical and mechanical (switches, locks, handles) registers a digital event, the periods of human *inactivity* will be as obvious to software as periods of activity. Software might also be able to provide a plausible model of a person's emotional and psychological state from all the observed physical activity and inactivity. This information could be evaluated automatically to dynamically adjust health insurance payments, carbon taxes, charge for services used, or even discipline for inappropriate behavior.

Similarly, on the daily commute to work, the car and the road system could monitor how the driver is behaving, whether the rules of the road were obeyed, and note the route taken for the purposes of warranty protection, law enforcement, and insurance and toll payments. If the journey is by public transportation, then automatic payment procedures or face-recognition software, or other biometric readers, would record the time and route of the journey for the purposes of billing and public safety. At work, keystrokes, access, and alterations to files, movements within and between buildings, and conversations at meetings and in corridors would all be automatically monitored and used to evaluate work efficiency, productivity, and standards, and to reshape behaviors to those required by the company. In the supermarket, shoppers would automatically be identified, their movement around the store would be tracked, and all the items picked would be monitored regardless of whether they were later purchased; and what is bought would be recorded. This is a world in which spaces of anonymity are negated by everyware and contemporary notions of privacy evaporates; as such, the "disappearance of disappearance" is a genuine possibility (Haggerty and Ericson 2000, 619).

In the world of everyware, intensive surveillance would not be confined to individuals, but also to the manufacture, distribution, use, and disposal of objects. For example, it has been hypothesized that the logical end point of coded objects are spimes (Sterling 2005). A *spime* is a wholly new kind object for which there is an entire recorded history stretching from design and manufacture to disposal/recycling. Such histories will include deep details on: (1) everything used to make, process, and distribute that object, plus protocols for safe and sustainable disposal, (2) everyone and everything that has come into contact with that spime during its lifetime, (3) the context of making and use, including labor relations, cost and profit margin, carbon tax, and patents. In other words, a spime is an object that has a full genealogy wherein the entire actor-network of a thing is knowable and indexical, which, Sterling (2005, 11) asserts, means they are "material instantiations of an immaterial system . . . [they] begin and end as data."

Although no spimes presently exist, there are projects and programs being developed that might be might be termed proto-spimes; that is, they invest objects with spime-like capacity, although their capacities exist external to the thing being recorded. For example, there have been a number of projects to make transparent the full extent of food production (see chapter 9; Buhr 2003; Popper 2007). With respect to agriculture, these are moving beyond existing farm-to-fork tracking systems to much more granular tracing that aims to follow livestock from conception (that is, recording both parents and over time the lineage of all animals and how they were reared) to the consumer's home (through farms, slaughterhouses, logistics chains, and supermarkets). In the home of the future, domestic practice would consist of a rhizomic assemblage of spimes and a computationally rich building fabric whose entire history of use and adaptation is known—and known in a very particular and precise way. Sterling (2005) views such spimes as empowering—as providing consumers with information they can use to make informed decisions. Depending on who has access to the information generated, they could also become rich sources of surveillance capta.

Sousveillance through Everyware

The MyLifeBits system is designed to store and manage a lifetime's worth of *everything*—at least everything that can be digitised.
—Jim Gemmell, Gordon Bell, and Roger Lueder

Sousveillance blends together ideas of personal empowerment and surveillance (Mann et al. 2003). It is the self-monitoring of one's personal life through surveillance technologies, consciously employed and controlled by an individual, with the resulting capta being used to help memorialize and manage one's life. The most common form of sousveillance under development is the notion of a life-log. A life-log is conceived as a form of everyware consisting of a unified, digital record an individual's experiences, captured multimodally through digital sensors and stored permanently as a personal multimedia archive. Activities will be seamlessly and unobtrusively captured by digital technologies that are always on, communicate with each other without human instruction or intervention, and are so pervasive that they cover all aspects of human activity and become so banal as to be unnoticed (CARPE 2004).

The aim of life-log developers is to provide a record of the past that includes every action, every event, every conversation, and every material expression of an individual's life—"the totality of information that flows through a human life" (Johnson 2003, 85)—with the ultimate goal being the simultaneous digitization of *all* cognitive inputs experienced by the brain (all five human senses), such that the life-log would be a digital *parallel* memory of the lived experiences of a person. This log would be augmented with capta not directly experienced, but held unconsciously as biological memories, such as physiological conditions inside the body (blood pressure and heart rate) and external conditions (orientation, temperature, and levels of pollution). All events would be accessible at a future date because a life-log would be a searchable and recallable archive (van Dijck 2005). Such life-logs will constitute new, pervasive sociospatial archives, because inherent in their construction will be a locational record; it will detail everywhere an individual has been.

In contrast to externally produced capta that constitutes surveillance, a life-log generates capta from an interior (or first-person) perspective, where the individual is seen through intimate technologies (that is, technologies that are in service to the individual, such as phones, car, fitness equipment, or wearable computers) with the capta pooled into a unified, multimedia archive that the person controls. Sousveillance is being complemented by scopophilic (the pleasure in looking and in being looked at) technologies—the conscious self-creation and public sharing of sousveillance, for example, through blogging and Web cams. At present, sousveillance capta is patchy in nature (in terms of what is actually captured), is not continuously collected (rather capta is only generated during use), and individual streams of capta are not being amalgamated into a single, unified life-log. Indeed, the retrieval and reuse of material memorialized is a complex set of practices.

The rationale for life-logging centers on changing the concept of personal computing from a computer for life to "memories for life" (Fitzgibbon and Reiter 2003). In particular, a life-log would: reduce physical clutter (there would be no need for photo albums, CDs, notepads, or books, because all would be stored in the life-log). The life-log would also allow the efficient managing of materialism and enhance domestic and individual productivity (it would be possible to know where every one of a person's possessions were and what conditions they were in). The life-log would enhance productivity and enjoyment of life by allowing the searching for and recalling of events and actions and enhance the management and recalling of frail memories, particularly in an aging population where there might be significant memory loss. The life-log would allow the self-monitoring of health conditions, stress levels, diet and fitness, and other aspects of daily life (systematizing and significantly deepening bodily performance monitoring regimes common across contemporary society; Schuurman 2004).

Significant progress is presently being made within the computer science community in exploring life-logging and the software tools needed to realize its vision. For example, an early project was that of Vemuri (n.d.), a researcher at the MIT Media Lab, who developed a personalized, sound logging system called "What was I thinking," that archives all of an individual's conversations and provides a means to usefully search the verbatim transcripts via visual interfaces. Another prototype, developed at the Microsoft Research Lab was SenseCam, a device which automatically took photographs of the person's environment in response to changing conditions (such as body motion, light levels, and temperature) (Williams and Wood 2004). It was "designed to act like a black box for the human body" (Twist 2004), with a custom-built digital camera worn like a necklace, with an ultra wide-angle lens that captured a 132 degree view in front of the wearer. The results of *SenseCam* was a timeline of hundreds of photographs that log activities and spaces as they are encountered throughout the day, which can be interrogated alongside the sensor logs.

Life-logs pose significant implications to the recording of the present, and thus how the past is recalled as opposed to how it is remembered (Allen 2008; Dodge and Kitchin 2007b). Like surveillance more generally, sousveillance also raises a number of social and ethical questions concerning who would own life-logged capta, how it could be used, and the limits to what is captured. In relation to ownership, while the capta within a life-log would be autobiographical, and would be held by the individual, there are questions concerning access and control. For example, who would have the right to access the life-log, other than the creator? To what extent could the material be sequestered for legal cases, and what would the legal status of such material be? Would capta take on the same status as biological memories? Or would they be seen as *more* objective and true? What would happen when a discrepancy arises between the statements of individuals and the life-log's capta? Would any third parties be able to have access, such as government security agencies or employers? Would access by third parties (including legal use) be restrictive or nonrestrictive (for example, would all capta be available, or only selected portions either by date or by recording medium)? Would other people captured by the life-log have a claim to access its contents (such as a partner, friends, or work colleagues)? What would happen to the life-log at death? What would the inheritance rights be? Who would have control of a child's life-log? Would life-logs be voluntary, or could pressure or mandatory measures by the state force people to adopt them?

The vision of life-logs is that they capture all possible capta, storing it forever. It is not clear, however, to what extent a life-log could be editable, if at all. Should a life-log be modifiable like a diary entry or should it be a photographic image? Should portions be open to selective, permanent erasing? Or just deletion from view, but with the prospect of recovery? Further, should these acts of erasing or deleting themselves be witnessed and remembered by the life-log? Are there events and actions that should be excluded from capture or should there at least be an option to suspend recording? Should you be able to press pause on the life-log? Would an act of deletion or suspension itself be considered a sign of guilt, if the life-log were to be used in a court of law? Do all the mundanities of life really need to be captured for all eternity, such as cleaning the house, walking the dog, or daydreaming in the office? As Oscar Wilde (1988, 80) stated, "One should absorb the color of life, but one should never remember its details. Details are always vulgar." In addition, to what extent would it be possible to dupe the log, to unsettle the authenticity of the record? There is also a case to made for the personal and communal benefits of forgetting events. Accordingly, Allen (2008, 57) warns that "not only might an individual's own life-log problematically preserve a record of bad luck and mistakes, the life-logs of others with whom the individual has come into contact might do the same. Yet people typically have a legitimate moral interest in distancing themselves from commonplace misfortunes and errors. In order to create that distance, they need to be safe from memory: they need to forget and need others to forget, too."

The degradation of biological memory through normal aging or through cognitive disorders are traumatic experiences, as the evidence from forms of dementia and mental illness illustrate. Taking this into consideration, what would be the impact of accidental or deliberate damage to, or alteration through the planting of false "memories" into the life-log? Moreover, could the life-log be stolen and used, perhaps in the same way as stolen passports or identity cards? What would be the consequences for the person whose life-log was stolen—both emotionally and materially?

Some questions about the real-life aspects of trying to live in a life-logged world are starting to be thought through and questioned, for example in the work of digital artists. One of these, Lucy Kimbell, through her web site (www.lucykimbell.com), "I measure therefore I am" has undertaken an exhaustive quantitative personal audit— which includes her stock market style evaluation called *LIX*, "a weekly index that tracked [her] performance between 2002 and 03 by measuring financial, emotional, social, and environmental factors." Multimedia artist Ellie Harrison's projects include *Gold Card Adventures*, a self-logging of all her public transport journeys for a year, and the *Eat 22* project where everything she ate for the year after her twenty-second birthday was self-photographed, logged, and displayed online (www.ellieharrison.com). Another work is Alberto Frigo's visual-statistics project that questions human beings' banal dependence on technology through a very exacting type of logging. The project is "an ongoing experiment consisting of photographing each time my right hand uses an object in order to create my autobiography for self-reflection and enforcing my identity" (Frigo 2004, 52).

The Dangers of Everyware

You had to live—did live, from habit that became instinct—in the assumption that every sound you made was overheard, and except in darkness, every movement scrutinised.
—George Orwell

As we have detailed above, and in chapter 5, the use of software in everyday life is changing the how governance unfolds. New forms of regulatory technologies are qualitatively and quantitatively transforming the nature of surveillance, both deepening the level of discipline, and actively reshaping individual behaviors. Given the potential of everyware to widen and deepen the oligoptical nature of surveillance, it seems pertinent to question whether the work of code across daily practices is inevitably leading to an automated form of Big Brother? Taken from Orwell's novel *Nineteen Eighty-Four*, Big Brother is the name of a system of totalitarian social control where people live within an almost perfect panopticon that renders them amenable to constant surveillance and self-discipline from fear of betrayal, and accordingly differential access to work and consumption.

It is certainly the case that the automated management produced within an everyware future has the potential for creating something like a Big Brother scenario. As examined in chapter 5, the rollout of surveillance technologies, based upon captabases and software algorithms, in recent years has significantly increased the generation of capta about whole populations and extended individual capta shadows through time and across everyday domains of living. While a capta shadow is inevitable and necessary to be able to function in contemporary society (for example, to work legitimately and pay taxes, to access government services, to have a bank account and borrow money, to legally own and drive a car, to travel internationally, to receive medical treatment, or to buy most commodities, Clarke 1994b; Lyon 2002), the amount and type of capta generated extends well beyond that needed to assess responsible citizenship and facilitate democratic participation. Further, becoming a subject of surveillance systems can be inadvertent, unknown, or against a person's wishes (Greenfield 2006).

This would be extended further in a world populated by everyware, and is likely to occur through technologies that were not initially envisioned as fulfilling such a role. Again, this process of "control creep" (Innes 2001), wherein capta generated for one purpose is kept and reused for another is already in evidence in today's society. Control creep can perhaps be best seen in action with regard to the intensification of security screening and surveillance, including the rise of intensive profiling and biometric authentication, whereby capta generated for one purpose is then used to profile passengers, or capta held by one agency is then shared with another that previously had no rights to access it (Lyon 2003). In the former case, existing administrative identification and record-keeping infrastructures are being remodeled as part of generalized anti-terror surveillance and risk-reduction apparatus. For example, the London Congestion Charge system was sold to the public on the basis that the capta on license plates, generated automatically from a grid of cameras, would only be used for administering congestion charge payments between 7 a.m. and 7 p.m. during weekdays. However, it is now used twenty-four hours a day and is also available as an effective surveillance system for all forms of crime under the rubric of tackling security issues (Ford 2007).

There are genuine reasons to be concerned about control creep and pervasive surveillance, especially when accompanied by legislation that gives states and companies ever more rights to monitor people unencumbered by independent oversight and effective rights of redress. As Andrejevic (2007) notes, legislation post-9/11 in the United States, for example, the USA PATRIOT Act (2001), gave the government extended powers to observe U.S. citizens while at the same time making the nature of that monitoring exempt from the Freedom of Information Act. At present, there are still opportunities to hide in the crowd, but if workable face recognition software could be developed to scan whole streets and identify its occupants, and cross-reference that to itineraries of where people should be, then the specter of Big Brother would take a significant step nearer to reality.

If life-logs are added to this mix and are made accessible to third parties, then the nature of an individual's capta shadow becomes all-encompassing, opening the way for highly invasive profiling, social sorting, and pernicious disciplining effects. Life-log capta could extend social sorting practices, allowing for preferential treatment of customers and clients that maximizes profits and maintains the status quo, and penalizes those that fit certain profiles (Gandy 1993; Graham 2005; Lyon 2003). Moreover, there is the potential for personal indiscretions, idiosyncratic interests, and minor infractions of the law to be identified and criminalized, thus encouraging more rigorous, self-disciplining behavior, and the development of an ultra-conservative society (Blanchette and Johnson 2002). When every action is recorded for perpetuity, in a seemingly objective manner, and it is likely that the consequences will be realized, then a panopticon starts to become possibility. To address these issues, Greenfield (2006, 235) suggests that everyware must:

- Default to a mode that ensures physical, psychic, and financial safety
- Be self-disclosing (people should know they are in the presence of everyware)
- Be conservative of face (people should not lose dignity due to everyware)
- Be conservative of time (everyware should not introduce undue complications into everyday operations)
- Be deniable (people must have the ability to opt out, always and at any point of systems they own)

We have previously contended that systems of pervasive computing should be engineered from the beginning to include elements of forgetting (Dodge and Kitchin 2007b; see chapter 11). We argued that "forgetting is not a weakness or a fallibility, but is an emancipatory process that will free life-logging from burdensome and pernicious disciplinary effects" (p. 441). While Greenfield's six point plan and our own "ethics of forgetting," are both laudable notions, the extent to which they will be built into future systems is doubtful, given the history of surveillance and how states treat their citizens and corporations their customers.

Beyond the dangers of pervasive surveillance, everyware creates a situation of over-reliance on a range of interlinked and interdependent technologies. A catastrophic failure of everyware could lead to widespread economic and social paralysis as multiple systems fail in a cascade without manual alternatives (the RISKS list posts a growing range of examples of the unforeseen problems and sometime subtle failures of current software systems, http://catless.ncl.ac.uk/Risks). At a more localized scale, any object that is networked is open to hacking and reconfiguration, potentially creating havoc with home and personal appliances (Mitchell 2004). In addition, there are dangers concerning identity theft whereby tokens of identity can be used to access financial and other records, potentially causing serious harm to the finances and status of the victim; harm that is presently difficult to repair. Collateral damage is also caused by errors in capta generation so that innocent victims end up on no-fly lists, or are barred entry to countries, or are denied access to services. Such errors are presently not uncommon. For example, as detailed in chapter 7, air travel captabases are known to have substantial biographical errors (typos, nonupdates, and missing or misleading fields) and biometric errors.

The rollout of everyware risks overcomplicating aspects of daily life that at present are relatively straightforward. For example, a typical home still largely consists of a set of relatively autonomous technologies that perform specific domestic tasks. In a smart home, where these technologies become interlinked and work in conjunction with one another a new layer of backgrounded complexity would be introduced in the running of the household in order to provide certain efficiencies and benefits. In this case, if the home management system were to fail, many domestic practices could not proceed as intended. We presently experience such moments during rare power outages that highlight how dependent many domestic practices are on the availability of electricity.

For McCullough (2004) one of the dangers of everyware is the potential for introducing new levels of frustration and inconvenience into basic operations of people's lives—a proliferation of autonomous annoyances (things constantly trying to interfere in and mediate daily lives). The reason why there was a successful transition from manual and mechanical labor to electrically powered work was that there were significant gains in effort expended, time, scale, and convenience. For example, the washing machine gave significant benefits over washing clothes by hand, and the electric oven gave benefits to cooking compared to an open fire. Going the next step, and adding computational power to the washing machine and oven would need to deliver additional benefits without making their use more cumbersome or inconvenient. An appliance that comes with a hefty "how to" booklet for a machine that replaces a relatively simple task suggests excessive functionality. A straightforward dial or a couple of selection switches are not improved by being replaced by an overwhelming choice of menus, options, and check boxes on a screen. It is likely in such scenarios that many people will simply fall back on default settings that seem to work, a point echoed with earlier rounds of complex electronic home technology, such as the VCR where large numbers of people failed to program them successfully, and simply used them as basic playback devices (Rode, Toye, and Blackwell 2004).

Given the wholesale transfer to digital information storage, including people's own personal records such as financial statements or photographs with sentimental value, risks also exist with respect to file safety and security. Relying on software to keep digital media safe is often compounded because most people are poor at maintaining systematic backups, or any backup at all, and where these records are stored on a networked device they become potentially vulnerable to unauthorized remote access and theft.

Other than consumer resistance along political or ethical lines, a critical problem that everyware has to overcome in order to become truly embedded as an everyday background to ordinary life, is to be flexible enough to be contextually adaptable to the messy, contingent, and fluid circumstances through which people's daily lives unfold. To be able to deal with the moment-to-moment ways that problems are encountered and solved is much more complex than the representational models and evaluative algorithms in present day software systems. For McCullough (2004) everyware needs to be context sensitive for it to be useful and successful. Perhaps somewhat paradoxically, everyware cannot operate in a universal fashion, as if all places and people are the same, but rather needs situational protocols able to handle subtleties of local circumstances. For Dourish (2001), this means everyware has to be a form of social computing—software systems that are designed with human context in mind. Developing such social computing represents an enormous technical challenge.

The Partiality of Everyware

The networks of control that snake their way through cities are necessarily oligoptic, not panoptic: they do not fit together. They will produce various spaces and times, but they cannot fill out the whole space of the city—in part because they cannot reach everywhere, in part because they therefore cannot know all spaces and times, and in part because many new spaces and times remain to be invented.

—Ash Amin and Nigel Thrift

Given some of the potential dangers of everyware, it is perhaps fortunate that the software technologies of everyware, for the foreseeable future, will be unable to produce a panopticon—there will always be gaps and blind spots for a variety of reasons. As such, systems of software-enabled surveillance remain, and will continue to remain, oligoptical in nature. Although they will be more efficient and powerful, they will still be open to vertical and horizontal fragmentation.

For everyware to work effectively and efficiently as coded assemblages, technologies must be able to internetwork and the capta held within systems must have a high degree of interoperability. As Greenfield (2006) notes, however, even environments that are highly saturated with software-enabled technology largely operate as a constellation of separate systems as there are few established protocols to enable internetworking. For example, in chapter 8, very few of the codejects we detailed can presently communicate and interact with each other automatically; they simply interface with the home's occupants, who can transcribe and translate settings and information as necessary. And yet, the various devices embedded within an environment need to be able to talk to each other if the system is to become more than the sum of its codeject parts (McCullough 2004). Even if they did work in harmony, Greenfield (2006) notes that any assemblage would be so densely woven and complex that in the event of a breakdown it might not be possible to diagnose where the fault lies. As new software is rolled out over time, new problems emerge concerning how to effectively interface these with a diversity of legacy systems. Critical to the success of everyware, then, is the ability of each system in the assemblage to self-recalibrate when new devices are added (McCullough 2004). This is no easy task, especially as altering legacy systems is difficult given that its code is old, has been worked on by many programmers over time, and it is unlikely that any one person understands it well enough to make significant changes (Ullman 1997). The difficulties of keeping a contemporary PC running efficiently and securely as it tackles all manner of tasks is a taste of the coming challenges of making everyware a reality.

If we consider the issue of interoperability, there are large variations in the form, units, and standards of capta generated by different software systems that severely limit the ability to use records from one system in another, or to marry details from two different captabases. This is compounded by the fact that most captabases have some degree of error caused by mistakes at the capture stage. Addressing the issue of capta interoperability is not a trivial exercise given the vast proliferation of agencies and companies around the globe producing new software products that generate voluminous quantities of capta, often creating new formats and standards (see figure 10.5). (This is often due in part to the economic strategy of product development that seeks to lock in customers.) Even if these organizations worked closely with each other to ensure compatibility with regard to things such as capta formats and ontologies (often difficult because they are commonly in competition with each other); and if further international capta standards and conventions were put in place; even if national and transnational capta infrastructures that provide common frameworks and standards across borders and platforms were created; and if detailed metacaptabases (capta about capta) that document how proper records are created by different agencies and their attributes were produced, there would still be significant gaps in capta coverage and interoperability that would limit surveillance to be oligoptic in nature, rather than panoptic.

The partiality of present forms of surveillence can be seen with respect to the governance of driver behavior, vehicles, and roads, which is uneven in nature and experienced unequally. At a basic level, there is a marked variation in the extent to which automated technologies are deployed within driving infrastructures. At the macroscale, there are large variations among cities and countries, depending on government policy, institutional will, and spending regimes. For example, Britain has embraced to a much greater degree the rolling out of such infrastructure than, say, Ireland. And within Britain, London has had a disproportionate investment in such systems compared to other cities. In part, this is because of the severe congestion in the city and its strategic economic importance to the nation, but also because of wider antiterrorist initiatives. At a more local scale, major highways are much more likely

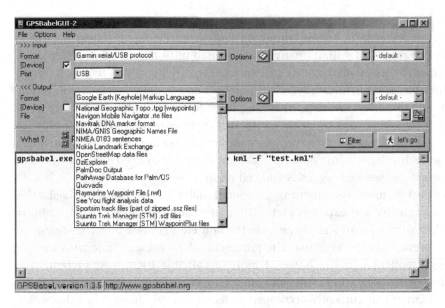

Figure 10.5

A prosaic example of the pragmatic constraints on everyware being built to handle the numerous formats for spatial capta, such as generated by GPS. Here, a purpose-built software tool called GPSBabel converts between many of the common formats.

to be surveyed and regulated through automated software systems than minor roads and residential streets. (These unwired places in the assemblage have often been subject to alternate, physical traffic calming, such as the disciplining of drivers through "dumb" features as road humps, chicanes, and width constrictions.) This is because the volume of traffic needs to be regulated with regard to flow and tolls. In addition, there is an uneven application across drivers and vehicles. For example, depending on age and previous penalties, drivers can be sorted by software with regard to insurance, or financing for buying vehicles. Newer and more expensive vehicles are more likely to be full of various coded systems relating to sophisticated engine management systems and GPS navigation tools (see Dodge and Kitchin 2007a). This partiality will continue for some time, if for no other reason than the cost to retrofit, monitor, and regulate the entire system, and the legacy effects of old vehicles and infrastructure.

We now look at the smart home example. The extent to which smart homes, as envisioned by some technologists, will come to fruition is doubtful. While it is evident that code is increasingly becoming part of everyday domestic life and does make a difference to how domestic practices unfold, any transition to the era of the smart home will take place over a long period of time (see chapter 8). With respect to the adoption of coded objects, many household tasks continue to be solved by analog appliances and tools that will, in many cases, be used until they need to be replaced. In other circumstances, coded objects are expensive luxury items that require a certain income, lifestyle, and technical literacy to purchase and operate (Rode 2006). Whole swaths of contemporary societies, including large segments in the West, live at or below the poverty line and only have sufficient income to meet essential bills for housing, fuel, and food. For these people, with little or no disposable income, many of the smart technologies being developed are not accessible or even desirable (though many personal gadgets such as iPods and cell phones are).

With respect to the development of computationally rich building materials, this will require extensive and expensive retrofitting of existing dwellings that is unlikely to be untaken without significant benefits to the household or else by force of external regulatory pressure (such as being a requirement of mortgage lenders/insurers or waste/energy reduction in the name of more sustainable living). At present, it is unlikely that such adaptations will offer such tempting benefits especially with the rapid redundancy that currently accompanies technological change. In other cases, people simply do not see the utility of living in homes that respond to them in new ways—they do not need or desire a home management system, they are content with their domesticity as it presently unfolds. Indeed, everyware sometimes seems like a technology that is being driven by what is technically feasible and the marketing engine of companies, rather than by a genuine demand among consumers. (To put this into perspective, the initial domestication of electricity also had to be heavily marketed as people did not see it as essential to daily life.) What this means is, as with the adoption of any set of technological innovations, the adoption of everyware will be uneven and unequal, both socially and geographically, depending on the person, the place, and changing circumstances.

Resisting Everyware

Everyware will also remain partial because its pernicious surveillance will be questioned and resisted by some people. Surveillance and automated management is contingent, relational, and negotiated in nature, and unfolds in multiple ways, shaped by how people interact with and resist the systems employed to survey and manage them. As Lyon (2007) notes, some people deliberately hide their faces from security cameras, falsify information, consciously switch devices off, and otherwise dissimulate, and negotiate with those that survey them. Surveillance is not a "static, relentless or unyielding process. . . . It is malleable, flexible, and the product of game-like processes . . . where the outcomes are far from determined in advance" (Lyon 2007, 165). Forms of resistance range from avoidance, partial compliance, subversion, and campaigning for wholesale change. Indeed, Marx (2003) details eleven different ways that surveillance is resisted by individuals (elements of which often work in unison).

Discovery   A person finding out if they are under surveillance (using some kind of detecting device).

Avoidance   The evasion of surveillance (taking a route that has no cameras) or not purchasing software-enabled versions of analog technologies.

Piggybacking   Using another person or object to avoid surveillance (following someone with a security pass through a secure door).

Switching   Using the identity of another person (using someone else's security pass to gain admittance through a secure door).

Distorting   Manipulating the results of surveillance so that they are misinterpreted (holding down a key so that it appears that a large number of keystrokes have been performed).

Blocking   Hiding a feature that might identify a person (wearing a hat or hooded sweatshirt that obscures the face).

Masking   Using a false identity (using a false name to access a web site).

Breaking/hacking   Vandalizing surveillance technology so it no longer works (placing something across the lens of a camera or attacking its supporting software with a virus).

Refusing   Refusing to impart a piece of information (refusing to fill out certain fields on an application).

Cooperation   A third party prevents or erases surveillance (a confederate removes the evidence of surveillance from the record).

Countersurveillance   Surveilling the surveillers in an effort to get them to limit their activities (making it widely known that a company is using surveillance to discriminate against customers; the aim of the counter-surveillance tactic would be to incite customers to move their business elsewhere).

Clearly these resistance techniques to surveillance depend, in part, on knowing when and where to deploy them. This is possible to some degree with partial and visible surveillance technologies, but much more problematic when software is used in capture systems where the practice is itself the means through which one is monitored (see chapter 5).

  If we examine systems which have heavily deployed software-enabled surveillance, all of these forms of resistance can be evidenced. For example, if we again consider the governance of driving and roads in the UK, an infrastructure that is heavily monitored and regulated through road taxes, licensing, insurance, and traffic management systems, we can see wholesale resistance and subversion in actions such as driving above the speed limit in unmonitored areas, avoiding routes that are actively monitored, driving a stolen vehicle, driving without paying tax and insurance, using false plates, using GPS enabled technologies to give advance warning of detection devices, vandalizing speed cameras, claiming that the vehicle was being driven by someone else, hacking car code to alter a vehicle's performance, and using homemade, illegal "traffic signal pre-emption devices" to alter traffic light sequences, and the vandalizing of cameras (Dodge and Kitchin 2007a). The extent to which the system is partial in its actions and effectiveness varies between activities, but as an illustration, estimates put the extent of uninsured driving in the UK at one vehicle in twenty (DfT 2004). These individual actions are being complemented by wider protests against some technologies, such as the vocal campaigns against speed cameras in the UK, which have argued that employment of automated management is more about local revenue raising than improving road safety.

Conclusion

In this chapter, we have considered how the current state of play with regard to the embedding of software into everyday life, might evolve into everyware—that is, the calculative capacity of code being distributed and available at any point on the planet. Everyware seeks to transform people's experience by producing interactions with software that "feel natural, spontaneous, human" (Greenfield 2006, 1). It is clear that the development of everyware will consist of the interweaving of a number of related forms of software—pervasive, ubiquitous, sentient, tangible, wearable computing—that all seek to transform how we interact and live with code. A core objective is to produce calm technology—software that people are comfortable using because it is so easy to interface with that it becomes a normal, unconscious practice. In so doing, it fades into the background, becoming part of the everyday experience. We have illustrated what such a future might look like by examining, in brief, everyware in relation to the discourses and materialities of empowerment, securitization, and sousveillance.

In the second part of the chapter, we examined some of the dangers and social risks associated with a state of everyware, and the extent to which everyware as envisioned by some commentators might come to fruition. Pervasive surveillance and sousveillance has the potential to produce a society that never forgets—that has a permanent sociospatial archive of trillions of events across a whole population, traceable through space and time; a detailed spatialization of the history of everything, everywhere. Paradoxically, everyware could well complicate life and introduce new technological hazards at the same time it seeks to make life simple and reduce risk. Some aspects of everyware are likely to become a standard part of everyday life, especially in cities, such as wireless access to networks. Cell phone coverage is already widespread in many countries, providing increasing seamless access to software systems regardless of location. The embedding of code into infrastructure and the rollout of smart management systems is likely to be much more uneven and unequal in access. The extent to which different software systems and captabases, produced for dissimilar reasons at different times, can become highly interoperable and adaptive to new additions is questionable. Further, aspects of everyware will be resisted in a variety of ways by individuals and communities. As a result, everyware, while striving to be universal in nature, will inevitably be partial.

11 A Manifesto for Software Studies

The longer a system has been running, the greater the number of programmers who have worked on it, the less any one person understands it.
—Ellen Ullman

You think you know your computer, but really all you know is a surface on your screen.
—Annette Schindler

More work is needed on understanding computer code and our current tools and methodologies are limited in trying to unpack its production, meaning, circulation and reception.
—David M. Berry

In this book, we have offered an analysis of software and its role in the unfolding practices of everyday life. We have not sought to provide a theory as to how computing and computation should be developed; rather, our aim has been to detail a set of ideas for thinking about software and its relations—how it is constitutive of, situated in, and does work in, the world. Strangely, this type of analysis has only begun to occur in the last decade or so, with the nascent formation of software studies. It is true that there has been plethora of research and literature about software, and the formation of new disciplines and fields such as computer science, human–computer interaction, artificial intelligence, Internet studies, information science, and software systems engineering, which have mirrored the development and growth of software-enabled technologies, systems, and products. And yet, these works are strangely silent in many respects, tending to focus on the development of software from an engineering-centered perspective and the social, economic, political, and cultural impacts of software-enabled technologies, as opposed to the software that enables such technologies. Where scholarship has examined in some depth the relations between software and people, it has tended to concentrate on individual cognitive and ergonomic aspects, drawing in particular from psychology and health-related disciplines, along with media research focused on the conceptualization of software in terms of social communication or economic transactions. Software studies differs from these other fields in that it focuses analysis explicitly on the conceptual nature, and productive capacity of software, and its work in the world, from a critical social scientific and cultural perspective. As Manovich (2004, 6) notes, "if we don't address software itself, we are in danger of always dealing with effects rather than causes, the output that appears on a computer screen rather than the programs and social cultures that produce this output."

By concentrating attention on the code itself, software studies seeks to create a theoretically and empirically rich understanding of software and its radically diverse constitution and growing contribution to social life. Rather than focus purely on the technical, it fuses the technical with the philosophical to raise questions about what software is, how it comes to be, its technicity, how it does work in the world, how the world does work on it, why it makes a difference to everyday life, the ethics of its work, and its supporting discourses. Software studies then tries to prise open the black boxes of algorithms, executable files, captabase structures, and information protocols to understand software as a new media that augments and automates society.

Code/Space and the literature we have drawn upon represent an initial foray into conceptualizing software as a vital source of social power. *Code/Space* further provides philosophical and analytical tools for making sense of code. Our aim has been to add to this growing body of knowledge in a general sense, considering in detail the nature of software, the relationship between code and objects, the effects of code on changing modes of governance, and how code can engender novel creative practices. We are also interested in exploring how code offers new possibilities to empower people. In so doing, we have argued for an ontogenetic conceptualization of software that works to destabilize the notion that code has a stable ontology, instead conceiving of code as contributing to unfolding practices; its work always in the process of becoming. Such a move recognizes that software is both a diversely created product and a key producer of social relations, with the relationship between software and society understood as a hybrid assemblage that is contingent, relational, productive, and made in the moment. In particular, we have argued for the creation of a set of knowledge that takes space, as well as time, seriously. Software is thoroughly spatial in its production and work, transducing complex spatialities.

Given the nascent state of software studies, there is much more work to be done to extend, deepen, and refine the analytical tools available for researchers and to explore and examine the various facets of software and everyday life. In the rest of this chapter, we set out a brief manifesto for the kinds of work we believe necessary in the coming years. This manifesto is inevitably preliminary and partial, framed by our own knowledge and ideological vision of the world. It is therefore also an invitation to others to reenvision and extend.

How Code Emerges

It seems to us that software is largely understood from an engineering and organizational point of view. Social analyses tend to focus on the consequences of computerization, rather than how software emerges and does work in the world. And yet, software is not simply a technical device. Software is both a product and a process. As we detailed in chapter 2, software is the product of a sociotechnical assemblage of knowledge, governmentality, practices, subjectivities, materialities, and the marketplace, embedded within contextual, ideological, and philosophical frames, and it does diverse and contingent work in the world.

In designing and writing software, developers make, on the one hand, critical, ontological decisions about what to capture, categorize, and represent in the world. On the other hand, developers make epistemological decisions about the relations between capta and how they should be processed to beckon into being actions in the world. Developers often unconsciously place a particular philosophical frame on the world that renders it amenable to the work of code and algorithms, thus realizing a specific system of thought to address a particular relational problem. As a consequence, the consistent and automated generation of precise forms of capta has become a tremendously important business because it provides the raw material that code works upon, often transducing it into information. But what does it mean for society when the capta and apparatus that underpins critical decision making is based on a constricted set of criteria designed to satisfy the limitations of algorithmic processing? What are the implications of reducing the world to a small ontological subset and a sequence of algorithms? Does the sensibility of a relatively small cadre of programmers become the overriding blueprint for future everyday social relations? Will defaults in code become the defaults for living? And what are the consequences of algorithmic processes that are so complex and opaque that even their designers are unsure as to how an outcome was arrived at (which seems to be the case for some pattern recognition software used in passenger profiling)? Indeed, unpredictable outcomes and unforeseen circumstances are a major cause of software glitches and system failures.

While we and others have made a start in exploring the nature of software, there is much research and appraisal to be done in terms of working through how to conceptualize code and its work. It seems to us that there is a critical need for more detailed ethnographic studies of how developers produce code, and the life of software projects, in order that we can build a better understanding of the ways in which software is diversely created and unfolds within contextual frames. At present, there are only a handful of in-depth studies that examine the complexities of how code is produced as a collaborative manufacture between programmers with diverse subjectivities, abilities, and worldviews, and corporations and institutions with particular philosophies, ambitions, and resources, and shaped by the market and the vagaries of investment finance. There is not enough research on how code is scripted through collective cycles of drafting, editing, compiling, and testing, or how it is produced in relation to a specification that is constantly being tweaked by programmers, shaped by outside audiences, and consumed by the public. There is also a need to develop a subarea of software studies—algorithm studies—that carefully unpicks the ways in which algorithms are products of knowledge about the world and how they produce knowledge that then is applied, altering the world in a recursive fashion.

An example of this type of research is Mackenzie's (2009) analysis of an esoteric but essential algorithm known as Viterbi that provides the guts of digital signal processing essential to the operation of cell phones, along with a growing array of other wireless devices that are at the vanguard of pervasive computing. He applies the Deleuzian notion of "envelopment" to conceptualize how this algorithm creates calculative spaces characterized by change that is always changing, what he calls "intensive movement." In other words, these are types of spaces in flux that cannot be mapped in certain terms, but can only be guessed at in probabilistic ways; they are spaces existing more in an unseen quantum universe than in the experienced fixity of Newtonian space. The enveloping radio spaces swirling around, between, and through the spaces populated by people's cell phones exhibit this intensive movement with ever changing patterns of congestion and contestation between signals that inevitably overlap, disrupt, and inhibit each other. Yet the Viterbi algorithm is able to make sense of the intensive movements in real time because it "assume[s] that we can only hope to determine the most probable series of sent signals" (Mackenzie 2009, 1303) which is at odds with "the images of strict determinism sometimes associated with digital technologies" (p. 1304). The work of this algorithm, which is now largely taken for granted, means that the phone in one's pocket receives only one clear connection, despite being in the midst of a cacophonous tumult of competing, continuously changing signals. In short, the Viterbi algorithm is creating the fundamental conditions in which communicative practices (a phone call or text) takes place.

How Code Performs

Code does work in the world. It has has technicity; it divulges and affords new kinds of automated agency, opening up new possibilities and determinations. Software is an increasingly capable actant performing in the world; it makes a difference to how people solve problems in a variety of intended and unintended ways, unfolding contingently and relationally with respect to prevalent conditions and contexts. While there has been voluminous research examining how computer technologies and digital infrastructures are reshaping everyday life, there has been relatively little focus on the role of software in such reconfigurations. That is not to say that what has been done is not useful and valuable. We simply find it surprising that there has not been much more research specifically focused on the messy and detailed enrollments and effects of code itself given the extent to which coded objects, infrastructures, and processes are ever more folded into everyday life, creating new coded assemblages. As a result, we believe that a core agenda for software studies is to produce detailed case studies of how software does work in the world, and to develop theoretical tools for describing how and explaining why, and the effects, of that work.

In this book, we have undertaken some broad brushstroke analysis with respect to how software is reshaping travel, home life, and consumption, but the kinds of study we are envisioning would be significantly more comprehensive and systematic pieces of work based on extensive fieldwork and empirical analysis that would tease out in detail the contextual ways in which code reshapes practices with respect to industry, transportation, consumption, governance, education, entertainment, and health. It would also need to be sensitive to place and scale, cultural histories, and modes of activity (for example, a study comparing the effects of code in rural Ireland and urban Manchester). Such in-depth code studies will provide a richness of observation and insight for scholars to better understand and explain how code makes a difference in those contexts. Again, we have sought to provide some initial theoretic insights and interpretations. We have argued that code makes a difference to the nature of objects because it imbues them with the capacity to do additional and new types of work. We have noted that code alters everyday spatiality because it has technicity to alternatively modulate how space unfolds. In addition, we have explored how code reconfigures governance because it enables new modes of regulation and automated management. We have further highlighted how code creates new forms of knowledge production, creative practice, and processes of innovation. We would consider these to be preliminary readings that require further refinement; initial forays to make sense of code's work. There is clearly much more to be done to sharpen and extend such interpretations, or to replace them with more nuanced and sophisticated insights.

How Code Seduces and Disciplines

We have made the case that code is rapidly moving to a state of pervasiveness in some aspects of daily life because it both seduces and disciplines people. Code interpellates people to its logic, wherein they voluntarily and willing submit to the agency of software. In fact, they often desire and embrace the framework of software, because it offers them real benefits with respect to convenience, efficiency, productivity, flexibility, and creativity. In short, software has the capacity to make society safer, healthier, richer, and more enjoyable. At the same time, code disciplines people by making them enact certain grammars of action and enforcing more pervasive modes of surveillance, automated management, and self-disciplining. People thus offset new forms of regulation against the benefits gained. As such, many consumers willingly trade aspects of their privacy for a service in the name of their own empowerment (Andrejevic 2007). Of course, such a trade works so long as consumers are aware that a trade is occurring and do feel empowered, the terms of service remain favorable, there is choice that enables them to transfer to another service, or people are content to live with the consequences of heightened forms of regulation. In some arenas, such as air travel and identity cards, this balance is constantly being renegotiated as the regulators push for ever greater compulsion to generate ever more capta.

One of the key factors in mediating this balance, and how people view and understand code, are the discursive regimes that surround it, and the work that it performs. There is a powerful and consistent set of discourses that promote and support the deployment of software across a whole series of domains. These discourses include safety, security, efficiency, anti-fraud, empowerment, productivity, reliability, flexibility, economic rationality, and competitive advantage. Some of these discourses gained significant robustness with increased securitization in the war on terror and the drive to stimulate economic growth through the creation of a so-called knowledge economy founded on software-enabled technologies. These ideas are challenging to counter because it seems counterintuitive to articulate a position that seems to be premised on being less safe, less secure, less productive, provide less choice, and more inconvenience. Such positions seem illogical and lacking common sense. That is not to say, however, that such discourses are not actively questioned and resisted by individuals, critical scholars, activist groups, and organizations, or that all parties promulgating such lines necessarily agree wholly on their aims or how certain goals are to be achieved. Indeed, it is often the case that there are significant internal differences between supposed allies, particularly where a software project cuts across competing agendas (for example, state security versus business flexibility).

To date, there has been relatively little research that has systematically examined how software seduces (or fails to seduce) people while simultaneously disciplining them. Further, there has not been enough detailed comparative exploration of the discursive regime of different software products and system configurations in separate locations (for example, Heathrow versus Dublin airport). Such research is necessary, we believe, if we are to more fully understand the role and effect of software in society. What is desirable are a number of in-depth case studies that examine how and why people adopt and submit to certain software products. This research should fully plot the complex and contingent ways that people understand and react to the discursive and affective fields surrounding software-enabled technologies. Further, this research should explore how people subtly balance the benefits of use against the negatives (the automated "gifts" associated with loyalty cards against profiling and targeted marketing); and how they both use and resist software-enabled technologies (submit to airport security but simultaneously question the rules, and perhaps transgress procedures in some way). Of course, this social scenario is complicated because much of the work of code remains hidden from view and people are subject to its processing without fully knowing what is being performed. Even when people are knowingly subjected to algorithmic profiling (for example, at an airport when an immigration officer swipes a machine-readable passport) they are in a subordinate position and lacking details on how to challenge the decision.

In addition, there is a need to examine the ways in which discursive regimes are assembled over time by a variety of vested interests—government, corporations, and civil society—through different forums such as advertising, media coverage, online media, letters, statements, signs, and staff training. It is also important to piece together how the dynamic of different voices internal to the regime unfolds, and how the discursive regime is supported by legislation and quasi-legal conventions that legitimate the governmentality that code enacts. Other avenues to explore include how the discourses promoted are countered by those that question their logic and social implications, and how the interchange between these sides unfolds to shape how software is developed, deployed, and received. As illustrated by the debates over issues such as identity cards and a national identity database (in the UK), and electronic voting machines (in Ireland), the discursive landscape around software can change markedly over time, and just because the technology is available, does not mean that it will necessarily be employed.

How to Code Ethically

Code and the prospect of an era of everyware raises manifold social, political, and ethical questions, not least with respect to the regulation of everyday life and the alteration of the conditions through which life unfolds. While code has the authority to empower individuals, at its logical extreme, individuals may come to live in an almost fully panopticon society, with internal sousveillance reflected into intensive endogenous surveillance.

Whether such a situation comes to pass, only time will tell; but it is important to think through the ethics of code: how should the world be captured in code to minimize negative impacts, and how might code do work in the world that is beneficial to the largest number of people? What capta can be generated with respect to individuals? How should such capta be stored and processed? How should such capta be employed? Who should have the power to use such capta? What would it be like to live in a world without anonymity or privacy? What would it mean to live in a society where there is a permanent and lifelong record of all manner of actions, deeds, and misdemeanors? To date, these kinds of questions have largely been avoided by many technologists because they are complex and difficult to think through and answer, but nonetheless these and related issues need to be examined in detail in order to consider how society and its spatialities should be managed and regulated. Elsewhere (Dodge and Kitchin 2007b) we have suggested that one path toward such an exploration is to construct an ethics of forgetting in relation to pervasive computing.

In such an ethics, we contend, the trend toward technologies that "store and manage a lifetime's worth of everything" should always be complemented by forgetting. Schacter (2001) details six forms of human forgetting, three concerned with loss, and three with error. Loss-based forgetting consists of transience (the loss of memory over time), absent-mindedness (the loss of memory due to distractedness at the time the memory relates to); and blocking (the temporary inability to remember—"it's on the tip of my tongue"). Error-based forgetting consists of misattribution (assigning a memory to the wrong source), suggestibility (memories that are implanted either by accident or surreptitiously), and bias (the unknowing or unconscious editing or rewriting of experiences). Schacter (2001) notes one other problem with memory—persistence, the recalling of events that would rather be forgotten.

Following the discussion in chapter 10, one can consider such forgetting in relation to ethical dilemmas posed by life-logging software whose developers seem to seek ubiquitous and "merciless memory" (Galloway 2003), and which seek to overcome both problems of loss and error in human memory. Life-log tools and software aim to produce a perfect digital record of events and activities that would not decay or fade; distractedness would be minimized through automated cross-referencing of life-log sources; and blocking would be minimized by intuitive retrieval and visualization capabilities. A life-log would minimize errors because the technology would not be open to misattribution, suggestibility, or bias—it would be an exact capta record of what the sensor witnessed and would not be open to reinterpretation and reworking. Moreover, the life-log would be augmented through the recording of detail beyond what an individual notices or knows. For example, each memory would be augmented by exact time-space coordinates, and possibly other environmental variables such as temperature, humidity, and physiological aspects such as heart rate. Moreover, it would add order, precision, completeness, multiple angles (taken from different sensor technologies to provide a multimedia memory), instantaneous recall of the whole archive, searchability, and filtering, and allow analysis (such as cross-referencing, charting of temporal development, producing value-added multimedia recollections, and plotting space-time patterns of activities) to what human memory or existing memory technologies (such as a photo album) can achieve. In other words, the life-log would not forget and would also augment through added detail.

Despite these qualities, which at first might appear to be significant benefits, we feel that the panoptic memory of such life-logs are highly problematic because they record without discretion. We see forgetting, therefore, not as a weakness or a fallibility, but as an emancipatory process that can free people from being swamped by excessive capta gathering and pernicious disciplinary effects. As Nietzsche suggests, forgetting will save humans from history (Ramadanovic 2001), because "forgetting turns out to be more benefit than bereavement, a mercy rather than malady . . . for no individual or collectivity can afford to remember everything" (Lowenthal 1999, xi). Forgetting allows people to be fallible, to evolve their social identities, to live with their conscience, to deal with "their demons," to move on from their past and build new lives, to reconcile their own paradoxes and contradictions, and to be part of society. This is why we suggest that a society with software systems that never forget and forgive has the potential to become a totalitarian regime.

Perhaps, in the process of designing and implementing more ethically orientated life-logging software, aspects of forgetting should be an integral part of any system. For us, this should happen from the bottom up and be a core feature of the life-log algorithms, rather than from the top down, wherein legislation or organizational policy is used to regulate "perfect" life-logs. So, rather than focus on the prescriptive needs for privacy protections to try to make everyware more ethically acceptable, we envision necessary processes of forgetting, following Schacter's (2001) six forms, that should be in-built into the code, ensuring a sufficient degree of imperfection, loss, and error. For us, this strategy of coding with ethics in mind would make the system humane and yet still useful.

Let us consider the case of a life-log of a journey across a city. Transience could be achieved by ensuring the fading or loss of details over time proportional to the length of time lapsed between capta generation and the present. Just as a person would simply start to forget parts of the journey, so the life-log captabase would gradually and subtly degrade the precision of the record with time.

Absent-mindedness could be ensured by having distractedness built into the sensing firmware of capta generation. The log would record the whole journey, but miss out certain pieces of capta because a recording media was switched off or was directed at something else.

Blocking could be incorporated at the time the life-log was being queried. At other times, the query could be answered with no problems.

Misattribution could be achieved algorithmically by the specific misrecording of part of an event, but not the whole event. For example, part of a journey would be randomly misattributed (having a coffee in Starbucks rather than Caffe Nero), but the overall journey in terms of traveling from A to B is correct. In other words, misattribution is meaningful in relation of time, space, and context. It is not the adding of false memories, but rather the tweaking of a past event.

Suggestibility could consist of the plausible rescripting of certain events after a particular time by software. Here, part of the journey would take a subtly different, but believable, route (taking street A rather than street B).

Lastly, bias could consist of rewriting all events based on pattern recognition; it could rescript the capta in line with past behavior, decisions, and preferences to create a record that would be consistent and plausible but subtly different. The journey could be an impression of the route rather than a perfect recording, highlighting the things seemingly more important; it would then become a memory and not a recording. Over time, the extent of suggestibility or bias could increase, adding a degree of uncertainty into the capta. Overall, then, a range of algorithmic strategies could be envisioned such as erasing, blurring, aggregating, injecting noise, perturbing data, and masking, that could be used to upset the life-log records.

While building fallibility into the system seemingly undermines life-logging, it seems to us that a fallible life-log, underpinned by an ethics of forgetting—an ethics that works at both the micro level (the individual level, being able to live with yourself) and the macro level (the collective level, being able to live in a society)—is the only way to ensure that people can forget, can rework their past, can achieve political growth and change based upon debate and negotiation, and can ensure that disciplining does not occur. Clearly, there is much scope for further normative thinking in terms of the fundamental design philosophies for everyware systems.

Full consideration of the ethics of code will also require other analyses that focus on the oversight and accountability of those employing code to enact forms of managerialism and regulation. To date, companies in the West such as cell phone operators and Internet service providers and content providers have mainly sought to use strategies of self-regulation to avoid overly punitive regulation by legislators. These are often accompanied by legal safeguards that determine what capta can be generated, stored, manipulated, used, and sold. As a result, data protection acts are already commonplace, as are legal standards regarding capta and its generation. However, given the range of new forms of capta such as life-logs, the potential misuses of such capta need to be charted, and the reach and effectiveness of such legislative control needs to be constantly monitored and amended accordingly. Indeed, the effectiveness of data projection laws has been limited for various reasons. These laws tend to be framed in ways inherently supportive of an institution's rights to collect data; compliance to regulation is often poorly policed; and enforcement for failures to comply typically do not relate to the individual damage caused. It is important that scholars undertake other such studies in normative ethics to fully consider how people want code as part of their lives. The alternative is, as Lessig (1999) notes, that code becomes law.

A Selection of Methods for Undertaking Software Studies

It would be unhelpful to be too prescriptive with regard to the detailed methodologies used to uncover the ways in which software emerges or how code works in the world.

Rather, we feel that a wide range of social science methodologies could be profitably brought to bear on the issue as appropriate to the philosophical lens used to understand the world. For us, that means using techniques that focus on the processes and practices of code, and which reveal its discursive and material constitution and effects. It also requires sensitivity to the issues of scale of observation necessary to capture the small moments of software transduction, and the hard-to-discern citational patterns of code. We are aware that in this book, we have mainly worked at the macro scale, mapping out at a relatively coarse level how software makes a difference to everyday life. This has been borne of necessity in order to provide a broad, accessible, and synoptic overview. There is, however, a pressing need for high quality analysis undertaken at the micro scale, mapping out the mundane and everyday practices of coding, and the embedding of software into everyday places. Analysis also needs to be undertaken into the ways that code mediates formerly analog activities including people's routine interactions, and how software vendors, the government, and other interest groups seek to promote and legitimate a coded approach to a diverse range of issues.

For us, the kinds of methods we would like to see applied include genealogies, ethnographies, observant participation, and envisioning using mapping and spatialization techniques. With respect to the first suggestion, we are interested in the creative application of a genealogical method from a Foucaultian perspective that seeks to trace out the contingent unfolding of a system of thought or set of actions rather than produce a rational, teleological historiography. In other words, we think there would be much merit in constructing as full as possible genealogies of the multiple, complex, and sometimes contradictory or paradoxical iterations of software projects—the evolution and contextual and contingent unfolding of ideas, decisions, constraints, actions, and actors that shaped their development. Through such an analysis, we can start to trace out over time the ways in which ontological frames emerge and become codified in algorithms, code has been produced, and software has seeped into everyday use.

Let us focus on the genealogy of algorithms. We believe it would be instructive to conduct a detailed archeology of how algorithms come to be constructed—to excavate the social lives of ideas into code—and how an algorithm then translates and mutates across projects to be reemployed in diverse ways. Such a genealogy would generate valuable insight into the coded production of knowledge; how concepts are molded into a capta ontology and translated from one medium to another; and how specific decisions at the point of programming influence the work the algorithm does.

The necessity of decoding the workings of obtuse algorithms at the heart of software systems, like cell phones, is difficult to achieve in ways that produce meaningful knowledge in a social science sense (Graham 2005, Mackenzie 2009). This is partly a problem of "black-boxing"—what Mackenzie (2009, 1299) describes as the "submersion of algorithms into commodity hardware." The obscurity of the operational logics of algorithms is apparent in many offline and online settings (Zook and Graham 2007 presents a critique of search engine ranking algorithms in this regard). Yet this is not the only issue, because as Mackenzie (2009, 1295) notes: "the algorithmic processes . . . offer a strong challenge for research. . . . In their somewhat stunning complexity, they seem to bear only a tangential relation to the powerful dynamics of belonging, participation, separation and exclusion typical of contemporary network cultures."

Ethnographic studies provide an in-depth, holistic analyses of social phenomena describing the many relations between actors and the material world they occupy. Empirical material is usually generated by participant observation undertaken over an extended period of time (several months or more) and in-depth interviews with a wide range of stakeholders. These interviews are complemented by other techniques such as a hermeneutic reading of related documents and artifacts (such as policy reports, manuals, e-mail exchanges, visual materials, and work spaces) and time diaries. In essence, an ethnography seeks an immersive understanding of the lifeworld of a community—its social relations, its rhythms, its cultural meanings, its patterns of power and decision-making—in order to comprehend how it is constituted and how it continuously unfolds. An example relating to software development is that conducted by Rosenberg (2007). For a period of two years, he followed a start-up company as they sought to bring a software product to market, sitting in staff meetings, making lengthy observations of the workers interacting with each other professionally and personally, interviewing key actors, and just generally "hanging round the place" as the team plotted, argued, coded, reprioritized, downsized, expanded within an ever shifting context of new ideas, investor confidence, personality clashes, and staff turnover. In so doing, Rosenberg soaked up sufficiently rich details that he was able to provide a convincing holistic account about the nature of software development as a messy, emergent process (rather than the idealized sequence set out in software engineering textbooks). This kind of study needs to be extended to investigating the production and employment of software in different arenas and practices, such as home, leisure, work, travel, and consumption.

These ethnographies, which are necessarily small scale and tightly focused, would be well complemented by wider-ranging observant participation. This is a method that we have employed extensively, examining the ways in which we ourselves interface with coded objects, infrastructures, and processes as a means to reflect on the nature of that interface. For example, in Kitchin and Dodge (2009) we used this technique in order to chart how the code/spaces of air travel are emergent, relational, contingent, and embodied in nature (rather than deterministic, fixed, universal, and mechanistic), and how these code/spaces are bought into being through the interplay of people and code. Our empirical material was derived through sustained observation of our own and other people's engagement with the software systems that are used to augment air travel. This consisted of spending significant periods of observation as we negotiated different airports and travel between them in order to chart the diverse means and ways of purchasing tickets, checking in, passing through security, hanging around departure lounges, navigating paths to gates, boarding planes, flying, collecting baggage, passing through customs and immigration, and exiting the airport. In so doing, we took detailed notes of events and transcripts of relevant conversations that we could then analyze and compare. Similarly, Ullman (1997) provides an effective self-autobiography of software development that draws extensively on her observant participation.

The power of envisioning methodologies is to reveal previously unknown spatial relationships and to effectively communicate the structure of complex processes. Mapping coded objects, infrastructures, and processes makes it possible to determine their deployment across space and time. Therefore, such a map reveals how particular locales take on the form of coded space or code/space.

Spatialization is a particular kind of visualization in which a spatial structure is applied to capta where no inherent or obvious structure exists in order to provide a means of inscribing and comprehending such capta (Dodge and Kitchin 2000, Skupin and Fabrikant 2003). Here, information attributes are transformed into a spatial structure through the application of concepts such as hierarchy and proximity (nearness/likeness). In previous research, we have documented and used such techniques extensively to examine the nature of several facets of the unseen Internet infrastructure and the social and semantic structures of online media (Dodge 2008, Dodge and Kitchin 2000, 2001). To date, however, mapping and spatialization has been relatively little used as an academic technique to examine the myriad of other ways in which software is being embedded in everyday life, although map interfaces regularly occur in management system interfaces for monitoring particular applications. We believe that together, mapping and spatialization can be used to reveal important insights into who owns and controls coded objects and infrastructure, who has access to them, and how they are being employed.

An example of the possibilities of using software to creatively map out aspects of the work of code, is an online mapping service to search and view different parts of the world. These interactions also leave new kinds of traces of their presence in the world. A pattern memory of their creation is preserved in automatically generated logs of the executing code. These logs can themselves be rendered visually, as maps revealing when and where people are mapping their worlds (see figure 11.1).

Another set of mapping techniques, employed to understand time geographies, also have the potential to reveal when and where people enroll elements of software to

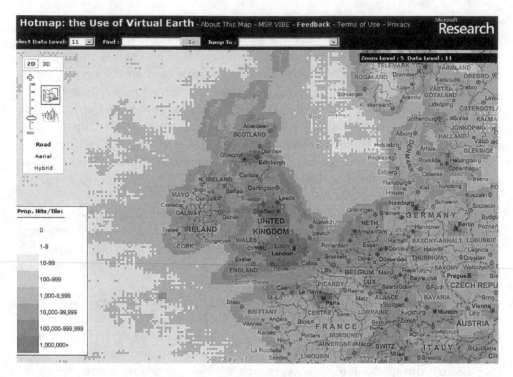

Figure 11.1
The potential to visualize how a mapping algorithm is employed using a simple heatmap approach developed by Fisher (2007). The intensity of colors represents the differential interest levels of users of Microsoft's Virtual Earth mapping system, http://hotmap.msresearch.us/

solve everyday problems. For example, research by a small cadre of human geographers analyzes how individuals rely on computers and online media in relation to the ordering of resources in time and physical/virtual access to spaces (see figure 11.2; Adams 2000; Ellegård and Vilhelmson 2004; Schwanen and Kwan 2008), although they typically do not go into sufficient detail to describe what particular algorithms and capta are at work and the exact nature of the transduction they cause.

These four methods are a subset of the wide range of possible ways of providing the empirical material to underpin theoretical explorations of software studies. As the field develops and grows, no doubt certain conventions will develop as to how research within the field should best be conducted. We would caution against the creation of such hegemonic formations. Instead, software studies needs to be open to a plurality of approaches and techniques, striving to use those tools that provide us with useful empirical material for making sense of the sociality and spatiality of code.

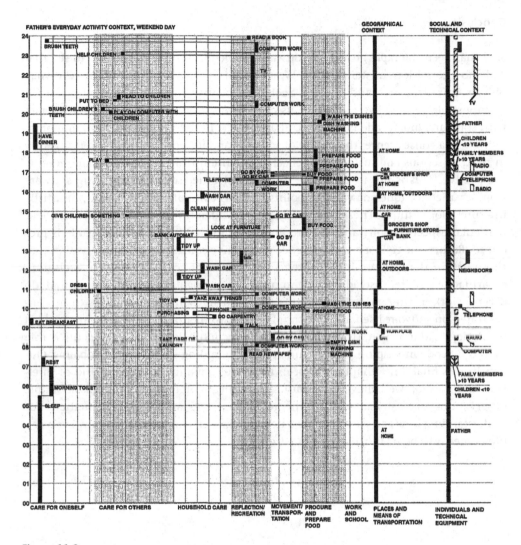

Figure 11.2
A linear visualization of ordering of daily activities through time including indications of when different ICTs are active. *Source*: Ellegård and Vilhelmson 2004, 286

Conclusion

Such has been the rapid growth of software-enabled technologies it is fair to say that code now conditions existence in the West—code is routinely embedded into everyday objects, infrastructures, and systems. Such is its pervasiveness that we would argue it is impossible to now live outside of its orbit (even if one does not directly interact with software, much code is engaged, at a distance, in the provision of contemporary living). As a consequence, the nature of software and its work in the world is urgently in need of serious and sustained intellectual attention from a critical social scientific perspective. This is not to denigrate the work of other scientists studying software from a variety of different vantage points, such as computer science, HCI, or artistic interpretation/critique. These studies and projects often reveal significant details about particular aspects of software, and are important in shaping how future code is produced. Rather, the call for a social science perspective comes from the observation that those within the software industry tend to conceive of code in a narrow, technical, or artifactual sense, instead of as complex and sociocultural productions that do diverse work in the world. Further, this proposed study requires analysis to be concentrated on software itself and not simply the first-order impacts of software-enabled technology. All too often, studies focus on such technologies, ignoring the critical role played by code in shaping their technicity and unfolding solutions to problems. Our aim in this final, brief chapter has been to set out a manifesto for the kind of intellectual endeavor we believe necessary. At the heart of this manifesto is a simple observation—*software matters*. The theoretical concepts and empirical methods for understanding how and why it matters need to reflect its importance in how everyday life comes into being in the twenty-first century.

Brief Glossary of Concepts

Ambient intelligence The capacity of material objects and physical environments to make context sensitive decisions and be responsive to the presence of people or things.

Automated management The regulation of people and things through processes that are at once automated (software enacted), automatic (the software performs the regulation without prompting or direction), and autonomous (regulation, discipline, and punishment are enacted by algorithms without human oversight).

Biometrics Biological (fingerprints, iris patterns, and DNA) and physiological (voice pattern, written signature, and walking style) characteristics employed to uniquely identify a person.

Capta Units that have been selected and harvested from the sum of all potential data. Here, *data* (derived from the Latin *dare*, meaning "to give") are the total sum of facts that an entity can potentially give. Capta is derived from the Latin *capere*, meaning to take. In other words, with respect to a person, data is everything that it is possible to know about that person, capta is what is selectively captured through measurement.

Captabase A collection of capta stored as fields, typically within a tabular form, that can easily be accessed, managed, updated, queried, and analyzed. Traditionally named a database, it has been renamed to recognize that it actually holds capta, not data.

Capta shadow The assemblage of all of the capta held across various captabases that refers to a specific person or object.

Code/space A space that is *dependent* on software for it to be transduced as intended. Here, the relationship between software and space is dyadic; they are mutually constituted, that is, produced through one another.

Coded assemblage A confluence of several different coded infrastructures and their coded objects and processes wherein they become integral to each other in the production of particular environments, for example, office complexes, transport systems, and shopping centers.

Coded infrastructure Networks that link coded objects together and infrastructures that are monitored and regulated, either fully or in part, by software.

Coded object   A material object in which code has been embedded, but where this software is incidental to the primary functioning of the object.

Coded processes   The transactions and flows of digital capta across coded infrastructures.

Coded space   A space that is transduced by software but is not dependent on software to function as intended. If the software fails, the space could still be transduced, but not as efficiently, effectively, or productively as if software had mediated the process.

Codeject   Material objects dependent upon software to function as required—the object and its code are thoroughly interdependent and nonseparable.

Control creep   A situation in which a software system and its capta, having been designed and implemented for one purpose, are subsequently utilized for an additional and potentially detrimental purpose.

Discursive regime   A set of interlocking discourses that provide the justification for, sustain, and reproduce a particular set of sociospatial conditions. The discourses of a discursive regime work to promote and make its message commonsense, but also to condition and discipline: their power is persuading people to their logic; to believe and act in relation to this logic.

Everyware   A future scenario in which computing power is much more widely distributed and unconstrained by geographical contexts—computation will be literally available everywhere with many computers existing for every person and where everyday objects are not simply computational devices, but are servers accessible across an Internet of things.

Firmware   Code that is stored permanently in read-only memory on a device, rather than being enacted through software that is accessible and potentially programmable by the end user.

Grammar of action   A highly formalized set of rules that ensures that a particular task is undertaken in a particular way given certain criteria and inputs.

Hardware   The physical components of a computer including digital circuitry within and across which software and firmware is executed.

Internet of things   A universal indexing mechanism for anything and everything that matters and a mechanism by which objects can connect to, transfer, and process information with each other and with people. In much the same way that the location of a web site can be looked up through its unique domain name from anywhere on the Internet, it is envisioned that the Internet of things will facilitate the same for any uniquely tagged object.

Life-log   A unified, digital record of the totality of an individual's experiences stored as a personal multimedia archive.

Logject   A material object that has a useful degree of awareness of itself and its relations with the world and which, by default, automatically record aspects of those relations in a log that is stored and can be recalled and used in the future.

Machine code   A kind of software that is expressed in a form that a CPU can process directly without translation or compilation.

Oligopticon   A sociospatial arrangement that renders people and places visible from fixed positions that have limited viewpoints onto the subject.

Ontogenesis   A form of ontological thinking that focuses not on what something is, but rather how something becomes. In so doing, it rejects the notion that objects or concepts are ontologically secure—fixable, definable, knowable—instead arguing that their ontological status is contingent, relational, and unfolding through practice.

Open-source software   Source and executable code that is developed individually or collectively and is distributed freely so that others can use and adapt it. The mode of authorship and licensing is often contrasted with proprietary software in which the source code is closely guarded and cannot be legally changed by others.

Pervasive computing   A mode of computation that consists of the wholesale embedding of software into everyday objects and infrastructures rendering them interactive and smart to varying degrees.

Panopticon   A sociospatial arrangement that seeks to render people and places visible to an all-seeing gaze and thus amenable to control by those operating the panopticon.

Sentient computing   A mode of computation in which coded objects and systems sense and react in a contextual fashion to an individual's presence.

Social sorting   The profiling and ranking of individuals based upon capta concerning them.

Source code   A set of coded instructions written in a programming language understandable by people but not directly by a computational device. It is compiled into machine code for use by a computer.

Sousveillance   The self-monitoring of one's personal life through surveillance technologies.

Surveillance   The action of identifying and monitoring of people's lives through the generation of capta concerning them and utilizing the capta to change their behavior in accordance with the institution performing the surveillance.

Tangible computing   A mode of computation that is controlled by natural modes of human communication, such as voice and gesture recognition and touch rather than directed typing on a keyboard or moving a mouse.

Technicity   The extent to which technologies mediate, supplement, and augment collective life; the unfolding or evolutive power of technologies to make things happen; to perform meaningful work in the world.

Transduction   The constant making anew of a domain in reiterative and transformative practices.

Ubiquitous computing   A mode of computation that will move seamlessly with a person who can access network services regardless of environmental context or physical location.

Wearable computing   A mode of computation migrates from specific devices such as PDAs to become embedded seamlessly into the clothes and accessories we wear.

Sources

The authors gratefully acknowledge the permission to draw upon portions of the following copyrighted material in this book. The material used from these papers has been wholly updated and extended; none is reproduced in full.

Kitchin, R. 2009. Space. In *International Encyclopedia of Human Geography*, edited by R. Kitchin and N. Thrift. Oxford: Elsevier. Reproduced with the permission of Elsevier Science Ltd.

Dodge, M., and R. Kitchin. 2009. Code, objects, and home space. *Environment and Planning A* 41 (6): 1344–1365. Reproduced with the permission of Pion Ltd.

Dodge, M., R. Kitchin, and M. Zook. 2009. How does software make space? *Environment and Planning A* 41 (6): 1283–1293. Reproduced with the permission of Pion Ltd.

Kitchin, R., and M. Dodge. 2009. Airport code/spaces. In Cwerner S, Kesselring S, Urry U (eds), *Aeromobilities* (Routledge, London), edited by S. Cwerner, S. Kesselring, and U. Urry. Reproduced with the permission of Taylor and Francis Ltd.

Dodge, M., and R. Kitchin. 2007. "Outlines of a world coming in existence": Pervasive computing and the ethics of forgetting. *Environment and Planning B: Planning and Design* 34 (3): 431–445. Reproduced with the permission of Pion Ltd.

Dodge, M., and R. Kitchin. 2007. The automatic management of drivers and driving spaces. *Geoforum* 38 (2): 264–275. Reproduced with the permission of Elsevier Science Ltd, Permagon Imprint.

Kitchin, R., and M. Dodge. 2006. Software and the mundane management of air travel. *First Monday* 7 (9) www.firstmonday.org/issues/special11_9/. Reproduced with the permission of First Monday.

Dodge, M., and R. Kitchin. 2005. Codes of life: Identification codes and the machine-readable world. *Environment and Planning D: Society and Space*, 23 (6): 851–881. Reproduced with the permission of Pion Ltd.

Dodge, M., and R. Kitchin. 2005. Code and the transduction of space. *Annals of the Association of American Geographers* 95 (1): 162–180. Reproduced with the permission of Blackwell.

Dodge, M., and R. Kitchin. 2004. Flying through code/space: The real virtuality of air travel. *Environment and Planning A* 36 (2): 195–211. Reproduced with the permission of Pion Ltd.

References

Aarts, E., R. Harwig, and M. Schuurmans. 2002. Ambient intelligence. In *The invisible future: The seamless integration of technology into everyday life*, edited by P. Denning, 235–250. New York: McGraw-Hill.

ACLU. 2004. *The seven problems with CAPPS II*. American Civil Liberties Union. www.aclu.org/ Privacy/Privacy.cfm?ID=15426&c=130.

Adams, P. C. 2000. Applications of a CAD-based accessibility model. In *Information, place and cyberspace: Issues in accessibility*, edited by D. G. Janelle and D. C. Hodge, 217–239. New York: Springer.

Adams, C. 2006. PowerPoint, habits of mind, and classroom culture. *Journal of Curriculum Studies* 38 (4): 389–411.

Aday, S., and S. Livingston. 2009. NGOs as intelligence agencies: The empowerment of transnational advocacy networks and the media by commercial remote sensing in the case of the Iranian nuclear program. *Geoforum* 40 (4): 514–522.

Addlesee, M., R. Curwen, S. Hodges, J. F. Newman, P. Steggles, A. Ward, and A. Hopper. 2001. Implementing a sentient computing system. *Computer* 34 (8): 50–56.

Adey, P. 2004. Secured and sorted mobilities: Examples from the airport. *Surveillance and Society* 1 (4): 500–519.

Adey, P. 2009. Facing airport security: Affect, biopolitics, and the preemptive securitisation of the mobile body. *Environment and Planning. D, Society and Space* 27: 274–295.

Agre, P. 1994. Surveillance and capture: Two models of privacy. *Information Society* 10 (2): 101–127.

Albrecht, K., and L. McIntyre. 2005. *Spychips: How major corporations and government plan to track your every move with RFID*. Nashville, TN: Nelson Current Publishers.

Aldrich, F. K. 2003. Smart homes: Past, present and future. In *Inside the smart home*, edited by R. Harper. London: Springer.

Allen, J. 2004. The whereabouts of power: Politics, government and space. *Geografiska Annaler B* 86: 19–32.

Allen, A. L. 2008. Dredging up the past: Lifelogging, memory, and surveillance. *University of Chicago Law Review* 75 (1): 47–74.

Al-Sudairy, M. A., and N. K. H. Tang. 2000. Information technology in Saudi Arabia's supermarket chains. *International Journal of Retail & Distribution Management* 28 (8): 341–356.

Althusser, L. 1971. *Lenin and philosophy and other essays*. Trans. B. Brewster. London: NLB.

Amin, A., and N. Thrift. 2002. *Cities: Reimagining the urban*. London: Polity.

Amoore, L., and A. Hall. 2009. Taking people apart: Digitised dissection and the body at the border. *Environment and Planning. D, Society & Space* 27 (3): 444–464.

Andrejevic, M. 2007. *iSpy: Surveillance and power in the interactive era*. Lawrence: University of Kansas.

Antić, D., and M. Fuller. 2006. The computation of space. *Transmedia*, Hogeschool Sint-Lukas, Brussels www.spc.org/fuller/texts/the-computation-of-space/.

Augé, M. 1995. *Non-places: Introduction to an anthropology of supermodernity*. Trans. J. Howe. London: Verso.

Baberg, T. W. 2001. Man-machine-interface in modern transport systems from an aviation safety perspective. *Aerospace Science and Technology* 5: 495–504.

Barnes, T. J., and M. Hannah. 2001. The place of numbers: Histories, geographies, and theories of quantification. *Environment and Planning. D, Society & Space* 19: 379–383.

Batty, M. 1997. The computable city. *International Planning Studies* 2: 155–173.

Beer, D., and R. Burrows. 2007. Sociology and, of and in Web 2.0: Some initial considerations, *Sociological Research Online* 12 (5) www.socresonline.org.uk/12/5/17.html

Bell, G., and P. Dourish. 2007. Back to the shed: Gendered visions of technology and domesticity. *Personal and Ubiquitous Computing* 11: 373–381.

Bennett, C. J. 2001. Cookies, web bugs, webcams and cue cats: Patterns of surveillance on the world wide web. *Ethics and Information Technology* 3 (3): 195–208.

Bennett, C. J. 2004. What happens when you buy an airline ticket (revisited): The collection and processing of passenger data post 9/11. *State Borders and Border Policing Workshop*, Kingston, Ontario. http://web.uvic.ca/polisci/bennett/queenspaper04.doc

Bennett, R. F., and C. J. Dodd. 2000. *Y2K aftermath—Crisis averted, Final Committee Report*, U.S. Senate Special Committee on the Year 2000 Technology Problem. www.senate.gov/~y2k/documents/final.pdf

Bergin, T. J. 2006. The proliferation and consolidation of word processing software: 1985–1995. *IEEE Annals of the History of Computing* 28 (4): 48–63.

Berry, D. M. 2004. The contestation of code: A preliminary investigation into the discourse or the free/libre and open source movements. *Critical Discourse Studies* 1 (1): 65–89.

Berry, D. M. 2008. A contribution towards a grammar of code. *Fibre Culture* 13 http://journal .fibreculture.org/issue13/issue13_berry.html

Blanchette, J.-F., and D. G. Johnson. 2002. Data retention and the panoptic society: The social benefits of forgetfulness. *Information Society* 18:33–45.

Bleecker, J. 2006. *Why things matter: A manifesto for networked objects—Cohabiting with pigeons, arphids and aibos in the Internet of things* www.nearfuturelaboratory.com/files/WhyThingsMatter .pdf

Blunt, A., and R. Dowling. 2006. *Home*. London: Routledge.

Bogard, W. 1996. *The simulation of surveillance: Hypercontrol in telematic societies*. Cambridge, MA: MIT Press.

Borgman, C. L. 2007. *Scholarship in the digital age*. Cambridge, MA: MIT Press.

Brand, S. 1995. The physicist. *Wired Magazine* September www.wired.com/wired/archive/3.09/ myhrvold_pr.html

Britcher, R. N. 1999. *The limits of software*. Reading, MA: Addison-Wesley.

Brooks, F. P. 1995. *The mythical man-month: Essays on software engineering*. Boston: Addison-Wesley.

Brown, B. 2006. The next line: Understanding programmers' work. *TeamEthno* (2): 25–33 www .teamethno-online.org.uk/Issue2

Budd, L., and P. Adey. 2009. The software-simulated airworld: Anticipatory code and affective aeromobilities. *Environment and Planning A* 41: 1366–1385.

Buhr, B. L. 2003. Traceability and information technology in the meat supply chain: Implications for firm organization and market structure. *Journal of Food Distribution Research* 34 (3): 13–26.

Burrows, R., and N. Gane. 2006. Geodemographics, software and class. *Sociology* 40 (5): 793–812.

Burton, I. 1963. The quantitative revolution and theoretical geography. *Canadian Geographer / Le Geographe Canadien* 7: 151–162.

Butler, J. 1990. *Gender trouble: Feminism and the subversion of identity*. London: Routledge.

Butler, D. L. 2001. Technogeopolitics and the struggle for control of world air routes, 1910–1928. *Political Geography* 20: 635–658.

Butler, D. 2006. Everything, everywhere. *Nature* 440: 402–405.

Campbell-Kelly, M. 2003. *From airline reservations to Sonic the Hedgehog: A history of the software industry*. Cambridge, MA: MIT Press.

Carlson, M. 2006. Tapping into TiVo: Digital video recorders and the transition from schedules to surveillance in television. *New Media & Society* 8 (1): 97–115.

CARPE. 2004. *First ACM Workshop on Continuous Archival and Retrieval of Personal Experiences* http://research.microsoft.com/CARPE2004

Castells, M. 1996. *Rise of the network society*. Oxford: Blackwell.

Charette, R. N. 2005. Why software fails. *IEEE Spectrum* 42 (9): 42–49.

Checkland, P., and S. Holwell. 1998. *Information, systems and information systems: Making sense of the field*. Chichester, UK: Wiley.

Clarke, R. 1994a. The digital persona and its application to data surveillance. *Information Society* 10 (2): 77–92 www.anu.edu.au/people/Roger.Clarke/DV/DigPersona.html

Clarke, R. 1994b. Human identification in information systems: management challenges and public policy issues. *Information Technology & People* 7 (4): 6–37.

Cosgrove, D. 1994. Contested global visions: One-world, whole-Earth and the Apollo space photographs. *Annals of the Association of American Geographers. Association of American Geographers* 82: 270–294.

Coupland, D. 1995. *Microserfs*. New York: HarperCollins.

Coupland, D. 2006. *JPod* London: Bloomsbury.

Cowan, R. S. 1983. *More work for father: The ironies of household technology from the open hearth to the microwave*. New York: Basic Books.

Computing Research Association. 2003. *Grand Research Challenges in Information Systems*. Washington, DC: Computing Research Association. www.cra.org/reports/gc.systems.pdf

Crabtree, A., T. Rodden, T. Hemmings, and S. Benford. 2003. Finding a place for ubicomp in the home. *Lecture Notes in Computer Science* 2864: 208–226.

Crabtree, A., P. Tolmie, T. Rodden, C. Greenhalgh, and S. Benford. 2007. Making the home network at home: Digital housekeeping. *Proceedings of the 10th European Conference on Computer-Supported Cooperative Work*.

Crampton, J. W. 2004. GIS and geographic governance: Reconstructing the choropleth map. *Cartographica* 39 (1): 41–53.

Crampton, J. W. 2009. Cartography: Maps 2.0. *Progress in Human Geography* 33 (1): 91–100.

Crane, D. 2008. Next-gen modular wearable computer systems being developed for U.S. Marine Corps. *Defense Review* www.defensereview.com

Crang, P. 1994. It's showtime: On the workplace geographies of display in a restaurant in South-east England. *Environment and Planning. D, Society & Space* 12: 675–704.

Crang, M. 2002. Between places: Producing hubs, flows, and networks. *Environment & Planning A* 34 (4): 569–574.

Crang, M., T. Crosbie, and S. Graham. 2006. Variable geometries of connection: Urban digital divides and the uses of information technology. *Urban Studies* 43 (13): 2551–2570.

Crang, M., and S. Graham. 2007. Sentient cities: Ambient intelligence and the politics of urban space. *Information Communication and Society* 10 (6): 789–817.

Crang, M., and N. Thrift. 2000. *Thinking space*. London: Routledge.

Curry, M. 1995. On space and spatial practice in contemporary geography. In *Concepts in Human Geography*, edited by C. Earle, K. Mathewson, and M. Kenzer, 3–32. Lanharn, MD: Rowman and Littlefield Publishers.

Curry, M. R. 1997. The digital individual and the private realm. *Annals of the Association of American Geographers* 87:681–699.

Curry, M. R., D. J. Philips, and P. M. Regan. 2004. Emergency response systems and the creeping legibility of people and places. *Information Society* 20:357–369.

Daniels, P. W., A. Leyshon, M. J. Bradshaw, and J. V. Beaverstock. 2006. *Geographies of the new economy: Critical reflections*. London: Routledge.

Danna, A., and O. H. Gandy. 2002. All that glitters is not gold: Digging beneath the surface of data mining. *Journal of Business Ethics* 40:373–386.

Davies, S. G. 1994. Touching Big Brother: How biometrics technology will fuse flesh and machine. *Information Technology & People* 7 (4): 38–47.

Davies, G. 1994. *A history of money: From ancient times to the present day*. Cardiff: University of Wales Press.

Dean, D. H. 2008. Shopper age and the use of self-service technologies. *Managing Service Quality* 18 (3): 225–238.

De Certeau, M. 1984. *The practice of everyday life*. Berkeley, CA: University of California Press.

Delaney, D., and H. Leitner. 1997. The political construction of scale. *Political Geography* 16 (2): 93–98.

Deleuze, G. 1992. Postscript on the societies of control. *October* 59:3–7.

Deleuze, G., and F. Guattari. 1987. *A thousand plateaus: Capitalism and schizophrenia*. Trans. B. Massumi Minneapolis: University of Minnesota Press.

Deloitte Research. 2002. *Mobilizing the machine: The coming embedded mobile revolution*. London: Deloitte Research.

Dennis, K. 2008. Sensoring the future: Complex geographies of connectivity and communication. *World Futures* 64:22–33.

Dery, K., R. Hall, and N. Wailes. 2006. ERPs as technologies-in-practice: Social construction, materiality and the role of organisational factors. *New Technology, Work and Employment* 21 (3): 229–241.

Desrosières, A. 1998. *The politics of large numbers: A history of statistical reasoning.* Trans. C. Naish Cambridge, MA: Harvard University Press.

DfT. 2004. *Uninsured driving in the UK. A report to the Secretary of State for Transport by Professor David Greenaway, University of Nottingham.* Department for Transport, August 11. www.dft.gov .uk/stellent/groups/dft_roads/documents/page/dft_roads_030393.hcsp

DHS. 2004. *US-VISIT program; Increment 2; Privacy impact Assessment.* Washington, DC: Department of Homeland Security. www.dhs.gov/interweb/assetlibrary/US-VISIT_PIA_09142004.pdf

Dobson, J. E., and P. F. Fisher. 2003. Geoslavery. *IEEE Technology and Society Magazine* (Spring): 47–52.

Dodge, M. 2008. *Understanding cyberspace cartographies.* Unpublished PhD Thesis Centre for Advanced Spatial Analysis, University College London.

Dodge, M., and R. Kitchin. 2000. *Mapping cyberspace.* London: Routledge.

Dodge, M., and R. Kitchin. 2001. *Atlas of cyberspace.* London: Addison-Wesley.

Dodge, M., and R. Kitchin. 2004. Flying through code/space: The real virtuality of air travel. *Environment & Planning A* 36 (2): 195–211.

Dodge, M., and R. Kitchin. 2005a. Code and the transduction of space. *Annals of the Association of American Geographers.* 95 (1): 162–180.

Dodge, M., and R. Kitchin. 2005b. Codes of life: Identification codes and the machine-readable world. *Environment and Planning. D, Society & Space* 23 (6): 851–881.

Dodge, M., and R. Kitchin. 2007a. The automatic management of drivers and driving spaces. *Geoforum* 38 (2): 264–275.

Dodge, M., and R. Kitchin. 2007b. "Outlines of a world coming into existence": Pervasive computing and the ethics of forgetting. *Environment and Planning. B, Planning & Design* 34 (3): 431–445.

Dodge, M., and R. Kitchin. 2009. Software, objects, and home space. *Environment & Planning A* 41 (6): 1344–1365.

Doel, M. 1999. *Poststructuralist geographies: The diabolical art of spatial science.* Edinburgh: Edinburgh University Press.

Dourish, P. 2001. *Where the action is.* Cambridge, MA: MIT Press.

Edwards, W. K., and R. E. Grinter. 2001. At home with ubiquitous computing: Seven challenges. *Proceedings of the Conference on Ubiquitous Computing (Ubicomp 2001).*

Ellegård, K., and B. Vilhelmson. 2004. Home as a pocket of local order: Everyday activities and the friction of distance. *Geografiska Annaler* 86 (4): 281–296.

Ferguson T., 2002. Have your objects call my object. *Harvard Business Review* June.

Fisher, D. 2007. How we watch the city: Popularity and online maps. *Workshop on Imaging the City, ACM CHI 2007 Conference* http://research.microsoft.com/~danyelf

Fishman, C. 1996. They write the right stuff. *FastCompany Magazine,* December. www.fastcom pany.com/online/06/writestuff.html

Fitzgibbon, A., and E. Reiter. 2003. *"Memories for life": Managing information over a human lifetime.* UK Computing Research Committee Grand Challenge proposal, May 22. www.nesc.ac.uk/esi/ events/Grand_Challenges/proposals/Memories.pdf

Ford, R. 2007. Terror police to track capital's cars. *The Times,* July 17. www.timesonline.co.uk/ tol/news/uk/crime/article2091023.ece

Foth, M. 2008. *Handbook of research on urban informatics: The practice and promise of the real-time city.* New York: Information Science Reference.

Foucault, M. 1977. *Discipline and punish.* London: Allen Lane.

Foucault, M. 1978. *The history of sexuality,* vol. 1. New York: Random House.

Friedberg, S. 2007. Supermarkets and imperial knowledge. *Cultural Geographies* 14 (3): 321–342.

Frigo, A. 2004. Storing, indexing and retrieving my autobiography. *Proceedings of Pervasive 2004 Workshop on Memory and Sharing of Experiences,* April 20.

Fuller, M. 2003. *Behind the blip: Essays on the culture of software.* New York: Autonomedia.

Fuller, M. 2005. *Media ecologies.* Cambridge, MA: MIT Press.

Fuller, M. 2008. *Software studies: A lexicon.* Cambridge, MA: MIT Press.

Fuller, G. 2009. > store > forward >: Architecture of a future tense. In *Aeromobilities,* edited by S. Cwerner, S. Kesselring, and J. Urry. London: Routledge.

Fuller, G., and R. Harley. 2004. *Aviopolis: A book about airports.* London: Blackdog Press.

Galloway, A. 2003. Towards the forgetting machine. *Purse Lip Square Jaw weblog,* December 17. www.purselipsquarejaw.org/ 2003_12_01_blogger_archives.php

Galloway, A. R. 2004. *Protocol: How control exists after decentralization.* Cambridge, MA: MIT Press.

Gandy, O. 1993. *The panoptic sort: A political economy of personal information.* Boulder, CO: Westview Press.

GE Infrastructure Security. 2007. *Entry3.* www.geindustrial.com/ge-interlogix/iontrack/prod _entryscan.html

Gemmell, J., R. Lueder, and G. Bell. 2003. The MyLifeBits lifetime store. *Proceedings of ACM SIGMM 2003 Workshop on Experiential Telepresence,* November 7. http://research.microsoft.com/~JGemmell/pubs/ETP2003.pdf

Gilheany, S. 2000. Projecting the cost of magnetic disk storage over the next 10 years. *Archivebuilders.com White Paper 22011v039.* www.archivebuilders.com/whitepapers/22011v039h.htm

Glass, R. L. 1998. *Software runaways.* London: Prentice Hall.

Goldsmith, J., and T. Wu. 2006. *Who control the Internet? Illusions of a borderless world.* New York: Oxford University Press.

Goodchild, M. F. 2007. Citizens as voluntary sensors: Spatial data infrastructure in the world of Web 2.0. *International Journal of Spatial Data Infrastructures Research* 2: 24–32.

Goodman, F. 2008. Rock's new economy: Making money when CDs don't sell. *Rolling Stone Magazine* May 29. www.rollingstone.com/news/story/20830491/rocks_new_economy_making_money_when_cds_dont_sell

Goss, J. 1995. "We know who you are and we know where you live": The instrumental rationality of geodemographics systems. *Economic Geography* 71:171–198.

Gottdiener, M. 2001. *Life in the air: Surviving the new culture of air travel.* Oxford: Rowman and Littlefield.

Graham, B. 1995. *Geography and air transport.* Chichester, UK: John Wiley.

Graham, S. 2002. CCTV: The stealthy emergence of a fifth utility? *Planning Theory & Practice* 3: 237–241.

Graham, S. D. N. 2005. Software-sorted geographies. *Progress in Human Geography* 29 (5): 562–580.

Graham, S. 2007. The city in the crosshairs: A conversation with Stephen Graham (Pt. 1). *Subtopia* blog posting, 6 August. http://subtopia.blogspot.com/2007/08/city-in-crosshairs-conversation-with.html

Graham, S., and S. Marvin. 1996. *Telecommunications and the city.* London: Routledge.

Graham, S., and S. Marvin. 2001. *Splintering urbanism: Networked infrastructures, technological mobilities and the urban condition.* London: Routledge.

Graham, S., and N. Thrift. 2007. Out of order: Understanding repair and maintenance. *Theory, Culture and Society* 24 (3): 1–25.

Graham, S., and D. Wood. 2003. Digitizing surveillance: Categorization, space, inequality. *Critical Social Policy* 23 (2): 227–248.

Gramelsberger, G. 2006. Story telling with code: Archaeology of climate modelling. *TeamEthno* 2: 77–84. www.teamethno-online.org.uk/Issue2.

Grant, D., B. Harley, and C. Wright. 2006. Editorial introduction: The work and organisational implications of Enterprise Resource Planning systems. *New Technology, Work and Employment* 21 (3): 196–198.

Greenfield, A. 2006. *Everyware: The dawning age of ubiquitous computing*. Boston: New Riders.

Grochowski, E., and R. D. Halem. 2003. Technological impact of magnetic hard disk drives on storage systems. *IBM Systems Journal* 42 (2): 338–346.

Haggerty, K., and R. Ericson. 2000. The surveillant assemblage. *British Journal of Sociology* 51 (4): 605–622.

Hand, M., and E. Shove. 2007. Condensing practices: Ways of living with a freezer. *Journal of Consumer Culture* 7: 79–104.

Hannah, M. 1997. Imperfect panopticism: Envisioning the construction of normal lives. In *Space and Social Theory*, edited by G. Benko and U. Strohmayer, 344–360. Oxford: Blackwell.

Hartshorne, R. 1959. *Perspective on the nature of geography*. Chicago: Rand McNally.

Harvey, D. 1969. *Explanation in geography*. Oxford: Blackwell.

Harvey, D. 1982. *The limits to capital*. Oxford: Blackwell.

Hayles, N. K. 2005. *My mother was a computer: Digital subjects and literary texts*. Chicago: University of Chicago Press.

Hayles, N. K. 2009. RFID: Human agency and meaning in information-intensive environments. *Theory, Culture & Society* 26 (2–3): 47–72.

Hitchings, R. 2004. At home with someone nonhuman. *Home Cultures* 1 (2): 169–186.

Holland, J. H. 1998. *Emergence: From chaos to order*. Oxford: Oxford University Press.

Hubbard, P., R. Kitchin, B. Bartley, and D. Fuller. 2002. *Thinking geographically: Space, theory and contemporary human geography*. London: Continuum.

Innes, M. 2001. Control creep. *Sociological Research Online* 6 (3). www.socresonline.org.uk/6/3/innes.html.

Jonas, A. E. G. 1994. The scale politics of spatiality. *Environment and Planning. D, Society & Space* 12 (3): 257–264.

Johnson, S. 2003. Offloading your memories. *The New York Times* December 14. www.nytimes.com/2003/12/14/magazine/14OFFLOADING.html.

Kalakota, R., and M. Robinson. 2000. *E-business: The roadmap to success*. Reading, MA: Addison-Wesley.

Kale, S. H. 2003. CRM in gaming: It's no crapshoot. *UNLV Gaming Research & Review Journal* 7 (2): 43–54.

Keefe, P. R. 2006. I spy. *Wired Magazine* February www.wired.com/wired/archive/14.02/spy_pr
.html.

Kitchin, R. 1998. *Cyberspace: The world in the wires*. Chichester, UK: Wiley.

Kitchin, R. 2009. Space. In *International encyclopedia of human geography*, edited by R. Kitchin and
N. Thrift. Oxford: Elsevier.

Kitchin, R., and M. Dodge. 2006. Software and the mundane management of air travel. *First
Monday* 11 (9) http://firstmonday.org/issues/special11_9/kitchin/.

Kitchin, R., and M. Dodge. 2009. Airport code/spaces. In *Aeromobilities*, edited by S. Cwerner, S.
Kesselring, and J. Urry. London: Routledge.

Knox, H., D. O'Doherty, T. Vurdubakis, and C. Westrup. 2005. Enacting airports: Space, movement and modes of ordering. *Evolution of Business Knowledge (EBK) Working Paper*, 2005/20 www
.ebkresearch.org/downloads/workingpapers/wp0520_knox_etal.pdf.

Knuth, D. E. 1974. Computer programming as an art. *Communications of the ACM* 17 (12): 667–
673.

Lane, S. N., C. J. Brookes, A. L. Heathwaite, and S. Reaney. 2006. Surveillant science: Challenges
for the management of rural environments emerging from the new generation diffuse pollution
models. *Journal of Agricultural Economics* 57: 239–257.

Latour, B. 1993. *We have never been modern*. New York: Harvester Wheatsheaf.

Lazer, D., A. Pentland, L. Adamic, S. Aral, A.-L. Barabasi, D. Brewer, N. Christakis, N. Contractor,
J. Fowler, M. Gutmann, T. Jebara, G. King, M. Macy, D. Roy, and M. Van Alstyne. 2009. Computational social science. *Science* 323: 721–723.

Leimbach, T. 2008. The SAP story: Evolution of SAP within the German software industry. *IEEE
Annals of the History of Computing* (October-December): 60–76.

Leitner, H. 2004. The politics of scales and networks of spatial connectivity. In *Scale and Geographic Inquiry*, edited by E. Sheppard and R. B. McMaster, 236–255. Oxford: Blackwell.

Lessig, L. 1999. *Code and other laws of cyberspace*. New York: Basic Books.

Leyden, J. 2005. Rise of the botnets. *TheRegister* March 15 www.theregister.co.uk/2005/03/15/
honeypot_botnet_study/.

Leyshon, A. 2009. The software slump?: Digital music, the democratisation of technology, and
the decline of the recording studio sector within the musical economy. *Environment & Planning
A* 41: 1309–1331.

Leyshon, A., S. French, and P. Signoretta. 2008. Financial exclusion and the geography of bank
and building society branch closure in Britain. *Transactions of the Institute of British Geographers
NS* 33: 447–465.

Leyshon, A., and N. Thrift. 1999. Lists come alive: Electronic systems of knowledge and the rise
of credit-scoring in retail banking. *Economy and Society* 28: 434–466.

Leyshon, A., P. Webb, S. French, N. Thrift, and L. Crewe. 2005. On the reproduction of the music industry after the Internet. *Media Culture & Society* 27 (2): 177–209.

Lillington, K, 2008. Software doctor's 999 service. *Irish Times*, Business This Week section, May 23.

Lockett, C. P., and A. G. Holland. 1991. Competitive advantage using information technology in retailing: Myth or reality? *International Review of Retail, Distribution and Consumer Research* 1 (3): 261–283.

Lowenthal, D. 1999. Preface. In *The Art of Forgetting*, edited by A. Forty and S. Küchler, xi–xiii. Oxford: Berg.

Lyon, D. 2002. Everyday surveillance: Personal data and social classifications. *Information Communication and Society* 5: 242–257.

Lyon, D. 2003. Surveillance as social sorting: Computer codes and mobile bodies. In *Surveillance as social sorting: Privacy, risk and digital discrimination*, edited by D. Lyon. London: Routledge.

Lyon, D. 2007. *Surveillance studies: An overview*. Cambridge: Polity.

Mackenzie, A. 2002. *Transductions: Bodies and machines at speed*. London: Continuum Press.

Mackenzie, A. 2003. *Transduction: Invention, Innovation and Collective Life*. Unpublished manuscript. www.lancs.ac.uk/staff/mackenza/papers/transduction.pdf.

Mackenzie, A. 2006. *Cutting code: Software and sociality*. New York: Peter Lang.

Mackenzie, A. 2008. Codecs. In *Software Studies*, edited by M. Fuller. Cambridge, MA: MIT Press, 48–55.

Mackenzie, A. 2009. Intensive movement in wireless digital signal processing: From calculation to envelopment. *Environment & Planning A* 41: 1294–1308.

MacKenzie, D. 2006. *An engine, not a camera: How financial models shape markets*. Cambridge, MA: MIT Press.

Mallett, S. 2004. Understanding home: A critical review of the literature. *Sociological Review* 52: 156–179.

Mann, S. 1998. Wearable computing as means for personal empowerment. *International Conference on Wearable Computing ICWC-98*, Fairfax VA http://wearcam.org/icwc/index.htm.

Mann S., J. Nolan, and B. Wellman. 2003. Sousveillance: Inventing and using wearable computing devices for data collection in surveillance environments. *Surveillance and Society* 1 (3): 331–355.

Manovich, L. 2000. *The language of new media*. Cambridge, MA: MIT Press.

Manovich, L. 2004. *Info-Aesthetics book proposal*, www.manovich.net/IE_MIT_proposal_2004.doc.

Manovich, L. 2008. *Software takes command*. http://lab.softwarestudies.com/2008/11/softbook .html (accessed November 20, 2009).

Markoff, J. 2007. Attack of the zombie computers is growing threat. *The New York Times* January 7 www.nytimes.com/2007/01/07/technology/07net.html.

Marontate, J. 2005. Digital recording and the reconfiguration of music as performance. *American Behavioral Scientist* 48 (11): 1422–1438.

Marples, G. 2009. *Credit card history.* www.thehistoryof.net/history-of-credit-cards.html.

Marston, S. A. 2000. The social construction of scale. *Progress in Human Geography* 24 (2): 219–242.

Marston, S. A., J. P. Jones, III, and K. Woodward. 2005. Human geography without scale. *Transactions of the Institute of British Geographers NS* 30: 416–432.

Martin, D., and J. Rooksby. 2006. Knowledge and reasoning about code in a large code base. *TeamEthno* 2: 3–12. www.teamethno-online.org.uk/Issue2/.

Marx, G. T. 2003. A tack in the shoe: Neutralizing and resisting the new surveillance. *Journal of Social Issues* 59 (2): 369–390.

Massey, D. 1994. *Space, place and gender.* London: Methuen.

McCullough, M. 2004. *Digital ground.* Cambridge, MA: MIT Press.

McNay, L. 1994. *Foucault: A critical introduction.* Oxford: Polity Press.

Miller, D. 2001. *Home possessions: Material culture behind closed doors.* Oxford: Berg.

Miller, R. B. 1968. Response time in man-computer conversational transactions. Proceedings of AFIPS Fall Joint Computer Conference 33, 267–277.

Miller, H. J., and J. Han. 2001. Geographic data mining and knowledge discovery: An overview. In *Geographic data mining and knowledge discovery*, edited by H. J. Miller and J. Han, 3–32. London: Taylor and Francis.

Mirapaul, M. 2003. Deliberately distorting the digital mechanism. *The New York Times* April 21. www.nytimes.com/2003/04/21/arts/design/21MIRA.html.

Mitchell, W. J. 1995. *City of bits: Space, place and the infobahn.* Cambridge, MA: MIT Press.

Mitchell, W. J. 2004. *ME++: The cyborg self and the networked city.* Cambridge, MA: MIT Press.

Morville, P. 2005. *Ambient findability: What we find changes who we become.* Sebastopol, CA: O'Reilly Media.

Murphy, A. J. 2007. Grounding the virtual: The material effects of electronic grocery shopping. *Geoforum* 38 (5): 941–953.

Murtaugh, M. 2008. Interactivity. In *Software studies*, edited by M. Fuller, 143–149. Cambridge, MA: MIT Press.

Nguyen, T. N. 2003. A bio-ecological framework for e-business software automation. www.csulb.edu/~tnnguyen/a%20bio-ecological%20framework%20for%20e-business%20software%20automat%85.pdf.

Nordhaus, W. D. 2002. *The progress of computing*, version 5.2.2, New Haven, CT: Yale University. http://nordhaus.econ.yale.edu/prog_030402_all.pdf.

Nova, N., and J. Bleecker. 2006. Blogjects and the new ecology of things. *Lift06 Workshop*. http://tecfa.unige.ch/~nova/blogject-lift06.pdf.

OECD. 2008. *OECD Information Technology Outlook 2008*. Paris: Organisation for Economic Co-operation and Development.

O'Reilly, T. 2005. *What is Web 2.0* http://oreilly.com/web2/archive/what-is-web-20.html.

Orwell, G. 1949/2004. *Ninety eighty four*. New York: World Publishing.

Osinski, M. 2009. My Manhattan Project: How I helped build the bomb that blew up Wall Street. *New York Magazine* March 29 www.nymag.com/news/business/55687/?partnerID=73272.

Page, L. 2007. US "Land Warrior" wearable-computing headed to Iraq. *TheRegister* April 19. www.theregister.co.uk/2007/04/19/us_fist_to_iraq_even_though_cancelled/.

Paglen, T., and A. C. Thompson. 2006. *Torture taxi: On the trail of the CIA's rendition flights*. Hoboken, NJ: Melville House.

Parks, L. 2007. Points of departure: The culture of US airport screening. *Journal of Visual Culture* 6 (2): 183–200.

Pascoe, D. 2001. *Airspaces*. London: Reaktion.

Pehrson, R. J. 1996. Software development for the Boeing 777. *CrossTalk, The Journal of Defense Software Engineering* January. www.stsc.hill.af.mil/crosstalk/1996/01/Boein777.asp.

Perkins, C., and M. Dodge. 2009. Satellite imagery and the spectacle of secret spaces. *Geoforum* 40 (4): 546–560.

Piet Zwart Institute. 2006. *Software studies workshop introduction*. February 26. http://pzwart.wdka.hro.nl/mdr/Seminars2/softstudworkshop/view.

Pollard, J. 2001. The global financial system: Worlds of monies? In *Human geography: Issues for the 21st Century*, edited by P. Daniels, M. Bradshaw, D. Shaw, and J. Sidaway. Harlow, UK: Prentice Hall.

Popper, D. E. 2007. Traceability: Tracking and privacy in the food system. *Geographical Review* 97 (3): 365–388.

Poulsen, K. 2006. Border security system left open. *Wired News* December 4. www.wired.com/science/discoveries/news/2006/04/70642.

Privacy International. 2004. *The enhanced U.S. border surveillance system: An assessment of the implications of US VISIT*. www.privacyinternational.org/issues/terrorism/rpt/dangers_of_visit.pdf.

Ramadanovic, P. 2001. From haunting to trauma: Nietzsche's active forgetting and Blanchot's writing of the disaster. *Postmodern Culture* 11 http://muse.jhu.edu/journals/pmc/v011/11.2ramadanovic.html.

Ratti, C., R. M. Pulselli, S. Williams, and D. Frenchman. 2006. Mobile landscapes: Using location data from cell phones for urban analysis. *Environment and Planning. B, Planning & Design* 33: 727–748.

Rensing, N. M., E. Westage, P. M. Zavracky, M. Chandler, K. R. Nobel, S. Helfter, M. Kinsky, M. Gold, and B. Martin. 2002. Threat response: A compelling application for wearable computing. *Proceedings of the Sixth International symposium on Wearable Computers.* http://ieeexplore.ieee.org/iel5/8353/26316/01167237.pdf?arnumber=1167237.

Rheingold, H. 1993. *The virtual community: Homesteading on the electronic frontier.* New York: Addison-Wesley.

Rheingold, H. 2002. *Smart mobs: The next social revolution.* Cambridge, MA: Perseus.

Risks List. 2003. Computer error grounds Japanese flights. *Forum on Risk to the Public in Computers and Related Systems* 22 (60). http://catless.ncl.ac.uk/Risks/22.60.html.

Ritzer, G. n.d. *Production, Consumption . . . Prosumption?* www.georgeritzer.com.

Rivlin G. 2002. The madness of King George. *Wired Magazine,* July. www.wired.com/wired/archive/10.07/gilder_pr.html.

Rode, J. A. 2006. Appliances for whom? Considering place. *Personal and Ubiquitous Computing* 10 (2–3): 90–94.

Rode, J. A., E. F. Toye, and A. F. Blackwell. 2004. The fuzzy felt ethnography—Understanding the programming patterns of domestic appliances. *Personal and Ubiquitous Computing* 8: 161–176.

Rooksby, J., and D. Martin. 2006. Ethnographies of code: Computer programs as the lived work of computer programming. *TeamEthno* 2 (1–2). www.teamethno-online.org.uk/Issue2/.

Rose, N. 1996. *Inventing our selves: Psychology, power and personhood.* Cambridge: Cambridge University Press.

Rose, G. 1999. Performing space. In *Human geography today,* edited by D. Massey, J. Allen, and P. Sarre, 247–259. Cambridge: Polity.

Rosenberg, S. 2007. *Dreaming in code: Two dozen programmers, three years, 4,732 bugs, and one quest for transcendent software.* New York: Three Rivers Press.

RSF. 2008. *Internet under surveillance.* Reporters without Borders. www.rsf.org.

Russell, B. 2004. *History of western philosophy,* 2nd ed. London: Routledge.

Savage, M., and R. Burrows. 2007. The coming crisis of empirical sociology. *Sociology* 41 (5): 885–899.

Schacter, D. L. 2001. *The seven sins of memory: How the mind forgets and remembers.* Boston: Houghton Mifflin.

Schaefer, F. K. 1953. Exceptionalism in geography: A methodological examination. *Annals of the Association of American Geographers.* 43: 226–249.

Schoenberger, C. R. 2002. The Internet of things. *Forbes Magazine* March 18. www.forbes.com/technology/forbes/2002/0318/155.html.

Schuurman, N. 2004. Databases and bodies: A cyborg update. *Environment & Planning A* 36: 1337–1340.

Schwanen, T., and M.-P. Kwan. 2008. The Internet, mobile phone and space-time constraints. *Geoforum* 39 (3): 1362–1377.

Sienkiewicz, S. 2001. *Credit cards and payment efficiency*. Discussion Paper, Payment Cards Center, Federal Reserve Bank of Philadelphia. www.philadelphiafed.org/payment-cards-center/publications/discussion-papers/2001/PaymentEfficiency_092001.pdf.

Sigala, M. 2005. Integrating customer relationship management in hotel operations: Managerial and operations implications. *International Journal of Hospitality Management* 24 (3): 391–413.

Simondon, G. 1989a. *Du mode d'existence des objets techniques*. Paris: Editions Aubier-Montaigne.

Simondon, G. 1989b. *L'individuation psychique et collective*. Paris: Editions Aubier-Montaigne.

Simondon, G. 1992. The genesis of the individual. In *Incorporations 6*, edited by J. Crary and S. Kwinter, 296–319New York: Zone Books.

Simondon, G. 1995. *L'Individu et sa genese physio-biologique*. Grenoble: Editions Jerome Millon.

Skupin, A., and S. I. Fabrikant. 2003. Spatialization methods: A cartographic research agenda for non-geographic information visualization. *Cartography and Geographic Information Science* 30 (2): 95–115.

Songdo. 2009a. www.songdo.com/page1992.aspx (accessed January 15, 2009).

Songdo. 2009b. *Home page*. www.songdo.com/default.aspx (accessed January 15, 2009).

Spiekermann, S., and F. Pallas. 2006. Technology paternalism—Wider implications of ubiquitous computing. *Poiesis & Praxis: International Journal of Ethics of Science and Technology Assessment* 4 (1): 6–18.

Spigel, L. 2005. Designing the smart house: Posthuman domesticity and conspicuous production. *European Journal of Cultural Studies* 8 (4): 405–426.

SPT. 2006. *Ideal process flow V2.0 report*. Simplifying Passenger Travel (SPT), December 1. www.spt.aero/files/downloads/21/IPF_V20_30_Nov_06.pdf.

Stalder, F. 2002. Privacy is not the antidote to surveillance. *Surveillance and Society* 1 (1): 120–124. www.surveillance-and-society.org/articles1/opinion.pdf.

Star, S. L., and K. Ruhleder. 1996. Steps towards an ecology of infrastructure: Design and access for large information space. *Information Systems Research* 7: 111–134.

Stein, J. 2009. Photoshopped images: The good, the bad and the ugly. *The Los Angeles Times* August 2. http://latimes.com/features/lifestyle/la-ig-photoshop2-2009aug02,0,3129812.story.

Sterling, B. 2002. When our environments become really smart. In *The invisible future: The seamless integration of technology into everyday eife*, edited by P. Denning, 251–276. New York: McGraw Hill.

Sterling, B. 2005. *Shaping things*. Cambridge, MA: MIT Press.

Stocker, G., and C. Schöpf, Eds. 2003. *Code: The language of our time*. Ostfildern, Germany: Hatje Cantz.

Tapscott, D., and A. D. Williams. 2006. *Wikinomics: How mass collaboration changes everything*. London: Atlantic Books.

Taylor, A., and L. Swan. 2005. Artful systems in the home. *Proceedings of the Conference on Human Factors and Computing systems (CHI '05)*, 641–650.

Thomas, D. 2005. Hacking the body: code, performance and corporeality. *New Media & Society* 7 (5): 647–662.

Thrift, N. 2003. Closer to the machine? Intelligent environments, new forms of possession and the rise of the supertoy. *Cultural Geographies* 10: 389–407.

Thrift, N. 2004a. Movement-space: The changing domain of thinking resulting from the development of new kinds of spatial awareness. *Economy and Society* 33 (4): 582–604.

Thrift, N. 2004b. Remembering the technological unconscious by foregrounding knowledges of position. *Environment and Planning. D, Society and Space* 22: 175–190.

Thrift, N. 2004c. Driving in the city. *Theory, Culture & Society* 21 (4/5): 41–59.

Thrift, N. 2007. *Non-representational theory*. London: Routledge.

Thrift, N., and S. French. 2002. The automatic production of space. *Transactions of the Institute of British Geographers* 27 (3): 309–335.

Top500. 2009. *The TOP500 Report for June 2009* www.top500.org/static/lists/2009/06/top500 _statistics.pdf.

Townsend, A. M. 2000. Life in the real-time city: Mobile telephones and urban metabolism. *Journal of Urban Technology* 7 (2): 85–104.

Townsend, A. 2003. *Wired/unwired: The urban geography of digital networks*. Unpublished PhD Thesis, Department of Urban and Regional Planning, MIT, Cambridge, MA.

Tufte, E. R. 2003. *The cognitive style of PowerPoint*. Cheshire, CT: Graphics Press.

Turkle, S. 1995. *Life on the screen: Identity in the age of the Internet*. New York: Simon & Schuster.

Twist, J. 2004. "Black box" cam for total recall. *BBC News Online* June 15 http://news.bbc.co.uk/1/ hi/technology/3797581.stm.

Uprichard, E., R. Burrows, and D. Byrne. 2008. SPSS as an "inscription device": From causality to description? *Sociological Review* 56 (4): 606–622.

UK Card Association. 2009. *Facts and figures.* www.theukcardsassociation.org.uk.

UK Home Office. 2004. *Cutting-edge technology to secure UK borders for 21ˢᵗ century.* www.gnn.gov .uk/content/detail.asp?NewsAreaID=2&ReleaseID=130801.

Ullman, E. 1997. *Close to the machine.* San Francisco: City Lights Books.

Urry, J. 2007. *Mobilities.* Cambridge: Polity.

U.S.-Canada Power System Outage Task Force. 2004. *Final Report on the August 14th Blackout in the United States and Canada.* https://reports.energy.gov.

van Dijck, J. 2005. From shoebox to performative agent: The computer as personal memory machine. *New Media & Society* 7 (3): 311–332.

van Kranenburg, R. 2008. *The Internet of things: A critique of ambient technology and the all-seeing network of RFID network notebooks.* http://networkcultures.org/wpmu/portal/publications/network -notebooks/the-internet-of-things/.

Van Zandt, J. P. 1944. *The geography of world air transport.* Washington, DC: The Brookings Institution.

Vemuri, S. n.d. *What was I thinking?* MIT.http://web.media.mit.edu/~vemuri/wwit/wwit overview.html.

Watkins, H. 2006. Beauty queen, bulletin board and browser: Rescripting the refrigerator. *Gender, Place and Culture* 13: 143–152.

Waldrop, M. M. 1994. *Complexity: The emerging science at the edge of order and chaos.* Harmond-sworth, Middlesex: Penguin Books.

Wardrip-Fruin, N. 2003. Introduction to surveillance and capture: Two models of privacy. *New Media Reader*, edited by N. Wardrip-Fruin and N. Montfort, 737–739. Cambridge, MA: MIT Press.

Washington, W. M., L. Buja, and A. Craig. 2009. The computational future for climate and earth system models: On the path to petaflop and beyond. *Philosophical Transactions of the Royal Society A* 367: 833–846.

Washington, W. M., R. Knutti, G. A. Meehl, H. Teng, C. Tebaldi, D. Lawrence, L. Buja, and W. G. Strand. 2009. How much climate change can be avoided by mitigation? *Geophysical Research Letters* 36 (L08703): 1–5.

Weiser, M. 1991. The computer for the 21st century. *Scientific American* 265 (3): 94–104.

Weiser, M., and J. Seely Brown. 1998. The coming age of calm technology. In *Beyond calculation: The next fifty years of computing*, edited by P. J. Denning and R. M. Metcalfe. New York: Springer.

Wellman, B., and C. A. Haythornthwaite. 2002. *The Internet in everyday life.* Chichester, UK: Wiley.

Wells, L. 1997. *Photography: A critical introduction.* London: Routledge.

Whatmore, S., and L. Thorne. 1997. Nourishing networks: Alternative geographies of food. In *Globalising food: Agrarian questions and global restructuring*, edited by D. Goodman and M. Watts, 287–304. London: Routledge.

Wheeler, J. O., Y. Aoyama, and B. Warf. 2000. *Cities in the telecommunications age: The fracturing of geographies*. New York: Routledge.

Whitelegge, M. 2004. Using geodemographic classifications in retail planning. Presentation to *CASA Research Methods* seminar, February 19. www.casa.ucl.ac.uk.

Wilde, O. 1891/1988. *The picture of Dorian Gray*. New York: W.W. Norton & Company.

Williams, L., and K. Wood. 2004. SenseCam: A photographic memory for everyone. *Microsoft Research Cambridge Open Day*, June 9 http://research.microsoft.com/hwsystems/SenseCam Overview/public.pps.

Wilson, M. I., and K. E. Corey. 2000. *Information tectonics: Space, place, and technology in an electronic age*. Chichester, UK: Wiley.

Wood, A. 2003. A rhetoric of ubiquity: Terminal space as omnitopia. *Communication Theory* 13 (3): 324–344.

Yourdon, E. 1997. *Death march*. Upper Saddle River, NJ: Prentice Hall.

Zook, M. A. 2005. *The geography of the Internet industry*. Oxford: Blackwell.

Zook, M., and M. Graham. 2007. The creative reconstruction of the internet: Google and the privatization of cyberspace and digiplace. *Geoforum* 38: 1322–1343.

Index